Derek Wilson is one of the UK's leading authors of history and historical fiction. In a writing career spanning 50 years, he has written over 70 books, featured on radio and television programmes, spoken at several major literary festivals and at the British Museum, Tate Gallery, British Library, Hampton Court Palace, Guildford Cathedral and other venues. Having graduated from Cambridge, where he studied history and theology, he has explored many aspects of the Reformation. Among his popular works are *Out of the Storm: The life of Martin Luther* (Hutchinson, 2007); *A Brief History of Henry VIII: Reformer and tyrant* (Robinson, 2009); *A Brief History of the English Reformation: Religion, politics and fear* (Robinson, 2012); and *Mrs Luther and Her Sisters: Women in the Reformation* (Lion Hudson, 2016). He currently lives in Devon, and writes for leading historical magazines. His most recent book is *Superstition and Science: Mystics, sceptics, truth-seekers and charlatans* (Robinson, 2017).

The
MAYFLOWER
PILGRIMS

Sifting fact from fable

DEREK WILSON

First published in Great Britain in 2019

Society for Promoting Christian Knowledge
36 Causton Street
London SW1P 4ST
www.spck.org.uk

British Library Cataloguing-in-Publication Data
A catalogue record for this book is available from the British Library

ISBN 978-0-281-07912-4
eBook ISBN 978-0-281-07914-8

1 3 5 7 9 10 8 6 4 2

Typeset by Falcon Oast Graphic Art Limited
First printed in Great Britain by TJ International
Subsequently digitally reprinted in Great Britain

eBook by Falcon Oast Graphic Art Limited

Produced on paper from sustainable forests

Contents

List of plates

Venetian navigator John Cabot.

Novum Testamentum Omne by Desiderius Erasmus.

The burning of Anne Askew in *Acts and Monuments* by John Foxe.

Memorial plaque to Robert Browne.

Tomb of Thomas and Faith St Paul (or St Poll).

Scrooby Manor.

Map of Leiden in the seventeenth century.

Plaque commemorating the English migrants to Leiden.

Sir Edwin Sandys and one of his pamphlets.

Memorial plaque to Catherine More's four children, disowned by her husband, Samuel, and shipped on the *Mayflower* as indentured servants.

Introduction

Is there such a thing as a Christian country? If so, what would it look like?

In 1520, most English people would have dismissed those questions as weird. It was perfectly obvious to them that they lived in a Christian country. Every community revolved round the parish church at its centre. The routines of its existence were governed as much by the cycle of religious festivals and holy days as by seed time and harvest. The nation was an integral part of Western Christendom. It owed allegiance to the pope in Rome, just as it owed allegiance to its earthly sovereign, Henry VIII, the second ruler of the house of Tudor, on whom Pope Leo X was about to bestow the honorific 'Defender of the Faith'. In that same year, a renegade monk in distant Saxony publicly burned a papal decree threatening him with excommunication for his disobedience, but that had nothing whatsoever to do with the men and women on Henry's island. Few of them had heard of Martin Luther. Fewer still were interested in what he had to say.

In 1620, a tiny group of English men, women and children turned their backs on their native land because they had decided it was *not* a Christian country. So strong were their convictions that they were ready to face the hazards of a transatlantic crossing in order to settle in a wild, untamed, largely unknown continent; a 'neutral' territory where they believed they could impose a perfect society, a truly Christian commonwealth. Where the 'Pilgrim Fathers' led, others followed.

Are we confronted here by a people of profound faith or naivety or spiritual arrogance or stupidity? Any clues to understanding these – undoubtedly courageous – pioneers lie in their prehistory. They were the products of 1520–1620, a century that had witnessed not just that unravelling of Catholic certainties we call the Reformation, nor the burgeoning of exciting and disturbing new rationalities we describe as the

Renaissance, but also a complete reassessment of the world in which the members of *Homo Europensis* lived and moved and had their being. The story of the first New England settlers has, of course, been told many times. However, chroniclers have tended to be too easily dazzled by what came after. The luxuriant growth that is the USA has seemed to necessitate the discovery of heroes and heroines, a process well underway by 1799:

> Hail, Pilgrim Fathers of our race!
> With grateful hearts your toils we trace;
> Again this Votive Day returns,
> And finds us bending o'er your urns.
>
> Jehovah's arm prepared the road;
> The Heathen vanished at his nod;
> He gave his vine a lasting root;
> He loads its goodly boughs with fruit.
>
> The hills are covered with its shade;
> Its thousand shoots like cedars spread;
> Its branches to the sea expand,
> And reach to broad Superior's strand.
>
> Of peace and truth the gladsome ray
> Smiles in our skies and cheers the day;
> And a new Empire's splendent wheels
> Roll o'er the top of Western hills.
>
> Hail, Pilgrim Fathers of our race:
> With grateful hearts your toils we trace;
> Oft as this Votive Day returns,
> We'll pay due honors to your urns.[1]

So Samuel Davis, the Massachusetts antiquary, wrote in his 'Ode for Forefathers' Day'. This is the stuff of legend, not history; a process, inspired by national pride, that looks for pioneers of stature. Inevitably, it distorts. If we really want to discover, as best we can, who the 1620 pioneers were, we need to probe their past, their heritage and their response to that heritage. And we also need some understanding of their context in the world they grew up in, the convictions they embraced, the assumptions they rejected and the changes with which they attempted – not always successfully – to cope. That is why the following narrative does not begin with the 180-ton *Mayflower*, after a series of false starts, clearing Plymouth harbour. Rather, it ends there.

The huddle of religious separatists on the ship's deck, watching their past disappear over the eastern horizon, believed they knew what a Christian commonwealth would be like and that, far from the satanic influences of the Old World, they could, under God, create it. We know that they were wrong. The communities they planted replicated the vices and the virtues of the ones they had left. The seeds of corruption lay within themselves. The perfect human society is a chimera. But we would do well to guard against cynical superiority. These pioneers were not alone in their determination to create a better world or in their belief that it was possible to do so. Political philosophers debated the nature of a Christian commonwealth. Many co-religionists of the emigrants stayed to challenge the existing regime. Some of those who left for America returned to join in the struggle of Parliament versus Crown. Idealists had several blueprints to choose from. Most of them related to construction in the Old World rather than the New.

Digging down to the roots of extremist religious separatism, while also analysing the soil within which they grew, perforce involves exploring several contemporaneous events and movements. Rather than investigating the various strands separately, I have tried to run them in parallel. This may make for a rather 'jerky' narrative, but I hope readers will gain an appreciation of how the events and movements combined or clashed, merged or rebounded. As Oscar Wilde observed, 'The truth is rarely pure and never simple.'

1
A new world

All Europeans thought geography and history to be *sub specie aeternitatis*. The Bible laid down fundamental truths about the planet, humanity's temporary residence in it and God's ultimate purpose for it: 'The earth is the LORD's . . . and they that dwell therein' (Psalm 24.1 KJV); 'this gospel of the kingdom shall be preached in all the world . . . and then shall the end come' (Matthew 24.14 KJV); 'I saw the new Jerusalem come down from God in heaven. A voice from the throne declared, "Now God's home is with mankind and they shall be his people"' (Revelation 21.2-3, paraphrased). This apocalyptic vision was fundamental to all Christians, Catholics and Protestants alike, but during the sixteenth century it, perforce, underwent reinterpretation as human knowledge of the planet changed.

Thinking people living in England in the early sixteenth century, when they reflected on the world they lived in, could scarcely avoid being aware of that change. Most obviously, this related to their physical environment. The planet on which they lived was not the one their forebears had inhabited. It was bigger, stranger, altogether more replete with marvels. If what mariners were reporting and geographers were calculating were true, old assumptions and convictions needed adjustment – perhaps they needed to be rejected. Yet more disturbing – or intriguing – or exciting, for those who permitted themselves to reflect on such things, were changing concepts of *spiritual* reality – the life of the human soul and its ultimate destiny. Daring innovators, proposing new understandings of Christian faith based solely on their reading of the Bible, were no less adventurous than the sailors who steered their fragile craft across uncharted oceans, as they dangerously departed the haven of traditional belief. The story we have to tell concerns men and women who shared a 'new world', in both senses.

Let us start that story a little over a hundred years before the 180-ton *Mayflower* slipped anchor in Southampton Water, her sails filling with a 'prosperous wind'. In 1516, no sane English captain would have set a westerly course from that haven in the confident hope of making landfall before his crew's food and water ran out. That does not mean English mariners were uninterested in transoceanic expeditions; simply that they lacked the knowledge, the experience and, more importantly, the backers for such speculative enterprises.

It was Bristol that provided the home base for England's more enterprising mariners. Annually, small fleets set out for the north-west Atlantic in pursuit of the shoals of cod that fed and bred in those waters. Fish made up an important part of the English diet and rewards could be substantial for those braving the icy waters. Some reached the coast of Newfoundland. The most significant discoveries are connected with the voyages of father and son John and Sebastian Cabot, Bristolians who hailed originally from Venice. Mystery and controversy surround the discoveries claimed by the Cabots or on their behalf by contemporary authors, but what is clear is that these were not just fishing expeditions. They were mercantile voyages, undertaken in the hope of discovering new lands with marketable resources or inhabitants with whom it would be possible to trade. The pioneers of overseas exploration were the Spanish and the Portuguese, who, on the cusp of the sixteenth century, crossed the ocean in lower latitudes, seeking seaways to the Orient. As we all know, they stumbled on the Americas and discovered the route around Africa to the lands of silks and spices. The Cabots' activities were contemporaneous and confined to northern waters, but they were pursuing the same objectives. Between 1494 and (possibly) 1516, the elder Cabot, and subsequently his son, coasted along the Newfoundland land mass. No one knew how far it extended to north or south; only that it presented a barrier preventing access to the potentially lucrative oriental markets. Sebastian ventured close to the Arctic Circle in search of a north-west passage, then followed the American coastline southwards, possibly as far as Chesapeake Bay. Much of this is conjecture, doubtless due in part to the explorer's desire to keep his discoveries secret.

For a few years, the attention of mariners and scholars was focused on the activities of Christopher Columbus, Amerigo Vespucci and

Juan del Cano (who completed the first circumnavigation of the earth after the death of the expedition's leader, Ferdinand Magellan). Gradually, the realization filtered through European society that the occupants of the Indo-European land mass shared their planet with a vast geographical entity called the 'New World'. The term itself came into existence in 1503 when the Florentine explorer Vespucci wrote a letter to his patron, Lorenzo de Medici, describing his adventures in the terrestrial paradise of the *Novum Mundum*. Within months, this epistle was translated into several vernaculars and was being rushed off printing presses throughout Europe. Readers were enthralled by the descriptions of strange peoples and a multitude of wondrous animals, birds, trees and flowers. Four years later, Martin Waldseemüller, a geographer from the Upper Rhineland, made a globe and wall-map that astonished everyone by being the first new representation of the world since the *Geographia* of Ptolemy, produced thirteen-and-a-half centuries earlier. It was accompanied by a text the full title of which revealed its breathtakingly spectacular claim: *Introduction to Cosmography With Certain Necessary Principles of Geometry and Astronomy to which are added the Four Voyages of Amerigo Vespucci, a Representation of the Entire World, both in the Solid and Projected on the Plane, including also Lands which were unknown to Ptolemy and have been Recently Discovered.* Waldseemüller may be said to have invented America, for, although he represented the New World as being contiguous with the Old World with no intervening Pacific Ocean, he did give that New World the name by which it would always be known – America – and he did map, with a remarkable degree of accuracy, its eastern seaboard.

These scholarly descriptions, combined with the travellers' tales brought back by sailors now venturing further across the great oceans and with the revelations of fabulous wealth just waiting to be torn from the earth of Central and South America, spurred generations of conquistadors and colonists to seek their fortunes in the New World. But more important in terms of this present study is the impact of all this on the imagination of Europeans. These revelations occurred during what cultural historian Jacques Barzun identified as 'the age of indispensable literacy'.[1] The print revolution had been gathering momentum for 50 years. No town of any importance in Europe was without at least one printworks and, by 1500, there were millions of books in circulation. Among them were many accounts of the wonders to be observed in exotic lands. Vespucci sought to impress his readers with paradisal visions reminiscent of the garden of Eden. In these regions, there were simple folk who painted their naked bodies. They possessed gold and wonder-working drugs:

> The soil is very pleasant and fruitful, full of immense woods and forests and is always green, for the foliage never drops off. The fruits are so many that they are numberless and entirely different from ours.
> The birds are so numerous and of so many different kinds, and of such various-coloured plumage that it is a marvel to behold them.
> What should I tell of the multitude of wild animals, the abundance of pumas, panthers ... of so many wolves, red deer, monkeys and felines, marmosets of many kinds, and many large snakes?[2]

The traveller, in his chronicling of wonders, did not hesitate to challenge preconceived ideas, though we may wonder if he appreciated that he was teetering on the edge of heresy when he commented that the animal species he observed were too numerous to have been accommodated on Noah's ark.

That reflection hauls us back to a truth which is absolutely fundamental to our understanding of the early voyages of discovery. For serious adventurers and scholars who commented on their exploits, what mattered more than the wonders they encountered (except insofar as these were evidences of the handiwork of the Creator) was how the New World was to be understood in relation to the outworking of the divine plan.

The major political reality of the sixteenth century that overshadowed all other interstate relations was the conflict between Christianity and Islam. Since the fall of Constantinople, capital of Eastern Christendom, in 1453, intermittent warfare had waged in the borderlands between the two religions. The Ottoman Turks pressed against the land borders of the Holy Roman Empire and, from bases on the North African littoral, menaced the Mediterranean sea coasts. The fightback was spearheaded by the rulers of Aragon and Castile who wanted to drive the Muslims from

Spain. For Christian rulers, the ultimate prize – if Bible prophecy was to be fulfilled and the Church's international mission was to be completed – was Jerusalem. When this was wrested from infidel hordes and the gospel proclaimed to those people in thrall to the Ottoman sultan, then, and only then, would the end come. Strategically, if the champions of the Christian faith were to get to grips with their enemy, they would have to overcome the formidable barrier that confronted them in the East. Their path was blocked either by Islamic territory or insurmountable sea and land barriers. That was why mariners and geographers sought routes to the Orient. Trade with the fabled lands of Cathay and Zipangu was, of course, a powerful lure, but the apocalyptic vision was seldom far below the surface of their thinking. Their knowledge of the world had changed, but the divine imperatives, as laid down in Scripture, still applied. The enemies of the cross had to be overpowered. Jerusalem had to be regained in readiness for the Second Coming. The gospel had to be preached to 'all people' so that the longed-for 'end time' could be hastened.[3]

Christopher Columbus was steeped in apocalyptic prophecy and the cause to which he devoted his life was gaining a leading position in the outworking of God's great design: 'God made me a messenger of the new heaven and the new earth of which he spoke in the Apocalypse of St John after having spoken of it through the mouth of Isaiah.'[4] So he wrote to a supporter at the Spanish court after his third voyage. It was no coincidence that, after years of hawking his grand vision around the monarchs of Europe, he eventually achieved the backing of Ferdinand and Isabella, who also interpreted their purge of Iberia as a part of the end-time scenario. To the end of his days, Columbus believed that he had made landfall on the coast of Asia so others following his lead would convert the indigenes. 'I believe that they would become Christians very easily,' he noted in his diary.[5] By converting the 'Indians' and making powerful allies among their rulers, it would be possible to converge on the infidel Turks from the east as well as the west and reclaim the Holy City in readiness for Armageddon. In his will, the mariner left a legacy to his son for the express purpose of establishing a fund for the reconquest of Jerusalem.

The discovery that the new-found continent was large and divided from Asia by yet another vast ocean put an end to this particular version of the last days, but in no way did it invalidate the biblical prophecy for Christian believers. Rather, it simply encouraged reinterpretation. There was nothing new in that. The Church has always been faced with the task of understanding past prophecy about future events in terms of present knowledge but, in what I am tempted to call the 'Reformnaissance', new questions and fresh enlightenments tumbled over one another, demanding reinterpretation of God's purposes for his creation. This was the century of Nostradamus, Mother Shipton, the Prophecies of Merlin and John Dee's conjurations. It was the age when everyone from kings and queens downwards consulted astrologers and when printed almanacs began to appear.

We might think that encounters with hitherto unknown or inaccessible races would have deterred the missionary endeavours of Christian commentators. Far from it. If preaching the gospel 'to every creature' was a prerequisite of the Second Coming, they reasoned, then the sooner preachers followed in the footsteps of explorers and conquistadors, the better. The Catholic Church responded warmly to this new challenge. As we shall see, by the time Protestant mariners began to explore 'heathen lands afar', the imperative to engage in holy mission had become somewhat less urgent. But the imaginations of English venturers were not dimmed; nor was their determination to reach (and exploit) those lands to which the arrogant Iberians laid exclusive claim.

It would not be until the reign of the first Elizabeth that a new breed of English sailors challenged the maritime supremacy of the Spanish and Portuguese pioneers and asserted their ownership of coastal and inland bases in the Caribbean and along the Atlantic seaboard. But though the practicalities of long-distance sailing and the establishment of faraway settlements proved, for the time being, too daunting, English ambitions were nonetheless fired by tales of strange lands and peoples. Just as the space race of the 1960s and 1970s gave a boost to sci-fi books and films, so, half a millennium ago, people were eager for (and largely uncritical of) stories of societies that might be found in lands the existence of which was now being discovered.

But phantasy cannot exist without reality. Unfamiliar marvels *are* marvels because they are unfamiliar – because they contrast with the world as we know it. It is but a short step from contrast to comparison, from what might exist in lands yet unexplored, to what could – or should – exist in one's own land. The best science-fiction adventures turn out to be reflections on terrestrial affairs, commentaries on the good and bad in human society. The year in which our story starts – 1516 – saw the publication of a book that is a literary ancestor of the time-and-space phantasy genre.

The lawyer and soon-to-be royal councillor Thomas More wrote *Utopia* (literally 'Nowhere'), a book that, at first sight, seemed to be a work of moral philosophy wrapped in a cloak of whimsy. The plot, such as it is, concerns the travels of the fictional Portuguese mariner Raphael Hythloday, a companion of Amerigo Vespucci, who continued his voyage after the Florentine had returned to Europe and discovered, in the South Atlantic, the island of Utopia. Its inhabitants had developed a peaceful and harmonious society that, if not perfect, exhibited a higher level of rational communal living than anything yet attained in Christian Europe. But to take *Utopia* as an erudite reflection on the world as it is and the world as it might be is to miss the darkness and bitterness at its heart. Seven years earlier, More had welcomed the accession of the youthful bon-vivant Henry VIII with a sycophantic coronation ode in which he contrasted the harsh, intrusive, avaricious regime of Henry VII with the prospect of a new, golden reign. He assured the new king, 'All are equally happy. All weigh their earlier losses against the advantages to come.'[6] It had not taken him long, however, to reassess his opinion of the second Tudor monarch. He confided to his son-in-law William Roper, 'I believe he doth as singularly favour me as any subject in his realm. However . . . I have no cause to be proud thereof, for if my head would win a castle in France, it would not fail to be struck off.'[7] In 1517, Henry VIII had yet to reveal the full bestiality of which he was capable, but to More, the signs of tyranny were clear.

Utopia is written in two parts. Book One is a conversation between More and Hythloday covering the condition of European society and the ills that need to be redressed – harsh laws, grasping landowners, warring monarchs and so on. By putting these complaints into the mouth of Hythloday, the author avoids the direct criticism that would certainly get him into trouble. The point is driven home when the participants debate the responsibility of royal advisers. Surely, More suggests, philosophers should seek to enter the councils of kings in order to guide them. Hythloday rejects this firmly. Numerous works of political philosophy had been written from classical times to his own day, but rulers rarely chose to be swayed by them. Why should the wise scholar pit himself against such wishful ignorance?

> If I should propose to any king wholesome decrees, doing my endeavour to pluck out of his mind the pernicious original causes of vice and naughtiness, think you not that I should forthwith either be driven away or else made a laughing stock?[8]

This was the dilemma facing many Renaissance orators and writers. If they remained aloof from the corrupting influence of politics, they might enjoy a certain amount of freedom to speak their mind, but would be unlikely to make much impact on contemporary mores. If they dirtied their hands in the dunghill of government, they might themselves become corrupted or end up as victims of the systems they were vainly seeking to reform. More's friend, the leading Christian philosopher of the age Desiderius Erasmus, chose the life of a wandering scholar. He survived. More attempted to guide Henry VIII into the 'paths of right-eousness'. He did not survive.

Book Two of *Utopia* is a detailed description of the government, econ-omy, religion and pastimes of the island state, in which, without the benefit of Christian revelation, the people live in harmony and mutual concern for one another. Just as modern tales of intergalactic travel high-light the ways in which human societies are failing, so the depiction of the Utopian commonwealth pointed up in detail the need for reform in the kingdoms of Western Christendom. Utopia is a land without differences of wealth and More derides the pride and presumption of hereditary nobles. Councillors, like magistrates, are elected and serve on an assembly that is summoned annually. A system of checks and bal-ances prevents the king from becoming too powerful. Religion for the Utopians is a mix of devotion, reason, moral restraint and charity:

> They define virtue to be life ordered according to nature, and that we be hereunto ordained of God, and that he doth follow the course

of nature which, in desiring and refusing things, is ruled by reason. Furthermore, that reason doth chiefly and principally kindle in men the love and veneration of the divine majesty . . . and also moveth us to help and further all others . . . For there was never man so earnest and careful a follower of virtue and hater of pleasure that would so enjoin your labours, vigils and fastings, but he would also exhort you to ease, lighten, and relieve, to your power, the lack and misery of others . . .[9]

For More, the objective of life in this world is to ensure 'the greatest good of the greatest number'. In matching up English life against this standard of 'commonwealth', More goes as far as he dares with his critique. While he writes of the responsibilities of those in office, he has little to say about maintaining the hierarchy. He exhorts devotion to God, but does not urge his readers to honour the king. He is even scathing about gambling and hunting, two pursuits particularly dear to Henry VIII. Yet, at the end of his discourse, as if to distance himself from any suggestion of political radicalism, he writes:

as I cannot agree and consent to all things that be said . . . so must I needs confess and grant that many things be in the Utopian weal public, which in our cities I may rather wish for than hope.[10]

More, as we all know, went on to become Lord Chancellor, reached the point at which he could not, in good conscience, endorse the king's religious policy and was, therefore, condemned to death. The story needs no retelling. What we are exploring here is the attitude of leading Tudor writers to the relationships of the individual, the Church and the State. Such matters formed a major preoccupation of Renaissance thinkers. As the politico-religious situation in England became increasingly tense, so More found himself further out on a limb. Eventually he parted company with his friend Erasmus.

The Dutch scholar, not tied to any existing regime, went further and deeper than More. Education was, for him, the fundamental necessity – radical education; education based on the Bible. In 1516, he published a Greek text of the New Testament, together with a new Latin translation that corrected certain errors in the Vulgate – the Church's 'infallible' Bible. Although he wrote in the scholars' lingua franca, Erasmus believed strongly in vernacular translations that would be available to everyone who could read:

> I would have the weakest woman read the Gospels and the Epistles of St Paul. I would have those words translated into all languages, so that, not only Scots and Irishmen, but Turks and Saracens might read them. I long for the ploughboy to sing them to himself as he follows the plough, the weaver to hum them to the tune of his shuttle, the traveller to beguile with them the dullness of his journey.[11]

It was a principle shared by most humanists (including Thomas More), but it would soon become a hot potato, especially in England. Although the Bible had appeared in other European languages, English church authorities had a morbid fear of the uncaged word of God. A whole century before the accession of Henry VIII, the Constitution of Oxford (1407-1409) had prohibited unauthorized translations (which, in effect, meant all translations) and sanctioned the punishment as heretics of any people found in possession of copies. The reason for their sensitivity was the persistence of England's native heresy, Lollardy. This was the name given to a ragbag of radical beliefs that were given intellectual substance in the teachings of John Wycliffe (1320-1384), an Oxford scholar who had criticized the pope, rejected some basic orthodox doctrines and inaugurated the production and distribution of a vernacular Bible. Despite sporadic persecution, Lollardy refused to disappear. It was kept alive by small groups of dissenters (for the most part tradespeople and farmers of modest means) who met in secret to study the forbidden text and were sustained by a network of preachers and colporteurs. The Lollards were a tiny minority of humble people, with little influence, who were yet a source of irritation to the Church establishment. For the most part, they were treated with disdain and derision, but sometimes they became the focus of irate sermons, were dragged into the church courts and, if unrepentant, were handed over to the secular authorities for burning.

One reason why the bishops were wary of the Lollards was because they became the mouthpiece of certain prejudices and criticisms that were widespread. It is quite impossible for us to take the religious temperature of the entire population of medieval England. The vast majority conformed outwardly. Many declared their apparent devotion by membership of religious guilds, undertaking pilgrimages and participating in all the standard rituals. But how deep or clearly thought out their convictions were must remain a mystery. By no means were they all the meek recipients of whatever their parish clergy told them or dumbly uncritical of those following a religious vocation. Anticlericalism could flare up at any time and in any place. In 1327, the townspeople sacked the great abbey of Bury St Edmunds. Two hundred years later, parish life was still occasionally upset, though not so spectacularly. When the vicar of Bideford refused to conduct the burial of a poor parishioner without payment of his mortuary fee – in this case a cow, which was the dead man's only possession – the local landowner, Sir William Caffin, ordered the recalcitrant priest to be placed in the open grave and earth to be shovelled in until the victim changed his mind. Church-state relations at all levels gave rise frequently to ill feeling and acts bordering on rebellion. In 1395, Lollards enumerated their principal grievances in 'Twelve Conclusions', pinned to the doors of Westminster Abbey and St Paul's Cathedral.

1 The Church is too much involved with temporal authority.
2 The ordination of bishops and priests has no scriptural warrant.
3 Clerical celibacy encourages the sin of sodomy.
4 The doctrine of transubstantiation leads to the idolatrous worship of bread and wine.
5 Clerical exorcism is a form of witchcraft.
6 Leading churchmen should not also be major officers of state.
7 Masses for the dead are merely a means of increasing church income.
8 Pilgrimages and veneration of relics are idolatry.
9 Auricular confession is blasphemous because only God can forgive sins.
10 'Holy' war is nonsense since Christ did not tell us to spread the faith by force of arms.
11 Female vows of chastity lead to abortions and concealed illegitimate births.

12 The creation of beautiful objects of worship is a misuse of craftsmen's time and talents.

The leaven of Lollard doubts and assertions working within the dough of English society could only be disturbing to the leaders of Church and State. The hierarchical nature of society was founded on and buttressed by religious sanctions deriving their authority from the declared purposes of God. Doubt that, and you were stumbling into the thickets not only of heresy but also of potential treason.

Erasmus wanted to have his cake and eat it. He passionately desired to see European society totally Christianized – but without changing its structure. Placing the Bible in the hands of everyone able to read (a constituency he ardently wanted to see expanded) would, he supposed, lead to a more comprehensive – and unified – understanding and experience of Christian truth. But if people were going to explore the word of God without the guidance or direction or control of the Church's 'experts', then they would be exercising choice in how to interpret it. Now, the Greek word for 'choice' is *hairesis* – heresy. This freedom to be guided directly by divine precepts was, in Erasmus's view, vital, largely because the teaching and conduct of so many Christian leaders, from the pope down, was scandalous and bore little relation to the 'philosophy' that Erasmus himself advocated and tried to live by. How, then, to prevent the doctrinal anarchy that such individualistic discipleship seemed to imply?

The answer (or *an* answer) proposed by this wandering scholar was to extend the disciplinary responsibility of temporal rulers and their law courts *and* to ensure that the rulers themselves were firmly grounded in Christian truth. In another book written during this remarkably fecund second decade of the century, Erasmus outlined how the leaders of Europe should be trained to be the guardians of faith in their dominions. *The Education of a Christian Prince* (1516) was a manual dedicated to the young Holy Roman Emperor Charles V. In an ideal world, Erasmus observed, rulers would be elected for their wisdom, piety and concern for the well-being of their subjects. The hereditary principle prevented the emergence of such a regime. The alternative, then, was education:

The mind of the future prince will have to be filled straight away, from the very cradle . . . with healthy thoughts while it is still open and undeveloped. And from then on the seeds of morality must be sown in the virgin soil of his infant soul, so that, with age and experience, they may gradually germinate and mature . . .[12]

In this way, the prevailing authoritarian structures could be made to work and the risk of peasant rebellion or baronial coup could be reduced. This idealistic regime depended on the magi of Western Christendom, the Christian humanist philosophers. It was their responsibility to educate princes and to influence kings by writing, preaching and, where they had opportunity, by whispering into their ears. They must be the seers, the truth-tellers of the age. They must be ready to challenge existing conventions and practices, as the prophets of old who railed in the name of God:

I hate your New Moon Festivals and holy days: they are a burden that I am tired of bearing. When you lift your hands in prayer, I will not look at you. No matter how much you pray, I will not listen, for your hands are covered with blood. Wash yourselves clean. Stop all this evil that I see you doing. Yes, stop doing evil and learn to do right. See that justice is done – help those who are oppressed, give orphans their rights, and defend widows.[13]

The comparison is an apt one. Just as, in ancient Israel, the independent prophets challenged kings, priests and cult prophets, so humanist philosophers brought a new perspective to religious thought and criticized not only the lax behaviour of monks and nuns, the ignorance of parish clergy, the notorious corruption of popes and cardinals, the pilgrimage 'racket' and the worship of images but also the arid 'scholasticism' that governed the teaching of theology in the universities. It was based on an approach to the gospel that led, through numerous layers of patristic commentaries and abstract speculation, to abstruse philosophical debate. Erasmus and his friends looked to the example of reformist kings such as Hezekiah and Josiah of old who listened to holy men and women, and modelled their regimes accordingly. But were the monarchs of the sixteenth century up to the challenge? Only time would tell.

While Erasmus, More and their coterie were discussing those things among themselves, yet another book appeared on the market that moved the whole debate to a higher (or, as some saw it, to a lower) level. A monk in distant Saxony, by the name of Martin Luther, challenged the practice of selling in the pope's name indulgence certificates granting remission from penalties in purgatory imposed for sins committed during terrestrial life. It was, ostensibly, a protest against a specific custom that, as many people recognized, had become a money-making racket, but, by implication, it questioned papal authority. Luther's *95 Theses* were printed on various presses in Latin and German. That was in the autumn of 1517. Within months they were being read in London and in August 1518 Luther expanded on his theses in *Explanations of the Disputation Concerning the Value of Indulgences*. The crisis now escalated with astonishing rapidity. Luther appeared to be giving theological gravitas not only to humanist demands for reform but also to anticlericalism, which was more widespread than those in authority had realized.

One victim of the gathering storm was the relationship between More and Erasmus. There was no dramatic falling out, but the two scholars found themselves on opposite sides of various debates. More wanted his friend to use his international celebrity to lead an anti-Evangelical crusade, but Erasmus was irenically inclined and would do nothing to ratchet up the conflict. He followed closely the reactions of German princes to Luther's initiative, believing stubbornly that politico-religious change to society could only be brought about by enlightened rulers. More looked to his ruler, Henry VIII, to take a pro-papal stand *against* change. In 1520, the Wittenberg monk issued his most vitriolic attack to date. His *Babylonian Captivity of the Church* was a swingeing denunciation of the Catholic sacramental system. More urged King Henry to enter the literary fray and helped him to write *A Defence of the Seven Sacraments* (1521), a clear statement of where England and its king stood in the big debate. In that same year, More and Erasmus met up in Bruges. Though More lived for a further 14 years, the two erstwhile reformist intellectuals never saw each other again.

During his remaining years, More became a man with a mission. He once explained to Erasmus his attitude towards heretics:

I find that breed of men absolutely loathsome, so much so that, unless they regain their senses, I want to be as hateful to them as anyone can possibly be; for my increasing experience with those men frightens me with the thought of what the world will suffer at their hands.[14]

More used his political position to encourage the detection and prosecution of Evangelicals and wielded his pen in vitriolic literary conflicts with Tyndale and others. It was to Tyndale that he exulted: 'The clergy doth denounce them and, as they be well worthy the temporality doth burn them; and after the fire of Smithfield, hell doth receive them, where the wretches burn forever.'[15]

Change, then, was inevitable and, to many thinking people, desirable but, if chaos were to be avoided, change had to be managed. The question that had to be addressed was: who should drive, control and channel changes – particularly in matters of religious belief and practice? Some would insist that it was up to the Church to put its own house in order. Others looked to the secular rulers, who alone wielded the power to enforce change on those reluctant to accept it. Luther began by appealing to the religious intellectual elite of his day. His *95 Theses* challenged the theological basis of the Church's penitential system. How conscious he was initially that he was attacking the authority of the pope to propound doctrine has been much debated. It was certainly Rome's negative reaction that forced a confrontation between *sola ecclesia* and *sola scriptura*. It then followed logically that if the members of the spirituality were not prepared to initiate change, the work would have to be taken over by the temporal rulers. But there was about Luther's gesture of defiance something very much more fundamental. The celebrated Wittenberg theses began with these words: 'When our Lord and Master Jesus Christ said, "Repent," He willed the entire life of believers to be one of repentance.'[16] Luther identified the necessary *change* that society so desperately needed as one that had to be established in the lives of individual believers. Every man, woman and child had their destiny in their own hands by responding in repentance and faith to the love of God revealed in Jesus Christ.

This was the breakthrough, the game-changer, the revolutionary principle backed by the word of God that forced people from their fears about hell and purgatory, and also from the traditional remedies for those fears offered by Catholic dogma but, ultimately, it failed to answer the desperate question 'What must I do to be saved?' The message of 'salvation by only faith' ran like rivers of fire through Western Christendom, giving people consent – divine consent – to challenge some teaching (and if 'some' why not 'all') of a Church that no longer commanded universal respect. In the second decade of the sixteenth century, unorthodox patterns of religious thought thus began to circulate among the upper echelons of English society, originated by Christian humanists and by Luther and his growing band of followers.

It would, of course, be absurd to suppose that the Pauline doctrine of salvation by faith was one that had been ignored by the Western Church for one-and-a-half millennia. It had always been a tall tree in the forest of Christian dogma, but it had been obscured in vigorous undergrowth. The doctrine of the Church had, for centuries, wrestled with the relationship between grace, faith, good works and sacraments. While theologians had threaded their way through the undergrowth, impatient bands of 'heretics', such as the Lollards, desperate for spiritual solace and critical of a priesthood that did not practise what it preached, scythed their own paths in search of an interiorized faith. Bible in hand, they hacked down clerical privilege and sacramental mystique and replaced them with common-sense interpretations of the holy text accessible to lay folk. Such were the spiritual ancestors of the Pilgrim Fathers. Thomas More would have been mortified to hear his name bracketed with the unlettered enemies of holy Church, but their aspirations were not dissimilar from his. Like him, Lollards yearned for a new world, a utopia where all were free to learn and live by the Christian gospel.

2

The idea of commonwealth

The reinvention of England intensified in the middle years of the sixteenth century. When Henry VIII 'discovered' (1532) that 'this realm of England is an empire entire of itself' and became the first leader of a major European power to break away from the spiritual EU that was Western Christendom, he had no idea of the enormous significance of what he had done. He had set the realm on a long, tortuous, hazardous and distressing journey towards an unknown destination. Half the landed wealth of England would change hands. Hundreds of men and women would be hanged, beheaded or burned to death. Iconoclastic tsunamis would strip age-honoured objects of 'superstition' from churches throughout the land. Sunday worshippers would become accustomed to the novelty of actually participating in the liturgy in their own tongue. The very monarchy Henry had thought to make all-powerful would be overthrown. But more fundamental to all this was the unintended liberty given to the king's subjects to think for themselves, to hold religious beliefs, not because they were the beliefs of their ancestors or because they devoutly embraced what their priests told them to embrace. They were, in the words of St Paul, 'working out their own salvation with fear and trembling' (Philippians 2.12). In the process, generations of sincere people would reach varying conclusions about their relationship with God, but they would also provide conflicting answers to such questions as, 'What is the State?', 'What is the Church?' and 'What is the relationship between the two?' In the process of agonizing over these fundamentals, a tiny minority of devout Christians would turn their backs on the blandishments of the all-too-familiar, irredeemably corrupt old world in order to establish, in virgin territory, the perfect society of the saints.

When Henry VIII came to the throne such a project would have been well beyond the range of intellectual radar. Renaissance writers and thinkers knew (or thought they knew) what the commonwealth was. If it was not functioning properly, the necessary adjustments were not difficult to identify. Manifestly, responsibility lay primarily with the Crown. So, at least, Edmund Dudley stated in his *Tree of Commonwealth* (1510): 'Our Lord grant that the prince shall renew the common wealth within this his realm, the which this long time hath been in some decay.'[1]

The author of this essay in sound government was not in the happiest of circumstances. Edmund Dudley, until recently councillor to the late King Henry VII, was in the Tower of London under sentence of death. We need not go into the details of his condemnation save to say that it was unjust. Dudley and his colleague Richard Empson were made the scapegoats for an unpopular regime. Dudley had been largely responsible for carrying out the rapacious policies of his royal master, but those policies had been entirely the king's. Henry VII was well versed in conveying to underlings the blame for immoral actions. His son would prove to be even more adept at passing the buck. As we have seen, many English people welcomed the change of regime, believing (or hoping) that the new 18-year-old king would not prove to be a chip off the old block. Dudley's little treatise was an offering to Henry VIII in which he dissociated himself as far as possible from the sins of the father and offered political advice to the son. What is significant is the author's dissection of the workings of a commonwealth.

Of course, the interrelationship of individuals in civil society, their respective rights and responsibilities, had featured prominently in philosophical discourse since the time of Socrates, but the twists and turns of history meant that the pack of ideas was time and again reshuffled. In late medieval Europe (that is, in Western Christendom), official theology/ philosophy stressed the divine ordering of society. The political structure was part of the eternal cosmos – a unity, pyramidal in structure. At its apex stood the triune Creator, Sustainer, Saviour and Judge. Then came the heavenly worshippers and mediators – ranks of angels and glorified saints, activating divine decrees, supporting mortal believers and interceding on their behalf before the throne of grace. The topmost layer of the earthly part of the pyramid was occupied by the pope, God's representative. Authority passed down from him through a hierarchy of bishops, clergy, monks, friars, anchorites and other religious functionaries to the wide base layer of the laity. Within this last band the gradation continued through the social classes from emperors and kings, nobles and gentry, right down to the humblest beggars dependent on their betters for any scraps that might ensure their survival. For all most folk knew, this was the way God had designed the 'humanity machine' to work and it was the responsibility of all mere mortals to act out their allotted roles (their vocations) so as not to interfere with the mechanism.

In no sense was Dudley an original thinker. For creative political philosophy we must turn to the writers of the Italian Renaissance and those influenced by them. What Dudley does is identify the problems confronting Henry VIII and his advisers. The ideal 'commonwealth' is, as the name implies, a state that works for the well-being of all its citizens. Since the template for such a state has been provided by God, there is no need for radical change (indeed, to propose such change would be sinful). The social hierarchy is a divine institution. All that is necessary is to make sure that it works properly. The prime responsibility lies with the king:

> For, as the subjects are bounden to their prince, so be all kings bounden to their subjects by the commandment of God them to maintain and support . . . though the people be subject to the king yet are they the people of God and God hath ordained their prince to protect them and they to obey their prince.[2]

Royal authority embraces religious reform, for it is the king's task 'not only [to] support and maintain his church and the true faith thereof . . . but also to see that such as he shall promote and set in Christ's Church . . . be both cunning [that is, well educated] and virtuous'.[3]

Dudley points out that religious and civil affairs in England are in a parlous state. He identifies the failings of the clergy, which had obviously not improved since the days of Wycliffe, and he is at one with the Christian humanists like More and Erasmus who were appalled at the moral failings and educational inadequacies of parish priests, monks and friars. Dudley was a close friend of John Colet, Dean of St Paul's, who in this same year (1510) observed in a famous sermon before his colleagues in the convocation of the province of Canterbury:

We are ... nowadays grieved of heretics, men mad with marvellous foolishness. But the heresies of them are not so pestilent and pernicious unto us and the people as the evil and wicked life of priests, the which, if we believe St Bernard, is a certain kind of heresy and chief of all and most perilous.[4]

Dudley is (though guardedly) also critical of the civil administration of the previous reign. The tree of commonwealth, he complained, is well-nigh utterly failed and dead.[5]

For Dudley, the tree of commonwealth is an established fact. It only needs careful tending to produce the fruits of true worship, prosperity, internal peace, honour, and example to other nations. There can be no question of replacing the unhealthy tree with another of a more robust species. Some of the Italian states were experimenting with republicanism and various types of aristocratic or mercantile cabals, but Dudley would not grasp the nettle of what to do if the tree was dead, if monarchy had morphed into tyranny, or official religious doctrine had fallen into error. He was not alone. How could perceptive critics of the regime suggest reform measures if the institution most obviously in need of reform was the monarchy itself? The poet and one-time tutor to Prince Henry during his father's reign, John Skelton, found the answer, in the 1520s, by attacking Cardinal Wolsey, the king's principal adviser, who wielded considerable power – and not only wielded it but abused it:

> It is a wondrous case
> That the king's grace
> Is toward him so minded
> And so far blinded,
> That he cannot perceive
> How he doth him deceive ...[6]

To blame the king's advisers was the only oblique way to criticize royal policy. Sometimes it could be of advantage to the sovereign himself. For example, Henry VIII was very happy to send Edmund Dudley to the block as a scapegoat. But it was not always safe for writers to use this escape route. In 1536-1537, when the Pilgrimage of Grace for the Commonwealth broke out in response to the Dissolution of the Monasteries and other aspects of religious policy, the leaders directed their ire at Thomas Cromwell, Wolsey's successor. But this did not save them from Henry's wrath and the ruthless suppression of their revolt. Small wonder that Skelton was far too canny to have his political critique printed, and it only circulated in handwritten form during his lifetime.

How could the commonwealth be rescued from a tyrant? If rebellion failed, it was folly for critics to speak out. One man who did dare to give Henry advice – though only from the safety of Antwerp – was William Tyndale. In 1527, while in exile and disgrace for producing his unauthorized English translation of the New Testament, he also wrote a treatise on government. On first examination it is difficult to see why the author might have felt nervous at his book falling into Henry's hands. Indeed, when the king did receive a copy, he was delighted with it. It was entitled *The Obedience of a Christian Man*, and in it the reformer gave his full weight to the concept of the hierarchical society, basing his argument squarely on Scripture. The thirteenth chapter of the letter to the Romans declared quite unequivocally:

Let every soul submit himself unto the authority of the higher powers. For there is no power but of God. The powers that be are ordained of God. Whosoever therefore resisteth power, resisteth the ordinance of God. And they that resist, shall receive to themselves damnation.

Expatiating on this, Tyndale explained that the king stood in the place of God, 'and representeth God himself and is without all comparison [superior to] his subjects; yet let him put off that, and become a brother, doing and leaving undone all things in respect of the commonwealth'.[7]

Tyndale was writing in the aftermath of the Peasants' War (1524-1525), a socio-religious German uprising, which had ended in a bloodbath and the slaughter of some 100,000 rebels. Some leaders of the ill-armed hordes who rose against their masters claimed divine sanction for challenging injustice and exploitation. Luther had been concerned to dissociate himself and his followers from the radicals and had denounced them in the most violent language. Tyndale, his English admirer, followed suit. For if there was one thing worse than tyranny, it was insurrection. At this stage of the Reformation there was no question in Evangelical circles of the divine ordering of society being challenged. If a ruler played the tyrant, his or her subjects had no other course but to submit, leaving all judgement in the hands of God, to whom alone sovereigns were responsible. For his part, Tyndale understood very well who he was dealing with. Henry might be pleased with some aspects of *The Obedience of a Christian Man*, but that would not make it safe for the exile to return. For Tyndale had made known his disapproval of the king's matrimonial manoeuvres, and for that Henry never forgave him.

There was only one man sufficiently committed to the commonwealth ideal and devious enough to bring about reform while, at the same time, serving the Tudor monster. He achieved this squaring of the circle by persuading Henry that the changes necessary for the well-being of the people were also in the king's best interests. The Pilgrims of Grace were quite right in blaming Thomas Cromwell for the religious changes they lamented. Cromwell's political and religious thinking had been shaped by two forces: political realism acquired during several years spent in Renaissance Florence, and Evangelical Christianity learned in the 1520s from the writings of Erasmus and Luther.

Some historians have suggested that Cromwell took Niccolò Machiavelli for his master. It is more likely that these two clear-headed pragmatists reached similar conclusions from their studies of the Medici, the Borgias and their enemies. Societies are best served by enlightened rulers who have the power to achieve beneficial policies, even if that means forcing the people to accept what they cannot immediately conceive to be in their best interests. The most momentous decade of the century was 1530–1540, the years of Cromwell's ascendancy. By his personal relationship with the king and his skilful manipulation of Parliament, he broke the link between the English Church and Rome, he put an end to a millennium of English monasticism, he supported Evangelical preachers and ran an effective propaganda machine, he worked for closer links with the Lutheran princes, and he masterminded several schemes of social reform. He even persuaded Henry to sanction an official English Bible (which, ironically, was in large measure based on the work of Tyndale).

These were all significant steps towards the achievement of a Christian commonwealth. Inevitably, Cromwell made many enemies. In 1540 they gained the upper hand with Henry and brought Cromwell to the block. But by then it was too late to reverse what had been begun.

That is not to say that some Reformation measures could not be cancelled, nor that England was, by 1540, a Protestant nation. What was more important than specific statutes, or the 'decluttering' of churches or the disappearance of ancient abbeys from the landscape, was a shaking up of people's beliefs and attitudes, a disorientation that affected the whole of society. As Greg Walker has observed:

> An earthquake may shake houses, break windows, even bring walls and bridges crashing to the ground, but the buildings can be rebuilt and all the damage is eventually made good. Similarly, the Henrician Reformation did not introduce any fundamental changes that were not subsequently reversed, revised, ameliorated, or adapted in later reigns. But those who experienced that Reformation, like those who have lived through an earthquake, were never quite the same thereafter. They never trod the ground with quite the same degree of confidence, never trusted with the same degree of blithe assurance to the solidity of bricks and mortar, and never again took their cultural heritage for granted in the ways they once had.[8]

A different metaphor might describe English religious energy built up like water behind a dam and only waiting for the opening of the sluice. That opening occurred in 1547, when Henry VIII died. At last, it seemed, years of confusion that had seen the execution, imprisonment or exile of both Catholics and Lutherans – those unable to adjust their beliefs to the bewildering toing and froing of royal policy – could now be consigned to history. An English Christian commonwealth could be established. The accession of the third Tudor was greeted with euphoria similar to that which had welcomed the second:

> the evangelical Reformation under Edward VI . . . was a movement of hope and moral fervour, capable of generating a mood of intense excitement, so intense that by 1549 thousands of people over

hundreds of square miles in south-east England were prepared to gather in 'the camping time'.[9]

These uprisings were expressions of social unrest, of long-standing rural discord between the haves and the have-nots. Yet, ironically, what they led to was the failure by an Evangelical, reformist regime to set up a Christian commonwealth. The king's uncle, Edward Seymour, Lord Protector, Duke of Somerset, embodying the principle that the godly prince should rule for the good of all his people, sent out commissioners to explore the grievances expressed by the rural underclass against major landholders who were encroaching on common land and in other ways infringing what were held by many people to be their ancient rights. He made a tentative start by disparking some royal forest and then introduced more far-reaching legislation into Parliament. But he lacked the dictatorial power of Henry VIII to enforce change. The vested interests represented in Lords and Commons rejected or simply ignored these reform measures. Out in the shires of eastern and southern England, members of the underclass, heartened by the official rhetoric, grew impatient at its slow implementation and took matters into their own hands. Marching under such titles as the 'Commonwealth of Kirk', they set about dismantling hedges, commandeering stock and emptying barns. Although the activists firmly rejected the accusation, they were denounced by the political elite as 'rebels'. Somerset thus faced pressure from both sides. He was trapped by the essential contradiction within the Evangelical social contract: the godly prince had to ensure the well-being of all his subjects but was expected to punish those who resisted divinely appointed rulers in pursuit of their own well-being. As the pressure mounted, he feverishly did deals with various groups of protesters. Then, when commonwealth zealots under the leadership of Robert Kett seized control of Norwich, England's second city, he was forced to send in troops (including German mercenaries). It was the end of the commonwealth experiment and, two and a half years later, the end of Edward Seymour, who was brought to the block by his powerful enemies.

However, the ideal of a just society going hand in hand with Evangelical religion did not die with him. Something really important happened in Edward's reign – something his father had refused to countenance. For the first time, English Evangelicals were free to be in contact with their Continental counterparts. The two most vibrant centres of reformed Christianity were Geneva and Zurich. The church leaders there had parted company with Wittenberg over their understanding of the presence of Christ in the communion service, and it was only in 1549 that John Calvin in Geneva and Heinrich Bullinger in Zurich had reached an accord on this thorny issue. For England's Evangelical theologians, the new access to the continent was timely. Several of them already had strong ties with friends in the major European centres of reform. Now (with the exception of the dwindling number of scholars who held fast to the teachings of the late Martin Luther who had died in 1546) they could make common cause in the pursuit of Europe-wide Reformation.

But what was now promoted by the reformist bishops, proclaimed by government-authorized preachers and enshrined in the first vernacular Book of Common Prayer (1549) was not accepted by all who called themselves Protestants. Everyone in the Evangelical underworld, suddenly free from censorship and the fear of interrogation, was able to enjoy and expound his or her own religious opinions. The result was ideological chaos, as the Edwardian Bishop of Gloucester, John Hooper, reported in a letter to Bullinger:

> The anabaptists . . . give me much trouble with their opinions respecting the incarnation of the Lord; for they deny altogether that Christ was born of the virgin Mary according to the flesh. They contend that a man who is reconciled to God is without sin, and free from all stain of concupiscence, and that nothing of the old Adam remains in his nature; and a man, they say, who is thus regenerate cannot sin. They add that all hope of pardon is taken away from those who, after having received the Holy Ghost, fall into sin. They maintain a fatal necessity, and that beyond and besides that will of his which he has revealed to us in the scriptures, God hath another will by which he altogether acts under some kind of necessity . . .
> There are some who deny that man is endued with a soul different from that of a beast, and subject to decay. Alas! Not only are those heresies reviving among us which were formerly dead and buried, but new ones are springing up every day. There are such libertines

and wretches, who are daring enough in their conventicles not only to deny that Christ is the Messiah and Saviour of the world, but also to call that blessed Seed a mischievous fellow and deceiver of the world. On the other hand, a great portion of the kingdom so adheres to the popish faction, as altogether to set at nought God and the lawful authority of the magistrates; so that I am greatly afraid of a rebellion and civil discord. May the Lord restrain restless spirits, and destroy the counsels of Achitophel![10]

The bishop was here using the word 'anabaptist' as a catch-all term to embrace the multiple shades of opinion on the radical wing of the Reformation. The rejection of infant baptism in favour of adult or believers' baptism was not the identifying mark of all Protestant extremists, except insofar as it symbolized dissociation from the concept of the state church. All Christians faced the challenge of being in the world but not of it. Luther, Calvin, Zwingli, Bullinger, Cranmer and other leaders within the mainstream Evangelical movement thought in terms of national churches, supported by civil authorities that, in the last analysis, had the right to compel all citizens to attend common worship and consent to common doctrine. For them, discipleship included the responsibility to *reform* society, to bring it into line with the moral imperatives of the kingdom of God. Radicals, by contrast, regarded all earthly states as irredeemable. For them the way of the cross was laid down in 2 Corinthians 6.14f.:

Do not try to work as equals with unbelievers, for it cannot be done. How can right and wrong be partners? How can light and darkness live together? How can Christ and the Devil agree? What does a believer have in common with an unbeliever? How can God's temple come to terms with pagan idols? . . . The Lord says, 'You must leave them and separate yourselves from them . . .'

On this basis (though, again, it must be stressed we should not generalize about beliefs held in the hydra-headed movement) we can identify common radical characteristics such as rejection of civil laws, pacifism, refusal to accept secular office, and disinclination to be bound by conventional worship.

Like so much in the Reformation debate, what was fundamentally at stake was *authority*. Once the concept of 'Christ's vicar', deputed to adjudicate on all matters of doctrine and practice, had been abandoned, decision-making became a personal affair. The believer was guided by the Bible (as he or she interpreted it) and/or the inner voice of the Holy Spirit. This insulated radicals from all the laws, customs, traditions and conventions that governed and framed the lives of their neighbours. Yet, having said that, we immediately have to recognize that personal revelation was *not*, in practice, the motivation for radicals. They could not help being pack animals. They formed groups, sometimes confederations, that inevitably came under the control of persuasive preachers, charismatic personalities or firebrand demagogues. Every sect developed its own doctrinal emphases, rules and methods of internal discipline, including excommunication.

When, in 1553, the boy king died, to be succeeded by his virulently Catholic half-sister, Mary Tudor, a significant number (perhaps as many as 800) of the staunchest individuals fled the realm. Whither could they go? To those Continental centres where 'Reformed' regimes had been established – where successful Christian commonwealths were flourishing. The impact of this migration is incalculable.

3

The genie out of the lamp

The availability of a vernacular Bible was far and away the most important single cause of all the disputes arising among English Christians, and their divisions into a variety of groups and sects. In this chapter, therefore, we step aside from the chronological development of our story to clarify which Bible versions partisans were reading (or not reading) and how they helped to shape arguments and reinforce prejudices.

William Tyndale, through his translation into English of the New Testament and parts of the Old Testament, established the pattern and set the tone of vernacular Scripture for the next 80 years. His contribution to the development of the national psyche would be utterly impossible to exaggerate. The English Bible, placed in the hands of every man and woman who could and would read it, became the most revolutionary book in the history of England. More than that: carried in the saddle-bags and cabin trunks of merchants, sailors, officials and missionaries, it became the main vehicle for conveying divine revelation to those parts of the world being opened up to European influence.

The 30-year-old scholar who travelled to Germany and the Low Countries seeking a publisher for his New Testament in 1524 was no revolutionary. Initially, his concern was to aid the process of English church reform from within by seeking the patronage of Bishop Tunstall of London, a scholar not inimical to progressive humanist thinking. Only when he drew a blank in his own country was Tyndale drawn irresistibly to Germany. We do not know whether he met Luther, but he certainly mingled with Lutheran scholars. When, at Worms in 1526, he arranged printing of the first edition of his New Testament, the book carried an epilogue explaining the Lutheran understanding of St Paul's teaching about law and grace. The impact was explosive. Because the debate started by the Wittenberg monk was one of the big issues of the day, entrepreneurs were not slow to see the market potential of the new book and were prepared to take serious risks smuggling it into England. The copies sold faster than the bishops' agents could sniff them out and destroy them, and that commercial fact alone indicates how potentially subversive Tyndale's New Testament was. In effect, it wrong-footed the ecclesiastical authorities. By 1530, they were burning not just vernacular Scriptures but also people who owned vernacular Scriptures. The message sent out seemed to be clear to most of the population: they could believe either the written word of God or officers of the Church, whose claim to base their authority on the word of God was now in doubt.

There were three reasons why this particular book was so effective in challenging traditional dogma. First of all, it was written in a fluent, idiomatic English that most literate people could easily understand. Second, it brought together readers of different kinds. Artisans raised on Lollard texts bought copies. Students in the universities acquired them. They found their way into the houses of the gentry and nobility, and even into the royal court. They were Trojan horses with Lutheran doctrine concealed in their bellies, for subsequent editions carried extensive Evangelical glosses. But finally, and most importantly of all, even without the additional commentaries, the plain text offered readings of the Greek that were at variance with those long regarded by Catholic expositors as infallible.

The very nature of the Church itself was called into question. The Greek *ecclesia*, translated as 'church' by St Jerome, Tyndale now rendered as 'assembly'. The word rendered as 'priest' in the Vulgate became in the new translation 'elder'. Instead of 'bishop', Tyndale reverted to the more generalized Greek concept of 'overseer'. More crucially, he went along with Luther in insisting that *metanoiete* meant 'repent' and not 'do penance'. No wonder the members of the ecclesiastical top brass were outraged. No wonder many people troubled by or critical of the state of the Church embraced this fresh understanding with relief and delight. It takes no leap of imagination to envisage a reader of Tyndale's New Testament thinking, 'Ah, now I see where we've all been going wrong,' and being elated by this fresh revelation.

So two concepts of 'Church' now existed in the public forum – images totally incompatible with each other. One reflected the world view of

St Jerome (c. AD 347–430) when a monolithic, newly Christianized empire was defending its borders against paganism, and regional bishops were taking their place alongside their civic counterparts in defining faith and protecting it from internal heresy and external persecution. The intervening 11 centuries had seen this union developed by popes and bishops who were, in effect, high priests of Christendom and, alongside emperors and kings, had triumphed over their spiritual and temporal foes. The other concept, advanced by the self-styled prophets of a new revelation, pointed out that the Church had been corrupted by power and needed to return to the simple gospel of apostolic times. Implicit in the reformers' message but not yet proclaimed with zealous confidence was the suggestion that the very structure of the Church needed to be brought into line with the Bible.

Yet more fundamental than such issues of exegesis was the encouragement of individualism. Intellectual freedom was not invented by the reformers. Questioning and disputation had, for centuries, been built into the structures of higher education, and Renaissance people were nothing if not inquisitive and speculating beings. But the idea that the individual was *totally* responsible for making his or her contract with God was an axe laid to the root of the concept of medieval society. There could be no Christian commonwealth if members were at liberty to believe or not believe in the basic tenets of the Christian faith. Or, to turn that proposition around, if people were free to interpret the Bible for themselves, then a Christian commonwealth could only exist among those who shared a common interpretation. In other words, there might exist within one nation several religious commonwealths. Those in positions of power in Church and State were essentially faced with the choice of enforcing 'official' doctrine or granting freedom of conscience in matters spiritual. It would take a long and sanguinary process to make the Western world ready to embrace religious toleration. In the 1520s and 1530s, the conservative reaction to the 'German heresy' was vehement, bitter and unyielding. Leading the charge in England for the teaching and authority of the ancient faith was Thomas More, who engaged in a vitriolic literary debate with Tyndale and carried out his own mini-Inquisition to bring heretics to the flames. The remainder of the sixteenth century witnessed increasing conflict between emancipated students of the word of God and those who were intent on imposing standard interpretations. This latter educational and hortatory process we will explore in the next chapter. First we will watch the genie of the Bible, now freed from the lamp of church–state control, perform its extraordinary magic.

There was no official opposition to the idea of vernacular Scripture. Translations existed in other countries, and Henry VIII had declared himself in favour of authorizing an English Bible – when the time was right. In reality what that meant was his realm could have its own version when it suited the king's political agenda to endorse one. Any such hypothetical translation would have to be approved by the church hierarchy. Now that the opposition had stolen a march on the bishops, that was going to be very difficult to achieve. In fact, a decade would pass before Henry's subjects were presented with a royally approved English version of Holy Writ. Then, in 1537, rather like the proverbial London bus, two came along together.

Much had changed in those tumultuous ten years. It might even be no exaggeration to say that everything had changed. Thomas Cromwell had replaced Thomas More as principal whisperer in the king's ear. The ex-Lord Chancellor had died under the headman's axe, and Catholic vigilantism was weakened by his passing (until such time as Henry should need to display his anti-heresy credentials). Cromwell planned his campaign with precision and executed it with tireless energy. He had masterminded England's breach with Rome and was edging foreign policy towards some kind of understanding with the German Protestant states. He began the assault on the monasteries, the major bastions of support for the papacy. He took every opportunity to insinuate reform-minded men into positions of influence in the court, in Parliament and in the shires. He commissioned Evangelical propaganda and patronized radical preachers. The one other thing needful, the coping stone of his strategy, was the English Bible. If he could persuade the king to sanction that, there could never be any going back. Place the word of God in every church and it would be very difficult for any subsequent reactionary regime to remove it. Even if it was banned, thousands of copies would remain in existence, read and cherished by generations of English men and women.

This was a project Cromwell had on the stocks for several years. He set the bishops to putting their heads together to come up with a new

Bible version, but progress was painfully slow and it may well be that the minister was not really interested in its success. He favoured initiatives being carried out by Evangelicals working abroad. In Antwerp he had his old friend, Miles Coverdale, tackling the project, and it was also engaging the talents of John Rogers, who was chaplain to the merchant community there. The fly in the ointment was Tyndale. Nothing would receive royal blessing that had about it the odour of the arch-heretic. But, at Henry's instigation, Tyndale had been betrayed into the hands of his enemies, and in the autumn of 1536 the pioneer translator was publicly executed near Brussels. Ironically, his death gave new life to his writings. Within months, while Henry enjoyed his reputation as a heresy-hunter, both Coverdale and Rogers published their versions (Rogers' under the pseudonym 'Thomas Matthew'), both of which were much reliant on Tyndale's version. The title page of both books lauded Henry VIII as God's appointed head of the Christian commonwealth, now graciously nurturing the spiritual life of his people. And the king commissioned a new mural for his privy chamber, which proclaimed that, thanks to Henry, 'religion is restored' and 'the doctrines of God have begun to be held in honour'.

The story of Tudor Bibles was far from over. There was much niggling against the Antwerp versions in conservative quarters. Cromwell, therefore, set in motion a belt-and-braces measure. Coverdale and a committee of scholars were instructed to produce a new text, based entirely on the best Greek and Hebrew documents, with annotations pointing out variants in the originals. It was to be an immaculate work of scholarship, avoiding the taint of Lutheran propaganda. The story of what came to be known as the Great Bible has all the elements of a spy thriller. Establishing an unimpeachable text in every parish church by royal authority was so important that Cromwell had it printed in Paris, where the best workshops were, and ploughed his own money into the production. For a while, it was kept secret from the Catholic officials. When they eventually swooped on the presses, Cromwell's agents managed to smuggle out plates and proof pages. The Great Bible was, some would say, the minister's greatest achievement. It was certainly his last. Within 15 months of the publication, in April 1539, Cromwell was dead, outwitted at last by his Catholic enemies and executed as a traitor.

His book did not fail him. It acted like adrenalin on the Evangelical community. Not only could believers read the Bible in the privacy of their own homes; they could also read it to their illiterate servants and share it with their neighbours without fear of the knock on the door in the middle of the night. Now a new word was added to the language – or, perhaps, a new nuance was added to an old word. A 'gospeller' was one ardent in the faith who went about to teach others from the 'plain word of God'. 'Gospeller' became a term of abuse for those enthusiasts before the equally opprobrious 'Puritan' was invented. Such activity was perceived as a threat because it raised the individual above society. For every reader, Scripture became *the* authority. There could be no debate. For example, when Anne Askew (burned for heresy in 1546) was pressed to say whether she accepted the official doctrine of Christ's real presence in the consecrated elements at the mass, she gave a telling reply. In the words of her own account:

I answered . . . the eternal son of God [does not] dwell there. In witness whereof I recited again the history of Bel, and the ix chapter of Daniel, the vii and xvii of Acts, and the xxiiii of Matthew, concluding thus: I neither wish death, nor yet fear his might, God have the praise thereof with thanks.[1]

Anne was no scholar, but she was a dedicated student of the Bible who could quote lengthy passages of it by heart.

Many people were in the grip of Bible mania. Not only was the book the subject of sermons and alehouse debate but also certain 'malicious minds' had 'taken upon them by printed ballads, rhymes, etc, subtly and craftily to instruct his Highness' people . . . untruly'. The words were from a statute of 1543: 'An Act for the Advancement of True Religion'. Henry was panicking. Having given permission for his people to put their trust in the Bible, not the pope, he discovered that some were putting their trust in the Bible, not the king. This Act – surely one of the most ridiculous in the history of Parliament – tried to legislate who was and who was not allowed to read the sacred text. No one below the rank of gentleman was permitted to read the Great Bible. Women were denied the privilege, though the regulation was subsequently relaxed in favour of ladies of breeding. Their menfolk were permitted to use Scripture but only for their private devotional purposes. A freedom granted, then withdrawn, is very much worse than a freedom denied. The Act provoked angry response. From the safety of Basel, one pamphleteer poured scorn on the idea of social hierarchy as a gauge for access to the word of God: 'there are more gentle fools than yeoman fools, number compared to number . . . whoever thou art that for any cause would keep poor men from the Scriptures, I say thou art one of the Pharisees' fools.'[2]

Two and a half years later, in an impassioned speech in Parliament, Henry made a plea for Christian unity. But what, exactly, were the English to unite behind? As Professor Marshall has observed:

> Henry wanted his people to travel with him, but the destination was bafflingly uncertain. His theology was a moving target, a work in progress, a nest of contradictions. The King spoke often of 'the Word of God', but didn't trust people to read the bible faithfully; he disallowed the authority of tradition, but retained his right to prescribe venerable ceremonies on a case-by-case basis . . .[3]

From this point the evolution of a united English Church based on written revelation became even more complicated. The nation had an authorized vernacular Bible and an anointed king who was supreme in Church and State. If Henry and his bishops had been able to come up with a reformed, non-Catholic liturgy and body of doctrine, backed by statute law, the majority of English people would have fallen into line, but new voices were increasingly heard in the theological debate. They came, not from Wittenberg and the north German Lutheran heartland, but from centres of 'Reformed' Protestantism, the Swiss cities of Geneva and Basel and the Rhineland towns of Strasbourg, Frankfurt and Wesel. As we have seen, links with the radicals in these places were already being forged in Henry VIII's reign, and during the minority of Edward VI teachers and preachers such as Peter Martyr, Martin Bucer and John à Lasco were encouraged to travel to England to take up influential positions. However, it was the exile of several hundred Evangelicals in the reign of Mary Tudor that pressed the accelerator of theological change.

At this point it is important to set the 1620 departure of the Pilgrim Fathers within what had become, over the preceding century, almost a *tradition* of religious migration. People always have travelled, and always will travel, to where they perceive the grass to be greener. Zealous scholars, for example, had long been accustomed to living peripatetically, seeking out the more prestigious teachers of the day and helped by the academic lingua franca of Latin. Merchants and bankers, of course, established foreign branches and some settled permanently abroad. Craftspeople – particularly Flemish textile workers – found it profitable to set up shop in England from the late fifteenth century. Now, however, a new breed of migrants became part of the fluidity of European life. Persecuted English Catholics sought Continental havens. Evangelicals from France and the Low Countries crossed the Channel in the other direction.

An example of how whole communities could be uprooted, transplanted and uprooted again, in these chaotic years, is furnished by Valérond Poullain and his Reformed congregation who travelled from Lille in 1551–1552. He gained permission for some 44 families, all following trades connected with the textile industry, to settle at Glastonbury. There they established their own church and were allowed the freedom to maintain their own patterns of worship. Their English sojourn was, unfortunately, brief. On the accession of Queen Mary the Glastonbury immigrants were given permission 'quietly to depart'. They resettled in Frankfurt where, within months, they were joined by some of their former English hosts.

And it is Frankfurt that provides the link with the next chapter in the story of the English Bible. One of the first immigrants to settle here was William Whittingham, a notable and much travelled scholar, who had made close study of the Lutheran and Calvinist styles of Reformation. Now that all restraints on Bible translation had been removed, it became the object of ongoing scholarship. Many fresh minds were being brought to bear on early texts in an effort to understand their finer nuances. Whittingham was one of those who devoted themselves to this painstaking task. It became apparent to him that the Great Bible could be improved on. The result of Whittingham's team emerged from the press in 1560 – the Geneva Bible. Why Geneva? Because Whittingham and his colleagues had moved on, both geographically and doctrinally. Initially they had discovered, as they thought, the perfect church. One of them described the Frankfurt congregation, in a letter to English friends, as totally without blemish and 'free from all dregs of superstitious ceremonies'.[4] Such a rosy view did not survive more than a few months. Discord broke out among the English exiles between those who wanted to continue using the 1552 Prayer Book and those who wished to see the vernacular liturgy further purified in line with other associates who took their lead from John Calvin. Factions polarized around the uncompromising John Knox and Richard Cox (who valued the link with his suffering friends in England above doctrinal niceties). In 1555, Knox and some of his supporters withdrew to Geneva. William Whittingham was of their number.[5]

There were excellent, practical reasons for continuing the translation work in Geneva. Calvin – himself a fine biblical scholar – was attracting some of the best linguists and theologians to the city. The Geneva Bible was a thorough revision of the Great Bible based on original texts. It was designed for personal study and, to that end, included novel features. Maps and illustrations helped clarify Holy Land topography and history, as well as stirring the imagination. Dividing the text into numbered verses helped readers locate passages and share them with others. Then there were the inevitable marginalia. Some notes provided clarification by explaining difficult words and by drawing attention to variant readings. But other notes were interpretative; that is, they put a Calvinist gloss on the text. Specifically, they attacked Catholic ceremonies and dogmas from which, in the editors' views, the English Church had not been sufficiently cleansed, and they took every opportunity to emphasize the Reformed doctrine of election (the action of a sovereign God in predetermining who should be saved – and who should not). Moreover, with the passage of time and the issuing of fresh editions, the tone of the marginalia became more trenchant. It is not surprising that this should be the case. The wars of religion on the nearer continent (1562-1598) were being fought with mounting hatred and fanaticism on both sides. Scotland was in the grip of a conflict also exacerbated by religious divisions. Ireland, where most subjects of the Crown were Catholic, refused to be pacified, and papal agents were engaged in various attempts to destabilize the regime.

Yet it was Calvinist winds – rather than those blowing from Rome – that most readily ruffled the feathers of the establishment after the accession of Queen Elizabeth in 1558: 'Satan is envious of our prosperity,' wrote Richard Cox, now Bishop of Ely, to a friend in 1573: 'It is not enough to have the papists our enemies, without stirring up men . . . who are labouring to bring about a revolution in our church.' Bishop Cox was alluding to a printed manifesto recently circulated:

Articles drawn up by certain Englishmen now disturbers of the state of the Anglican church:

I. The names and functions of archbishops, bishops and other officials, ought to be altogether abolished.

II. The election of the ministers of the word and sacraments should be restored to the people, as not belonging to the episcopal office.

III. No one ought to be confined to set forms of prayer.

IV. No sacrament ought to be administered without being preceded by a sermon, preached, and not read . . .

VI. All the ministers of the church ought to be equal, not one superior to another.

VII. They condemn the order of confirmation, in which the bishops lay their hands upon the children on their repeating the catechism, and pray the Lord that he may vouchsafe to increase in them the knowledge of his word and godliness . . .

IX. They cannot endure the reading of the holy scriptures in the church.[6]

Cox's complaint was directed not at Calvinist predestinarianism (with which many English clergy agreed) but at the determination to see the formularies and rituals of the Church of England remodelled in accordance with those of the Church of Geneva.

When the writer drew attention to Reformed objections to the 'reading of the holy scriptures in the church', he was referring to the latest round in the 'battle of the Bibles'. For sheer scholarship, the Geneva Bible had outshone the Great Bible but, rather than endorse it with all its radical elements, the Elizabethan regime produced yet another translation. Created by an episcopal committee, it was appropriately called the Bishops' Bible.

The new book, essentially a revision of the Great Bible, bore all the hallmarks of being made by a committee. It was very varied in quality and it failed to win the hearts of the people. Even though no licence was given until 1575 for the Geneva Bible to be printed in England, it far outsold its rivals. Between 1560 and 1644 the Geneva Bible appeared in over 140 editions. Most households throughout the land acquired a copy. It had a formative impact on the language, being quoted and referenced by authors and poets from Shakespeare to Milton. The Bishops' Bible, by contrast, though officially used in worship, could not boast more than 65 imprints between 1568 and 1633.

Whittingham's Bible was not the only link connecting the prosaic life of an English parish with the 'heaven on earth' of the Genevan state church:

> The people are everywhere exceedingly inclined to the better part. The practice of joining in church music has very much conduced to this. For as soon as they had once commenced singing in public, in only one little church in London, immediately not only the churches in the neighbourhood, but even the towns far distant, began to vie with each other in the same practice. You may now see at Paul's Cross, after the service, six thousand persons, old and young, of both sexes, all singing together and praising God.[7]

So reported John Jewel, Bishop of Salisbury, in March 1560. He was probably being a tad optimistic, but there is no doubt that congregational singing of the Psalms, a custom brought back by the returning Marian exiles, proved popular as an educational as well as devotional device through which words of Scripture lodged themselves in the minds of worshippers. In 1562, Thomas Sternhold, John Hopkins and others produced the first complete psalter, which presented the Psalms in ballad metre and set them to melodies imported from France and the Netherlands or borrowed from popular songs of the day. There was a world of cultural difference between these novelties and the worship music of the Chapel Royal beloved of the queen. Differences of style were as important as differences of theological substance. Queen Elizabeth, who loved the motets of Thomas Tallis and William Byrd, dismissed the new music as 'Geneva jigs' and regarded those who sang them as what today might be called 'happy-clappies'.

The king who came to the throne as James I in 1603 shared his predecessor's loathing of all things Genevan, including the Bible: 'I could never yet see a Bible well-translated in English; but I think that of all, that Geneva is the worst . . . in the Geneva translation, some notes are partisan, untrue, seditious and savouring of traitorous conceits.'[8]

The main outcome of the 1604 Hampton Court Conference, summoned by James, was – as is well known – the King James or Authorized Version (KJV). It was a thorough revision of the Bishops' Bible carried out by a committee of 47 'safe' scholars. Like its predecessors, it was the only version approved for use in churches. Crucially, it was devoid of glosses. It would be wrong, however, to assume that England now possessed a universally beloved standard text. Many people still stuck rigidly to the Geneva Bible. Not until well into the second half of the seventeenth century could the KJV be said to have won the battle of the books.

There is one more episode in the adventure of the English Bible that needs to be mentioned. It is a footnote to the story of Puritan New World settlement, but it does emphasize the irresistible power of the demand for vernacular Scripture. About 1561 an English Catholic seminary was established at Douai in the Netherlands and relocated to Rheims in France in 1578. Here priests were trained to be sent to England to minister to Catholic recusants and to be a spearhead for the reconversion of the nation. It was here that yet another English Bible was conceived. It was a translation from the Vulgate. The New Testament appeared in 1582, and the entire canon in 1610. After half a century of resistance to making the word of God easily available to lay people, Catholic authorities did have some explaining to do. They insisted that people should only resort to the holy text under the guidance of their clergy, and they stressed that the issue of the Douai-Rheims Version did not involve a change of Catholic teaching or 'pastoral practice':

we do not publish this translation upon any erroneous opinion of necessity, or that the holy Scriptures should always be in our mother tongue, or that Scriptures ought or were ordained by God to be read indifferently of all, or could even be easily understood of everyone that reads or hears them in a known language: or that they were not often through man's malice or infirmity, pernicious and very harmful to many: or that we generally and absolutely deemed it more convenient in itself, and more agreeable to God's word and honor or edification of the faithful, to have them turned into vulgar tongues than to be kept and studied only in the ecclesiastical learned languages. Not for these nor any similar causes do we translate this sacred book. Rather we do so upon special consideration of the present time, state, and condition of our country, unto which a diversity of things are either necessary or profitable and therapeutic, now, rather than in a time of peace in the Church where such things were neither much required nor perhaps entirely tolerable.[9]

The genie was well and truly out of the bottle. All basically educated English people could now read the foundation Christian text and in a version of their choice. But, whatever translation readers opted for, it still did not speak with 100 per cent crystal clarity. It had always needed to be explained, expounded, interpreted. In that regard, nothing had changed. Different groups of English believers still looked to their chosen leaders to shed light on the word of God. Preaching was still important – perhaps even more so, now that the growth of Christian diversity had become irrevocably established and shaped by hortatory styles imported from abroad.

4

Home truths from abroad

As we pick up our story again in the 1550s, it would be difficult to over-emphasize the traumatic impact of Mary Tudor's reign on educated English Protestants. The reimposition of Catholicism was for Protestants a heart-rending experience and one that lived long in the memory, not only of those who experienced it, but also of their children and children's children. It taught them that what they valued as religious truth is a fragile flower easily crushed and one that must be protected at all costs. With the benefit of hindsight, we know that the pro-papal reactionary regime came to an end after a little more than five years and that the reign of childless Queen Mary was superseded by that of her humanist-Evangelical half-sister. Contemporaries did not enjoy that comforting foreknowledge. To them it seemed that the Reformation had been stopped in its tracks. Although some Evangelicals did harbour thoughts of rebellion, there were only two things the 'godly' could practically do. Writing in the very early days of the new regime, a foreign observer remarked to a friend in Zurich:

> we must expect things more atrocious, unless God in his mercy look upon that church, on behalf of which I do not think I have any need to request your prayers; for you know from your own experience how excellent are the members of Christ in that country.[1]

Apart from the minority who did go into exile, English Evangelicals could only suffer for their faith (perhaps accepting persecution as divine chastening) and look for support to their co-religionists abroad. As matters turned out, this set the pattern, not just for the years 1553–1558, but also for the reign of Elizabeth I that followed – and beyond. Reaction to the Marian regime established thought patterns for years to come.

By the time Mary died in November 1558, religious allegiance among her subjects fell into five categories. The majority 'went with the flow'. Their consciences were not overburdened with theological niceties and they supported the life of their parish churches with all their traditional trappings. Then there were those who heartily rejoiced to see the back of the New Learning and hoped that the ups and downs of the last two decades were, at last, over. On the other side of the religious fence were the rebels. Some had taken up arms with Thomas Wyatt, who led an unsuccessful rising in 1554, but many more showed, in other ways, their disagreement with the papalist, pro-Spanish regime. They absented themselves from mass and mumbled in alehouses. Some went further and ended up in jail. More than 300 chose imprisonment or death. A minority, to whom we will return, left England for more congenial foreign havens. That left the 'Nicodemites'. These were Protestants who were deeply opposed to the regime but who would not forsake home, family and country for faith's sake. They worshipped with their Catholic neighbours and were careful not to draw attention to themselves.

'Nicodemite' was a term of contempt invented by John Calvin, the French theologian emerging as the fashionable leader of Protestant thinkers. This lawyer-cum-humanist scholar had developed a ruthlessly logical, black-and-white doctrinal programme that left no room for compromise, toleration or half measures. He had nothing but contempt for Protestants living in Catholic lands who outwardly conformed to the prevailing regimes. He branded them 'Nicodemites', after the prominent Jew, Nicodemus, who visited Jesus secretly by night because he did not want to be suspected of being a follower of the Messiah (John 3.1-21). But before we explore more closely John Calvin's teaching and why it was so influential, we need to understand the world into which it was born. Throughout the middle years of the century, Europe became *mouvementé* as groups and individuals responded to religious and political pressures, seeking places where they could settle, permanently or temporarily. The Church has never been without heresies. Most of them have tended to be regional in nature, and we can locate the affected areas on a map with a reasonable degree of accuracy. But from the 1520s onwards unorthodox belief became much more international – or, perhaps, 'intranational' would be a better word. Displaced believers seeking havens crossed frontiers and settled in other lands. English Catholics relocated to France. French Huguenots migrated to England. German Lutherans crossed the Baltic to Scandinavia. Anabaptists from the Spanish Netherlands found refuge in Saxony. English Protestants moved to the Swiss cantons. Some put down roots in their chosen havens. Others lived in what they hoped would be only a brief exile in centres where they could study at the feet of eminent theologians and plan the restoration of 'true religion' in their homeland. Most English Protestant exiles tended to make their homes in the Swiss or free imperial cities such as Geneva, Zurich, Strasbourg, Frankfurt and Basel, municipalities that fiercely guarded their independence from the neighbouring major powers.

In these nurseries of what came to be the 'Reformed' tradition, there was a basic doctrinal consensus but also a level of disagreement over some issues of faith and practice that boded ill for future harmony. Most Protestants were slow to be weaned from the principle of the state church. They accepted that rulers had the right to decide the religion of their subjects. The first assertion of the doctrine of holy resistance was aired in Magdeburg in 1550. The emperor Charles V, having won a crushing victory over the rebellious Lutheran princes in Germany, attempted to enforce a blanket return to Catholic orthodoxy, but the Protestants were not to be easily brought to heel and, in the peace negotiations that followed, Charles was obliged to offer concessions. However, the abandonment of certain customs and the toning down of contentious dogmas did not go far enough for the Protestants – hardly surprising since they were required to forswear justification by only faith and to agree to accept transubstantiation. By a large majority vote, they rejected the emperor's compromise document, the Augsburg Interim. Magdeburg was one of the hotspots of protest and the city's defiance was declared in several pamphlets. They reiterated the old fundamental belief that the powers that be are ordained by God and should, thus, be obeyed, *but* now they added a new caveat: if a ruler tried to abolish true religion, it was made clear by that act that he or she was not God's deputy. Such a ruler might, thus, lawfully be deposed. Shortly afterwards, the tide of war turned against the emperor, so the new teaching was not put to the test, but a vital 'balloon' had been released into the intellectual sky: personal conscience was now the arbiter, not only of personal obedience, but also of corporate action. If a body of Christians believed their ruler to be acting against their understanding of the will of God, they might use any means to remove him or her from office. For a few years, the full impact of this was not felt, but the balloon was still hovering and influencing public debate whenever church–state relations were under discussion.

The leading contender in the debate was John Calvin, the brilliant Parisian lawyer who was destined to become the Aquinas of Evangelicalism. His journey to theology took him through humanism and the law. His study of the classics and of legal niceties produced a cast of mind that was both profound and precisionist. It was an upsurge of violence in 1534 that thrust the 25-year-old intellectual out of the study and into the public arena. Up to this time, the French king, Francis I, had adopted a tolerant attitude towards Lutherans and other dissenters, largely out of deference to his much loved sister, Margaret of Navarre, who was greatly in sympathy with the reform movement and the patron of several Evangelical and humanist scholars. Then, in October 1534, a group of hot-headed dissidents distributed posters in Paris and other towns denouncing the Catholic doctrine of the mass. This 'Affair of the Placards' provoked great anger in establishment quarters and re-awakened the fear of social unrest, which was always a light sleeper.

Calvin was not involved in the demonstration, but he found it politic to move across the border into Genevan territory. Here he preached sermons and wrote books to encourage the French Protestants (Huguenots). In 1536, he published what began simply as a catechism designed to establish the main elements of Evangelical doctrine and help readers to distinguish them from papistical 'falsehood', but which developed into his history-changing magnum opus. *Institutes of the Christian Religion* was an instant success, and over the next 24 years four new editions were published, each longer than its predecessors, emerging finally as a monumental, detailed statement of Protestant belief. This seminal work, which dotted every theological 'i' and crossed every theological 't', leaving no wriggle room for the individual intellect, became a second Bible for Calvinists and was accepted widely by Evangelical regimes throughout Europe. It placed in their hands a resource that provided readers, preachers and teachers with not only the arguments to cast at their opponents but also the certainty to strengthen their resistance. It offered not finely reasoned evidence for their faith but the assurance that they were the elect of God who must inevitably triumph over all adversaries. Calvin's unyielding rigidity could not avoid provoking opposition from within Protestant ranks, and for a time he was banished from Geneva. But by 1541 he was back stronger than before and devoting his intellectual gifts to a new politico-religious structure for Church and State – in effect a complete rethinking of the concept of a Christian commonwealth.

It was, he claimed, self-evident from the New Testament that God intended the establishment of states governed by civil and ecclesiastical authorities working in perfect harmony. Under the rule of saints, the Church of Christ would be fully visible to all observers. The *raison d'être* of the Christian state was to ensure:

> That idolatry, blasphemy of the Name of God and against His truth and other scandals to religion, be not publicly set forth and broadcast among the people; that public peace be not troubled, that each be secured in what is his own, that men's intercourse may be without fraud and violence, in fine that among Christians there may be some public and visible form of religion and that humanity be settled among men.[2]

Calvin's utopia was no less authoritarian than any other contemporary European state. In fact, the lives of citizens were more closely monitored than those of people in any neighbouring principality. They had to be, because Geneva's populace was not just under civil law but under the law of God, and those in power were there to enforce obedience to the divine diktat, not only *pro bono publico*, but for the good of every citizen's eternal soul.

Calvin's Geneva was not a theocracy. Rather it was an attempt to balance the rights and responsibilities of the civic and religious leaders. Thus, he was at one with all Catholic and mainstream Protestant teachers in his fear of the anarchy that complete tolerance tended to encourage, and he upheld obedience to secular authority insofar as conscience allowed. In most states, any Christians who found themselves at odds with legally appointed rulers might offer only passive disobedience and must be prepared to suffer the consequences. *But* in Geneva, and other places that accepted the Genevan model, such conflict could not exist. Any members who disagreed with the hierarchy were, quite simply, *wrong*. The civic and church overseers acted in parallel and, theoretically, in harmony. The elected Civic Council was the supreme law-making and enforcing body. The parallel ecclesiastical institution was the Consistory, comprising pastors, teachers, elders and deacons who maintained pastoral oversight of the religious and moral life of the state. The collaboration of Council and Consistory produced a system that, in effect, differed little from that of the Inquisition.[3] Though Geneva never developed the mechanism of persecution instigated by the Sacred Office, the same methods of enforcing orthodoxy were employed: prying into citizens' lives, encouraging informers, excommunicating offenders and, in very rare cases, imposing the death penalty. The powers of the Consistory were breathtakingly wide:

Men and women were examined as to their religious knowledge, their criticisms of ministers, their absences from sermons, their use of charms, their family quarrels, as well as to more serious offences. Other examples, from the later activity of the Consistory in Calvin's time, show disciplinary procedure against a widow who prayed a 'requiescat in pace' on her husband's grave; for having fortunes told by gipsies; against a goldsmith for making a chalice; for saying that the incoming of French refugees had raised the cost of living and that a minister had declared that all those who had died earlier (i.e. before the Reformation) were damned; for dancing . . . against a woman of seventy who was about to marry a man of twenty-five; for declaring the Pope to be a good man; making a noise during a sermon, laughing during preaching; criticising Geneva for putting men to death on account of differences in religion; or singing a song defamatory of Calvin.[4]

For precisionists seeking heaven on earth, Calvin's polity seemed to fit the bill. John Knox, the firebrand Scottish reformer, thought it 'the most perfect school of Christ that ever was in the earth since the days of the apostles'.[5] Others, however, took the view enunciated in the next century by John Milton. He vigorously opposed the oppressive measures taken by community leaders who dared

> To force our consciences that Christ set free,
> And ride us with a classic hierarchy.

In the poet's opinion, 'New presbyter is but old priest writ large.'[6] It was a fair assessment: no regimen could force people to agree on what is right, and to do what is right. In Geneva and other places where the Calvinist package was accepted, there were frequent tensions between civic and church leaders and between government and people. However, we must keep at the back of our minds the fact that this was an authoritarian age in which societies were held together by power hierarchies. An infallible system of salvation, underpinned by an intricate theology and imposed by powerful or charismatic leaders, appealed (and continues to appeal in religious cults) to people unable or unwilling to examine the small print for themselves. Some of the *Mayflower* passengers would later fall into this category.

There were certainly very real flaws in a system that vested in one body the determination of the will of God for the state and all individual members thereof, and in another body the enforcement of the will of God. Thus, for example, candidates for public office (including membership of the Council) had to be approved by the Consistory and could be excommunicated by the Consistory. No one who fell foul of the church authorities could enjoy full citizenship rights. To be known to deviate from the doctrine laid down by Calvin was, in essence, to be banished from Geneva. This was rigid, ice-cold, sharp-edged Christianity.

Having discovered and established *the* divine blueprint for the Christian state, Calvin sought to imprint it on the minds of future generations and to spread it far beyond the walls of Geneva. In 1559, he persuaded the Civic Council to set up the Academy, an educational establishment in two parts – a preparatory school for the sons of citizens and a centre of high learning to which all were welcomed. This was arguably the reformer's greatest single achievement. It was an instant success, boasting 2,000 students within five years. Young men came from all over Protestant Europe, not only to master Latin, Greek, Hebrew and biblical studies, but also to absorb the ethos of the state church. Discipline was strict and punishments were administered in public. The day began and ended with prayers, and attendance at sermons by Calvin and other preachers was mandatory. For intellectual rigour, the Genevan Academy matched anything being imparted in Jesuit colleges. In fact, the two rival systems were very much in competition for the minds of believers. The Catholic college of Douai in the Spanish Netherlands was founded at about the same time, and both institutions were dedicated to providing their respective missionary movements with leaders equipped to win (or win back) the nations of Europe. As graduates from Geneva returned to England, Scotland, France, the Netherlands and elsewhere, they took with them two things: a detailed Reformed theology, including a crystalline church polity, and a sense of belonging to an international brotherhood of like-minded pastors and teachers.

However, the returning English exiles in 1559–1560 had some serious issues to contend with. One was that they did *not* all belong to 'an international brotherhood of like-minded pastors and teachers'. That is to say that, while they all broadly accepted the Calvinist schema, some of them had misgivings about aspects of it. Freed from the state-church structure in England, the settlers in various centres had established, not without internal conflicts, congregations with rules and rituals of their own devising, and doctrines based on their own interpretations of the word of God. The most fractious group was the emigrant church at Frankfurt. Under the leadership of first Richard Cox and later Robert Horne (both Cambridge theologians), the assembly used a form of worship based on the second Edwardian Prayer Book (1552). Others, however, wanted to adopt a wholly Calvinist order of service. The most virulent protester was the Scot John Knox, who eventually left with his followers for the more congenial atmosphere of Geneva. Desperate to prevent further fragmentation, Horne appealed to Bullinger to chair a conference that would draw up a church order acceptable to all the exiled English groups:

> we are in hopes that master Calvin will come back again, and that he will have both yourself and other learned men as his companions . . . of his labours in this business. May the eternal Lord God grant this through Christ, that you may, some time or other, being

assembled in the fear of God (with Christ presiding in your council) set forth at length a pure confession without any stain of error, to the confusion of the adversaries, the peace of the church, and the glory of God . . .[7]

The conference never happened. Conflict became increasingly acrimonious, and in January 1557 the congregation sacked Horne, decreeing that the 'church was above the pastor and not the pastor above the church'.[8]

Another difficulty facing the returnees was their relationship with the 'Nicodemites'. As early as 1552 Calvin poured searing vitriol on those who shunned martyrdom by refusing to challenge 'godless' regimes. His *Quatre sermons* of that year was soon translated into English. This attempt to put backbone into Protestants living under a papal regime could be understood, though it might seem to us to be, at the very least, an uncharitable attack from someone living well away from the war zone. What is harder to accept is the reprinting of *Quatre sermons* four times during Elizabeth's reign. Calvinist propagandists threw the Nicodemite taunt at all Protestants who accepted a religious settlement not fashioned, in every detail, after the Genevan model. One such, William Fuller, a member of the Earl of Leicester's entourage (and a distant relative) who had succoured Elizabeth in the dark days of her half-sister's reign, presumed on this connection in 1585 to admonish his sovereign by pointing out that God had preserved her despite the fact that she was 'unworthy by reason of your yielding to that idolatry'.[9] It is not to be wondered at that the queen found Puritans utterly obnoxious.

Technically, Calvin was quite right in identifying and naming Nicodemism insofar as it applied to Protestants living under papal regimes who survived by keeping their faith hidden and dutifully attending mass. There was nothing new about it. For the best part of 200 years, thousands of Lollards had survived by outward conformity. They could and did claim that what some regarded as clandestine – even dishonest – behaviour had kept alive for future generations their understanding of Christian truth. Lollardy was one of the very few medieval heresies that had not been persecuted into oblivion. The difference with Edwardian Evangelicalism was that its ranks included many leaders in Church and State, from the captive princess downwards. It was understandable that the new queen would advance several of them to her Council and her episcopate. Not only did they understand her position; they also shared her conviction that 'the powers that be are ordained of God' (Romans 13.1 KJV), that they have the right to establish the national religion and that they should be obeyed. Now that this burden had fallen on her shoulders, she wanted her Church to be run by men of varying shades of Protestant opinion who could unite around core beliefs and practices and display a measure of toleration and compromise regarding *adiaphora* ('things indifferent').

This posed a problem for those who hoped to see a Calvinistic paradise established in their own land similar to those pertaining in the Continental centres of reform: could they accept positions in Elizabeth's Church alongside fellow labourers who were 'in God's cause so faint and courageless that they will not open their lips to speak for Christ' (as the divine and poet Thomas Drant commented in a sermon preached at court in 1570)?[10] One man smitten in conscience on his return from Strasbourg was Thomas Sampson. Should he, he wondered, accept high office in Elizabeth's tainted Church? He turned for advice to his friend, the Italian-born and much travelled Peter Martyr Vermigli. In reply, Vermigli urged the Englishman to put principle before preferment:

> You are afraid on both sides: for if you reject the ministry, you seem to let go an opportunity of directing things in a proper manner; while, if you undertake the offered function, you have just and good cause to fear lest you should appear to assent to those ordinances, which not only impair and weaken the pure worship of God, but also corrupt and marvellously bring it to decay; although they may seem to have but little weight and importance in the eyes of men who are but faintly disposed towards the gospel; for they count all such things as matters of indifference. But will any one who is somewhat better instructed in religion, when he sees you, a messenger of Christ and zealous trumpeter of the gospel, arrayed in these vestments, praying at an altar before the image of the crucifix, repeating holy words, and distributing the sacraments – will any one, I say, not think that these rites are not only tolerated, but also approved by you?[11]

Sampson was something of a pain in the neck to his foreign friends. Nor was he alone. Heinrich Bullinger, leader of the Protestants in Zurich, was weary of the correspondence generated by tender-conscienced English clergy seeking his advice. Writing to another colleague, he described Sampson as 'a man of a captious and unquiet disposition'. And he went on to observe: 'England has many characters of this sort, who cannot be at rest, who can never be satisfied, and who have always something or other to complain about.'[12]

Those of a precisionist disposition wanting to reassure themselves that undiluted Calvinism *could* be transplanted looked across the Scottish border at the experiment being carried out by John Knox. He had lost no time in returning to his native land from Geneva and making his uncompromising stance very clear. In a round robin to his supporters he declared, 'We are persuaded that everything our adversaries do is diabolical.'[13] This followed logically from the conviction that he was in possession of the truth, based on his interpretation of Scripture. But who was to say that that interpretation was correct? The only answer he deigned to give was that it was manifest to all who read the Bible. In 1558, Knox wrote his most notorious pamphlet, *The First Blast of the Trumpet against the Monstrous Regiment of Women*. Since Holy Writ made it quite clear that women were subservient to men, it was not surprising that evil prevailed in states where the roles were reversed. Knox had in mind England under the Catholic tyranny of Mary Tudor, and Scotland where the French-trained teenage Mary Stuart was queen. She was being brought up in France, and the woman acting as regent during her minority was Mary of Guise. His timing could not have been worse. Within weeks England had a Protestant monarch back on the throne, but that monarch also happened to be a woman, Elizabeth Tudor. She retaliated by refusing him entry to her domain in his journey northward. From his arrival in May 1559 until his death in November 1572, Knox consistently preached his uncompromising message in a nation sundered by civil war between Catholic nobles supported by France and their Protestant foes aided and abetted more circumspectly by the English government. This is not the place to rehearse again the well-known tragedy of Mary Stuart's complex personal and political relationships, which ended with her being a troublesome 'guest' of the Protestant queen south of the border. What is pertinent to the present study is the religious regime that was Knox's legacy to his country.

By 1572, all obvious aspects of the Roman Church had been removed. The pope and the mass had been jettisoned. Churches had been cleansed of 'idolatrous' clutter. The sermon had become the main feature of worship, and the word of God faithfully preached was backed up by the *Book of Discipline* designed to cover every aspect of private and corporate life:

> Drunkenness, excess (be it in apparel or in eating and drinking), fornication, oppression of the poor by exactions, deceiving of them in buying and selling by wrong mete or measure, wanton words and licentious living, tending to slander, do properly appertain to the Church of God to punish, the same as God's word commendeth.[14]

Courts were set up staffed by committees of ministers to supervise and enforce this holy regime. At grass-roots level a *Presbyterian* system was established; that is to say that church life was in the hands of groups of local ministers, meeting in regional bodies (*presbyteries*) and national 'parliaments' (*synods* and *assemblies*). A full-blown presbyterian system would have consigned episcopacy to the rubbish bin, along with all the other trappings of papistry, and some Scottish Protestants were all for this further stage of reform. But though the Protestant element in the Scottish nobility was strong, there was little appetite for ridding the realm of bishops, who were seen as a valuable prop to the Crown, currently worn by the young Mary Stuart. Full-blown Presbyterianism would be a long time coming, but church government was slowly moving in that direction.

In England, meanwhile, the choice was not between Elizabeth's halfway house and Presbyterian polity. As well as those who had lived in satisfactory exile under Lutheran regimes or the less rigid church-state systems pertaining in the Swiss and German city states, there were English churchmen who took pride in the pattern of civic and ecclesiastical rule that had evolved over the centuries – a pattern that involved representations of the *people* in the work of government. Parliament had slowly chipped away at the power of both autocratic monarchs and ecclesiastical courts. If, then, all rule in this world derives from God, where did the will of the people fit in?

That question was being asked and discussed in many places where Protestants met. It would be a mistake to confine our thinking on such matters to the full-blown theories advanced in the works of major theologians. As men and women in these years of mounting religious conflict struggled to square political reality with biblical revelation, many ideas were exchanged, not all of which made their mark in the written records. One such that did briefly appear in print in a little-known book came from the pen of John Ponet, the former Bishop of Winchester, who fled to Strasbourg, where he died in 1556. His last work – printed anonymously – was well in advance of its time as far as the history of political thought was concerned, and its significance would not be appreciated for a hundred years. Ponet, who may have been involved in Thomas Wyatt's rebellion against Mary Tudor, was faced with the problem of how God-fearing subjects could give their allegiance to a ruler who, though rightfully instituted and anointed as God's appointee, yet behaved tyrannically and enacted laws at variance with the will of God as laid out in the Bible. Ponet averred that sovereigns who showed themselves to be enemies of God should be removed from office. How could that be squared with the biblical assertion that the powers that be were ordained by God and must therefore be either obeyed or only passively resisted? Ponet's answer was that authority was conferred, not on any individual or group, but on the people as a whole, and that they were empowered to choose what manner of regime they should live under. Where there was a king, he was only a member of the commonwealth, and the commonwealth was not dependent on him for its existence.

Ponet's *Shorte Treatise on politike Power* was not an influential volume in its own day. It could not be, as long as political thinkers were unwilling to let loose the anchor of divine-right monarchy. Its importance lies in the fact that the politico-religious tumult of the sixteenth century was forcing people to seek eagerly – desperately even – religious principles that would tear out the manifestly evil weeds infesting European society without uprooting with them the essential God-given law.

Such anxieties still haunted the dreams of those in authority in the 1560s. Hatred of tyranny and fears of rebellion now unleashed the Wars of Religion in France and the Low Countries. The backlash against Calvinist success was not slow in coming. In August 1572, Europe was rocked by news of the St Bartholomew's Day Massacre, an explosion of undiluted hatred against the Huguenots that began in Paris, spread like an uncontrollable inferno through the country and did not abate until it had claimed some 13,000 lives. Pope Gregory XIII sent his congratulations to the French king and had a medal struck depicting an avenging angel brandishing a sword and the legend 'Huguenots slaughtered'. Across the border in the Spanish Netherlands the military governor, the Duke of Alva, hailed these events as proof that 'God has been pleased to change and rearrange matters in the way that he knows will favour the conservatives of the true church and advance this holy service and His glory'.[15] Alva, too, was involved in the suppression of 'heretical rebels' involving the merciless slaughter of men, women and children. The Eighty Years' War (1568–1648) would eventually split the Low Countries into an independent, Protestant Dutch Republic in the north and a reduced, Catholic Spanish Netherlands comprising, more or less, modern Belgium, Luxemburg and Nord-Pas-de-Calais.

To most English people it must have seemed obvious that their government could not avoid taking sides, but this was the one thing Elizabeth was resolved *not* to do. 'Consider with yourselves the bitter storms and troubles of your neighbours,' she commented to Parliament in 1576, 'the true cause whereof I will not attribute to princes (God forbid I should) since these misfortunes may proceed as well from sins among the people.'[16] Nothing could induce the queen to risk friction with her fellow monarchs. In 1570, Pope Pius V declared in a papal bull that he had deprived her of her 'pretended title' and that all English Catholics were absolved from their allegiance to her. Since 1567 Elizabeth had become the reluctant hostess of Mary Queen of Scots, who had been forced to abdicate and flee for her life across the border. Thereafter she became the focus of plots aimed at unseating Elizabeth, several of which were supported by papal and Spanish intrigues. Within months of Pius V's *Regnans in Excelsis* broadside, three leading noblemen had led an open rebellion, seized the city of Durham and made a bid to rescue Mary Stuart. Year on year, Catholic priests were being smuggled into the country from the seminary in Douai where they were trained for the reconversion of England.

Despite all this, Elizabeth remained more sensitive to the activities of the Puritan network, with its 'cells' throughout the country and its continuing contacts with the Reformed European churches. She simply loathed the people to whom the derogatory word 'Puritan' was now being attached. What was it about the Puritans that she found so objectionable? Undoubtedly, part of her response was aesthetic. Stripped-down church interiors, unadorned altars and simple congregational singing was not at all to her taste. She liked a certain amount of adornment in religious ritual. She refused to remove crucifixes from her chapel and gave her patronage to the known Catholic composer William Byrd, appointed to the Chapel Royal in 1572. Also, the political pressure she was under from Calvinistic advisers cut across her theological convictions about monarchy. As King Philip of Spain not only relentlessly continued his attack on the Protestants of the Low Countries, but also assumed the role of Counter-Reformation champion committed to restoring to papal obedience those states that had fallen into heresy, the queen was urged to nail her Protestant colours to the mast and provide military aid to her co-religionists. As ever more shocking news arrived from France from Huguenot escapees pouring into England, her advisers begged her to make strong representations to the French king. Such appeals went completely against the grain for Elizabeth. How could she, an anointed sovereign and God's deputy in England, show solidarity with people who were rising up against their divinely nominated rulers? At one Council meeting she lost patience with her most trusted adviser, Secretary William Cecil, and told him to stop blathering on about the plight of his 'brothers in Christ'.[17]

But what really touched a raw nerve for the queen was Puritan preaching. We will explore in the next chapter how organized programmes of Puritan sermonizing developed during the reign, but from its early days it was something that stuck in Elizabeth's craw. Theologians who had reacted against the regime of 'Bloody Mary' and gone on to develop their church-and-state doctrines in the 'capital cities' of the Reformation did not hold back when proclaiming their views about the relationship between state rulers and ministers of the gospel. On 25 February 1570, the same day that Pius V issued his notorious attack on Elizabeth, the Cambridge divine Edward Dering preached at court a sermon denouncing the clergy as ignorant 'dumb dogs' and drawing attention to general ecclesiastical malfunction. But he did not stop there; he reminded the queen of her disciplinary responsibility as shepherd of the flock and of his own responsibility to guide and, if necessary, to upbraid her. 'I should lead you along in the Spirit as God did the prophet Ezekiel,' he informed Her Majesty. Warming to his subject of clerical abuses, Dering declaimed:

> you in the meanwhile that all these whoredoms are committed, you at whose hands God will require it, you sit still and are careless, let men do as they list. It toucheth not belike your commonwealth, and therefore you are so well contented to let all alone . . . God is a righteous God; He will one day call you to your reckoning.[18]

No less than the pope's minions, it seemed, Puritan spokesmen were setting themselves up as judges over the crowned heads of Europe. But while Elizabeth's Catholic subjects met and talked and worshipped in secret, Dering and his like challenged her to her face. Small wonder that she felt threatened by Puritan disobedience.

The frustration felt by Puritans was that she was, indeed, determined to 'let all alone'. She had reinstated the English Church much as it had been in Edward VI's reign, reissued the 1549 Prayer Book, and sacked bishops and clergy not prepared to use it. As far as she was concerned, that was that. Like her father and her siblings before her, the queen wanted religious unity, with all her subjects adhering to the state church. And like Henry, Edward and Mary, she was indulging in a pipe dream. Militant Puritans were no less strangers to reality. Even if they could all have agreed on those aspects of church life most in need of reform, it would have been impossible to accommodate them within one state church – certainly not without a measure of toleration they were temperamentally unable to embrace. But they could not agree what to attack. They had no coordinated strategy.

The first anti-establishment campaign launched by some was the vestiarian controversy. More powerful than words in identifying, shaping and declaring orthodox belief was the garb of clergy officiating at public worship. There was an obvious world of difference between the priest in his mass vestments, or even in simple cassock and surplice, and the minister in his plain preaching gown. To some Puritans, elaborate dress and ritual smacked of papistical priestcraft. Equally objectionable to some Evangelicals were certain aspects of orthodox ceremonial. Kneeling at Holy Communion suggested adoration of the elements. The use of wafers rather than ordinary bread similarly suggested that there was something intrinsically 'holy' about the elements. Some Puritans even objected to the sign of the cross being made in baptism. There were others who wanted to dig even deeper beneath the foundations of Elizabeth's Church. Insisting that the New Testament provided a pattern of ecclesiastical structure and organization for all lives and all places, they clamoured for a Presbyterian ecclesiology. Where major landowners or powerful town corporations held the advowsons, there was little bishops could do to prevent them instituting 'radical' incumbents if they were so inclined. By the 1570s, a stalemate situation prevailed. Attempts by Puritans to use Parliament to effect change were stymied by the queen, who simply refused to endorse any radical legislation. She relied on the bishops to discipline nonconformist clergy, but they were in many areas baulked by leaders in the shires who were supporters of further reform.

Sometimes the conflict turned nasty. The atrocities on the continent inflamed passions, driving extremists on both sides to drastic action. As well as Catholic plots against the queen, savage acts were carried out by Puritans. In October 1573, the mariner Sir John Hawkins was murderously attacked in the lawyers' quarter of the capital because he was mistaken for one of Elizabeth's ministers. This provoked a royal response in the form of a proclamation demanding tougher measures against clergy refusing to use the approved Prayer Book or criticizing it from the pulpit. As a result, offenders were thrown into prison. Some died there.

Puritan propagandists utilized the popular press to such good effect that a vigorous pamphlet war was now in full swing. *An Admonition to the Parliament* and *A Second Admonition to the Parliament* made scurrilous attacks on individual bishops and called for the abolition of episcopacy and its replacement by a Presbyterian system. The public debate was joined by two Cambridge academics who emerged as its pro and anti figureheads. Thomas Cartwright was a fellow of Trinity College and Lady Margaret Professor of Divinity. He used his position to wage war on the ecclesiastical establishment and accused it of departing from the New Testament pattern of church structure. John Whitgift, Master of Trinity, took the opposite viewpoint and it served him very well. His defence of the ecclesiastical status quo won him royal favour and promotion. He became vice chancellor of the university and, not content with engaging Cartwright in debate, deprived him of his fellowship and his professional chair. One of Whitgift's more temperate diatribes against the Puritans indicates his contempt and condescension:

> How much better had it been for them to have proceeded in teaching necessary points of doctrine, and exhorting to obedience, to concord, to godly life and conversation, than thus, with no small rejoicing of the wicked, great offence of the weak gospellers, marvellous grief of the queen's majesty and other that have the care of government, frowardly to disquiet and disturb the church, trouble the happy peace of the commonweal, and hazard the whole state of religion, they shall one day (if not too late) well understand.[19]

The implied threat of those last few words is telling. Whitgift, the establishment man, was furious at what seemed to him to be the arrogance of anyone who questioned the system. Little, if anything, separated him from Professor Cartwright in terms of central doctrine. In matters of soteriology, both men were Calvinists, even to the point of accepting predestination. But any attack on the episcopal ordering of the English Church was, in Whitgift's view, not only an affront to the bishops; it was also an insult to the queen. It was the old authority issue all over again. The Presbyterians turned to the New Testament and discovered therein a pattern of ministerial oversight for the Church of Christ in all ages. The vice chancellor looked on that same written word of God through spectacles tinted by church history and the freedom granted to succeeding ages to regulate their own affairs.

Whitgift's clouded vision enabled him to see nothing beyond the near-perfect state of the Elizabethan Church, the Puritan movement as its sole enemy, and the need to crush that movement utterly. He could not or would not recognize that this 'movement' was multihued, that not all Puritans were agitators for a Presbyterian system, that there was room for debate, and that a hard-line stance would, inevitably, turn some moderate reformists into intractable opponents. When he became Archbishop of Canterbury in 1584 he was one of the few anti-Puritans among Elizabeth's senior advisers, but the important point was that he and the queen saw eye to eye in church affairs. He became her instrument in undermining the disturbing influence of idealists. As Professor Collinson observed, Whitgift's policy

> was the product of a tidy, schoolmasterly mind which could tolerate no deviation from a rigidly conceived standard of clerical obedience. For the sake of what was surely an unattainable degree of uniformity, he made it more difficult to deal effectively with the hard core of extremists . . .[20]

Before this, Cartwright had deemed it wise to spend several years abroad visiting Reformed churches and writing or translating controversial books and pamphlets. When he did return, in 1585, without royal permission, he was quickly clapped in prison. Fortunately, he did not lack for powerful supporters. It was Elizabeth's most trusted adviser, William Cecil, and her closest friend, Robert Dudley, Earl of Leicester, who interceded for him, and the earl provided generously for the ageing firebrand by appointing him as Master of Leicester Hospital in Warwick. Thus protected, Cartwright resumed his preaching career throughout the Midlands, where, it was reported, his sermons attracted crowds and were a constant irritation to the church hierarchy. Whitgift had clipped his wings but not grounded him.

The strident tone of the Puritan pamphlets and their extreme demands probably did their cause more harm than good. Several of the 'old guard', the ex-exiles, disassociated themselves from this extremism. In 1573, Edwin Sandys, Bishop of London, certainly no enemy of Puritanism, complained to a friend in Zurich of a new generation of 'foolish young men' who were seeking 'the complete overthrow and routing up of our whole ecclesiastical polity'.[21] He was certainly not alone. With the passage of time the mood of the engagement was changing. While some activists were frustrated at not being able to replicate in England the regime of Geneva or Zurich, others acknowledged that their country was different and would have to find its own route to the promised land. It was also clear that the Continental churches their friends so much admired had their own problems. Calvin had worked tirelessly to realize his vision of a Christian commonwealth, but his work was unfinished at his death in 1564. Geneva and the other Protestant city states were caught up in the religious wars and, as well as external enemies, were dealing with an upsurge of Anabaptism at home while also trying to preserve doctrinal unity.

Change could only be brought about legally by the queen in Parliament, and more might be achieved by persuasion and gradualism than by hot-headed confrontation. The Puritans did not lack for substantial men ready to seek election to the lower house. They campaigned determinedly in elections to the parliaments of 1572, 1581 and 1584, and to a large measure set the tone in the House of Commons. But politically they were no match for the queen. Elizabeth insisted that religion fell within her prerogative. Over and again she baulked the progressives by vetoing their proposals or simply refusing to allow them to debate sensitive issues.

However, with international tension mounting, even Elizabeth could not sit on the fence indefinitely.

5
Lollardy to lectureships

Not that I intend to reprove the study of Scripture, for I extol it and praise it above all other study, so [long as] it be used . . . with modesty and charity, with patience and [toleration], till God send them a true instructor, not infected with wilful and newfangled heresies, from which I pray God to defend you all, and send you teachers [imbued] with such science as may instruct you in truth, by which you may attain to joys everlasting.[1]

Aye, there's the rub. The open Bible intended by Wycliffe, Tyndale, Cromwell and other champions of vernacular Scripture to clarify Christian witness had to be interpreted, explained and applied to contemporary situations. On a day-to-day basis, this was the task of preachers – men who used their own knowledge and spiritual insight, but also their own personality and prejudices, to impress their hearers. God's 'PR men' were not all endowed with 'modesty, charity, patience and toleration'. Nor, in a sense, should they have been. Roger Edgeworth, the Catholic-inclined priest who exhorted his flock around 1540 in the words quoted above, was a traditionalist who saw anarchy in any departure from the message endorsed by the ecclesiastical hierarchy. But the Bible *is* anarchic. Jesus himself had said that he came to bring not peace but a sword (Matthew 10.34f.) and 1,500 years of church history had abundantly endorsed his prophecy. In the sixteenth century, 'Reformation' almost became synonymous with a battle of pulpits. Within a few years of Edgeworth's appeal for expositors not to rock the Catholic boat, Hugh Latimer, the most famous preacher of the age, was intriguing his congregation with a very different message:

And now I would ask a strange question: who is the most diligentest bishop and prelate in all England, that passeth all the rest in doing his office? I can tell, for I know him who it is; I know him well. But now I think I see you listening and hearkening that I should name him. There is one that passeth all the other, and is the most diligent prelate and preacher in all England. And will you know who it is? I will tell you: it is the devil. He is the most diligent preacher of all other; he is never out of his diocess; he is never from his cure; ye shall never find him unoccupied; he is ever in his parish; he keepeth residence at all times; ye shall never find him out of the way, call for him when you will he is ever at home; the diligentest preacher in all the realm . . .[2]

The importance – indeed, the very nature – of preaching changed in the early sixteenth century. Thereafter, it contributed in new and powerful ways to the religious dynamic of Tudor and early Stuart England. If the printed Bible was the principal agent of spiritual revolution, impassioned preaching ran it a close second. Revolution, of course, is only evolution speeded up. Reading the runes of what was happening in the religious life of the nation as the Yorkist age gave way to the Tudor is far from easy.

Hitherto sermons had not been part of the standard fare of regular worship. Parish clergy were supposed to preach four times a year and on prescribed subjects, but the requirement was honoured more in the breach than the observance. Some incumbents fulfilled the letter of the law by reading from published collections of homilies. Others simply did not bother – particularly if they were non-resident clergy who paid curates to perform the bare minimum of parish duties. It may be that many people did not miss what they had never had. One Yorkshire churchwarden was probably not a lone voice when he complained that when a sermon was advertised most parishioners voted with their feet! However, the situation was not viewed favourably in the upper levels of the ecclesiastical establishment. Bishops frequently deplored the intellectual poverty of the secular clergy, few of whom could compose and deliver an address in the vernacular. To some extent the lack of education and exhortation was made up by the professionals. Most of the Church's official 'prophets' (that is, forthtellers rather than foretellers) belonged to the mendicant orders. Franciscans, Dominicans and Augustinian friars were licensed to travel from marketplace to church to private home, proclaiming 'Thus says the Lord'. Many of them pulled in the crowds by their gifted oratory. People who avoided the uninspired messages from their parish pulpit flocked to hear the entertaining 'soapbox' oratory of the friar on the village green.

One attraction of the friars was their reformist zeal. They were often critical of the current status quo and, particularly, were noted for their opposition to the secular clergy. As late as 1515 Henry Standish, Warden of the London Greyfriars (Franciscans), was denounced as a heretic for supporting the call of the House of Commons for restriction to the benefit of clergy, which exempted those in holy orders from prosecution in the civil courts. Standish, an avowed enemy of Erasmus, was by no stretch of the imagination unorthodox in his theology, but he was dauntless in exposing the gap between theory and practice, between the hard demands of the gospel and the privileges and powers claimed by the ecclesiastical establishment. In that, he touched an exposed nerve, the tingling of which was felt by many lay people. It has long been thought that Lollardy, the English heresy, was the stock on to which Continental reformism was grafted, but that is not, perhaps, the most helpful metaphor. Professor Marshall suggests something more apposite: 'The early Reformation in England had a sympathetic Lollard godmother, but its parents were orthodox and Catholic.'3 Friars and other official preachers were at one with lay critics in exposing ecclesiastical shortcomings. Nor were all church leaders indifferent to complaints about clergy who were ignorant, or lazy, or immoral, or avaricious, or ambitious or arrogant. In 1510 (or possibly 1512 – scholarly opinion differs), no less a person than John Colet, Dean of St Paul's, warned his colleagues in the southern convocation that the ill living of many clergy was a bigger threat to the Church than heresy.

Having observed that regular preaching was a non-event throughout much of the land, we are confronted by a physical reality that appears to give the lie to that observation. The half-century from 1480 to 1530 was a 'boom' period for the provision of pulpits and pews in hundreds of churches. Ornate structures of stone or wood were created to dignify the preaching of the word. And many congregations no longer had to stand in their rush-strewn naves or take stools to sit on. For the first time, we find records of pew rents paid by the more substantial members of the community to enable them to listen to lengthy sermons in relative comfort. Does this betoken the normalization of preaching or simply increased expenditure on beautifying churches in a relatively prosperous period of history? Were pulpits merely part of the new fashion, so that parishioners felt the need to keep up with the Joneses?

There is no doubt that some places did have long traditions of preaching. These tended to be in cities and larger towns, where congregations were made up in no small part by the families of merchants and craftsmen – widely travelled, well-to-do, better educated and more sophisticated than the dwellers in rural areas. The most famous venue was the outdoor pulpit beside St Paul's Cathedral, where people regularly flocked to listen to celebrity preachers, but similar events occurred in Norwich, York, Bristol and other major urban centres. It was around this time that a new phenomenon began to appear in the religious life of the people: sponsored sermons. It was commonplace for well-to-do members of society to make bequests in their wills for the performance of masses for the repose of their souls, but some testators were making provision for the spiritual well-being of others. In 1523, John Bridgeman of Exeter left five shillings a year 'to be paid unto the preacher that maketh the sermon on Easter Even'.[4] In 1526, James Wilford of the London parish of St Bartholomew the Less made provision for an annual Good Friday sermon.[5] Dame Elizabeth Thurston, wife of a prominent London merchant, opened a memorial fund for a specific brand of university students whom she wished to encourage – 'pulpit men'.[6]

The vast majority of regular preachers and the majority of congregations who enjoyed their ministrations were not radical in their handling of received doctrine. We cannot quantify the adherents of heretical beliefs or beliefs tending towards heresy in the pre-Reformation years. Nor is it important for us to do so. What matters is that something important happened when the philosophical and exegetical disputes of the university lecture hall 'escaped' into the marketplace and the tavern, and mingled with the unsophisticated reasoning of semi-educated folk untrained in the scholarly abstractions of the schools, with the scepticism of people leaning towards anticlericalism, and with the yearning of those who longed for a closer walk with God. The resulting conflict was an example of the oft-repeated contention between the specialist and the man or woman 'in the street', the powerful and the powerless, the door-keepers of human aspiration and those eager for access. The increased emphasis on preaching gave ordinary people the right to enter the debate.

And in the 1520s some of them received encouragement from no less a person than the king. He had embarked on his campaign to get rid of his wife and was not going to let the pope or his English minions stand in his way. This is not the place to describe again Henry VIII's 'Great Matter', save to say that, in dethroning the pope from headship of the English Church, he and his Mister Fix-it, Thomas Cromwell, had to persuade the people that his course was just. This called for an extensive public-relations campaign. The government needed writers, artists *and preachers* to point out the failings of the clergy and to challenge the doctrine on which their authority was based. Cromwell, Archbishop Thomas Cranmer and other reform-minded bishops licensed orators to pro-claim the official line. Under cover of explaining the Act of Supremacy, a harlequin assortment of pulpiteers proclaimed a bewildering variety of 'truths' embracing anticlericalism and snippets of theology culled from the writings of Continental reformers.

In 1536, John Longland, Bishop of Lincoln, had a bone to pick with Archbishop Cranmer:

Swynnerton has been preaching in these parts and offends the people, for he lacks learning, knowledge of his doctors and discre-tion, and as some report, his living is not all of the best . . . His sermons are not fruitful but rather seditious . . . He resorts to light people and to their houses, who leave their worldly labour and read English books all day so that they fall into poverty and idleness and assemble many times together. There have been robberies lately, and some conjecture they are committed by such idle people . . .[7]

Though little is known about Thomas Swinnerton, he is an interesting bridge figure linking the early critics of the religious establishment to the proclaimers of doctrinal novelties gleaned from Continental reform-ers. He appears to have had no English university training but did travel to Wittenberg where he drank at the Lutheran spring. He was back in England by the time Henry VIII's break with Rome was being pushed through Parliament, and he offered to write in defence of government policy. Swinnerton's anti-papal pamphlets (published anonymously) obviously impressed Cromwell and Cranmer, and in 1535 the archbishop licensed him to preach throughout the kingdom. Despite the complaints of diocesans such as Longland, Swinnerton was protected by the Reformation leaders and he was appointed to a curacy in Ipswich. There he continued his literary activities, which began to display Calvinistic influence. His ministry was appreciated by at least one Ipswich citizen. A wealthy merchant, Robert Cutler, funded his preaching activities and arranged for him to substitute sermons for requiem masses. Cranmer later moved Swinnerton to Kent to play a leading role in the evangelization of that county. There he remained until the reign of Mary Tudor, when he joined the stream of radical activists emigrating to the continent.

Swinnerton was just one preacher among many now authorized to spread a theology at odds with accepted conventions. Traditionalist bishops were not slow to respond by licensing men of their own party to refute the spread of 'heresy'. Soon a pulpit war was raging.

Whatever the impact of all this was on public opinion – and we can never accurately assess that – one thing is clear: preaching assumed a new importance. It was controversial and frequently confrontational. And, like a bruising wrestling bout, it was, doubtless, entertaining for many spectators. In the spring of 1533, the people of Bristol crowded into their churches to hear the slanging matches between Hugh Latimer and the no-less-extrovert William Heberden and their respective supporting casts. We do not have a printed version of the sermons delivered in these verbal combats, but a letter written afterwards by Latimer in response to his critics reveals something of their tone. Here Latimer defends his attack on payment for masses to be said for those in purgatory:

Provision for purgatory hath brought thousands to hell. Debts have not been paid; restitution of evil-gotten goods and lands hath not been made; Christian people are neglected and suffered to perish; last wills unfulfilled and broken; God's ordinances set aside. Thus we have gone to hell with masses, dirges, and ringing of many a bell. And unless we do what God hath commanded us, though our soul-priests sing till they be blear-eyed, say till they have worn their tongues to the stumps, neither their singings nor their sayings shall bring us out of hell, whither we shall go for contemning of God's forbiddings. Purgatory's iniquity hath replenished hell, and left heaven almost empty. If purgatory were purged of all that it hath gotten by setting aside restitution, and robbing of Christ, it would be but a poor purgatory; so poor, that it should not be able to feed so fat, and trick up so many idle and slothful lubbers.[8]

The ranks of radical preachers were being swelled by members of the intellectual elite. Ardent radicals from the universities were appearing in pulpits across much of England, offering well-reasoned arguments in support of their dissentient beliefs. Lollardy had begun in Oxford, way back in the late fourteenth century, when John Wycliffe, sometime Master of Balliol College, set in train unofficial Bible translation and promoted the written word of God as a rival authority to the pope in matters of doctrine and practice. The university had been subsequently purged of error, but Oxford's college heads remained sensitive about heresy and it was in Cambridge that the new wave of radical religion appeared in the sixteenth century. It was natural that the fashionable academic novelties should be discussed there and that banned books should be read because they *were* banned. But advocates of radical doctrine were soon going further, convinced that biblical truth should be publicly proclaimed and commonly held error should be challenged. It was at Christmas 1525 (months before Tyndale's New Testament became available) that Robert Barnes, head of the local Augustinian friars (the same order as that to which Luther belonged), delivered a sermon in which he attacked clerical abuses from a public Cambridge pulpit.

About the same time, another member of the Cambridge set of radical intellectuals was granted a licence to preach throughout the diocese of Ely. Thomas Bilney of Trinity Hall lost no time in denouncing the pilgrimage racket and other clerical abuses. When summoned before Thomas Wolsey, Bilney satisfied the cardinal that he did not share the damnable heresies of Luther. However, he was soon in trouble again, was forced to recant his 'errors', and was confined for several months to the Tower of London. But he was a broken man, suffering agonies for his denial of what he believed to be true. On his release in 1529 he deliberately resumed preaching, knowing that this would lead to his death as a relapsed heretic. On 19 August 1531 he was burned at Norwich. The university had its first martyr. But the contest was far from over. 'Little Bilney' was a popular figure in Cambridge, admired for his gentleness and personal piety. Others shared his beliefs, and some were ready to follow his lead. Bilney's travel companion, Thomas Arthur, when under interrogation had told his examiners:

> Though men be restrained to preach nowadays (which is against God's Laws) yet I may preach . . . by the authority of God, by which authority every man may preach, and there is neither bishop nor ordinary, nor yet the pope, that may make any law to hinder any man to preach the gospel . . . If I should suffer persecution for the preaching of the gospel yet there are seven thousand more that would preach the gospel of God as I do now.[9]

It was a wild exaggeration, but there was a growing number of men prepared to go into the pulpit and proclaim their faith.

As a result, more people were asking fundamental questions about the nature of the Church and, specifically, the role of the clergy. Was the priest a sacramental agent, like the Levites of old, concerned with rituals and sacrifices, or did he stand in the prophetic tradition among those whose task it was to enlighten the minds of men and women about the reality of God and his dealings with humankind? Perhaps he was called on to be both. If so, which responsibility was the greater? The scattered Lollards were in no doubt about the answers to these questions as they gathered round their handwritten copies of the Scriptures. But one did not have to be a religious rebel to re-evaluate traditional teaching. One of the most popular books around the turn of the century was the anonymous *Dives and Pauper*, which urged that, given a choice between attending mass and hearing a sermon, the simple believer should choose the latter. It questioned much of what passed for 'church magic'. Increasingly the sacramental and the prophetic came into conflict. Those who advocated the absolute necessity of regular instruction from the word of God found a ready audience in pragmatic, commonsensical, workaday English folk who did not understand or who mistrusted the philosophical niceties of theological debate. Thus, traditional teaching insisted that, by consecration, the priest at the altar transformed bread into the flesh of Christ, but many hearers were relieved when preachers exploded this mystery and assured them that 'what looks like bread, smells like bread and tastes like bread is bread'.

It was the reign of Edward VI that saw the Protestant Reformation established by law in England, and preaching became a major element of government policy. Within months a law had been passed ordering a pulpit to be set up in every church where one did not exist before. New homilies were issued to ensure that pulpits were used, and used to endorse the Evangelical programme of the new regime. The boy king, under the supervision of the regent, Edward Seymour, Duke of Somerset, led the way. At a recently built pulpit in the privy garden at Whitehall Palace regular sermons were delivered to as many hearers as could crowd into the designated space. Historians have often attributed to vandals the iconoclasm that swept through the land, tearing down statues and whitewashing painted images, but such orgies of destruction, whether spontaneous or orchestrated by England's new masters, were egged on by pulpit oratory. The violent start to the new reign has to be seen as one expression of euphoria – the hope shared by thousands of people that a bright new day was dawning. Somerset and his supporters promised, not just a clear-cut religious programme after years of Henrician confusion, but also widespread social reform – the creation of the perfect Christian commonwealth in which old grievances would be removed, exploitation of the poor by the rich would end, and all could live in harmony. Such a utopian vision was a powerful intoxicant. Rebellion broke out in eastern England, led by radicals determined to gain by force what the government was promising and not delivering, but in the west reactionaries also took up arms, believing that only the overthrow of the reformers and a return to Catholic tradition could restore peace and order.

All political and religious groups in England shared this desire for peace and order, but they meant different things by it. Where they were in accord was in the use of the pulpit to present their agendas for the transformation and perfection of society. This was evidence of a major new phenomenon – the growing importance of public opinion. The ongoing Reformation, and the reaction of Counter-Reformation, could no longer be simply imposed by leaders in Church and State. The people had to be persuaded and won over. Everyone with a vested interest, therefore, sponsored preachers – the Council, the bishops, municipal corporations, wealthy individuals in the shires and the towns. It is here that we encounter the origins of what would emerge as Puritan lectures, classes, exercises and prophesyings.

As the reign of the last Tudor monarch got into its stride, the central issue in the nation's religious life was what it always had been – authority. In this regard, England's breakaway from papal control had changed nothing. There was still confrontation between the power vested in human agents and the power of God's word written. On one side in Elizabeth's England stood Crown and Mitre; on the other side stood the vernacular Bible. Few contemporaries would have agreed to express the state of affairs so starkly. All involved parties were loud in voicing their allegiance to Holy Writ. Richard Hooker, the arch-defender of the Elizabethan settlement, firmly asserted the primacy of Scripture, and his *Laws of Ecclesiastical Polity* (1594-1597) was a brave attempt to demonstrate that the official Church by law established was deeply rooted in the word of God. But what Hooker was writing was an apologia, a defence of the status quo. It placed tradition and reason on the witness stand as well as the Bible to show that the Church of England was the 'true Church' – or, at least, the 'true Church' for England. Like Aquinas's *Summa* and Calvin's *Institutes*, Hooker's *Laws* was a piece of systematic theology designed to undergird an authoritarian church regime. As Professor MacCulloch has quipped: 'one feels that if the parliamentary legislation of 1559 had laid down that English clergy were to preach standing on their heads, then Hooker would have found a theological reason for justifying it.'[10] However, those who opposed episcopal authoritarianism (whether or not they clung by their fingernails to Church of England membership) also claimed to belong to the 'true Church' as revealed in Scripture. And, of course, the separatists – those who distanced themselves from the state religion – did exactly the same.

Yet what all partisans failed to understand – or, at least, failed to acknowledge – was that the conflict was not Bible versus ecclesiastical authority, but various interpretations of the Bible against one another. In effect, that meant ideological warfare between the men who were interpreting the text, namely the preachers. Most church leaders of all stamps deplored the woeful ignorance of the populace and were convinced that it should be addressed. Nor were they alone. As we have seen, in many localities there was a popular demand for that religious instruction that was lacking in the routines of the established Church. It is therefore not surprising that, as early as the 1560s, clergy 'schools' were springing up spontaneously in some dioceses. They followed a pattern that had been observed and enjoyed by the Marian exiles in their European havens, but we do not need to trace a direct link to the continent. Puritans establishing 'lectureships' or 'prophesyings' within the national Church were doing essentially what the heretics of earlier generations had done: gathering round the word. The underground was, at last, breaking into the overground.

'Prophesyings' were exegetical sermons, the word being taken from 1 Corinthians 14, in which Paul had instructed church members to voice in the assembly the inspired messages they had received from God. This was regarded as licence by many enthusiasts, as Bishop Sandys of London, himself a Puritan sympathizer, complained:

> New orators are rising up from among us, foolish young men, who while they despise authority, and admit of no superior, are seeking the complete overthrow and rooting up of our whole ecclesiastical polity, so piously constituted and confirmed, and established by the entire consent of most excellent men; and are striving to shape out for us, I know not what new platform of a church. And you would not imagine with what approbation this new face of things is regarded, as well by the people as the nobility. The people are fond of change, and seek after liberty; the nobility [seek for] what is useful. These good folks promise both, and that in abundance.[11]

Sandys was particularly concerned that prophesyings were being used to promote the Presbyterian form of church governance, but the catalogue of unofficial doctrines being aired was obviously wide. The bishops were in a quandary: they were acutely aware of their responsibility to meet the need and demand for preaching, but they also knew they had to silence the wilder spirits. And they had another major problem: the queen disliked sermons. She thought of most preachers as troublemakers and tarred with the same brush. None of her subjects, she believed, needed to be on the receiving end of more than three or four sermons a year. But, as Sandys observed, the general populace did not agree with such short rations. Gifted speakers, whether delivering their oratory from the church pulpit or parish cross, were in demand. Such entertainment had been in short supply ever since Elizabeth's father had done away with the orders of preaching friars whose performance had enlivened many a market day, and there was a ready audience for a new generation of eloquent tub-thumpers. But, as any monarch knew, political unrest often began in unauthorized gatherings. The queen had some reason to be wary.

Because the word 'prophesying' was, in any official circles, like a red rag to a bull, it generally came to be replaced by the more neutral term 'lecture'. Many such orations were set up in churches already known for radical tendencies. Within a year of Elizabeth's accession, one was recorded as having been begun at St Anthony's in Budge Row, a fashionable London church popular with many of the merchant fraternity. The disapproving chronicler of this innovation noted that the service was 'after Geneva fashion'. The congregation gathered at 5 a.m. and sang metrical psalms until the hour-long address began at 6 a.m. It was quite normal for worship to take place before the working day began. In the provinces, lectureships usually occurred on market days when the preacher could be assured of a large congregation drawn from the surrounding countryside. The preachers' fees were met by wealthy patrons, by bequests in wills, by merchant guilds or by town corporations. It was not usual for the extra responsibility of weekday lectures to be undertaken, in whole or part, by the incumbent of the parish in which the lecture was held. Some speakers were itinerants, supported by patrons such as the Dowager Duchess of Suffolk and the Earl of Leicester, prominent champions of the reformed cause. Such popular 'celebrity' preachers were outside the parochial system and thus not subject to episcopal oversight, a fact that provoked increasing conflict as the reign wore on.

However, it was not the intention of the radical leadership, early in the reign, to impose on the Church a body of independent preachers like the old mendicant orders. They wanted to *reform* the system, not abandon it. Some of the lectureships were maintained by groups of local clergy who took it in turns to preach once or twice weekly, in a town church that was the focal point of the campaign. Precise details varied from place to place, as did the strength of the pressure applied in the hope of securing radical doctrinal change. Few towns experienced a more forthright attempt at 'Genevafying' than Northampton. The corporation required that a sermon be preached at the Sunday service and that all citizens be required to attend. There was to be no singing or organ music. Young people were to receive instruction in Calvin's Catechism. It was ordained that every Thursday there should be a lecture to be attended by the mayor, the council and all prominent townspeople, after which, in response to God's word, an informal court would be held 'for the correction of discords made in the town as for notorious blasphemy, whoredom and drunkenness'. Concerned as they were to improve the standard of the parish clergy, the town fathers insisted that every Saturday there should be 'an exercise of ministers . . . about the interpretation of Scripture'.[12]

These 'exercises' were what the name suggests: theological workouts where groups of local clergy met to hone their hortatory skills. They varied from place to place but were essentially meetings at which the members took it in turns to preach on a given text. Sometimes lay people were admitted to these gatherings and the responses of the folk in the pews were valued. Just how influential the reactions of listeners could be is well illustrated by the colourful career of Walter Travers (c. 1548–1635). He was a domestic chaplain to William Cecil and a dyed-in-the-wool, nonconformist Puritan. In 1581 he was appointed Lecturer at the London Temple, the lawyers' church, close by the Inns of Court. The legal fraternity was traditionally inclined to religious radicalism, and two years later the senior members recommended Travers to replace the ailing Master of the Temple. The anti-Puritan Archbishop Whitgift ignored them and appointed arch-conservative Richard Hooker. The congregation insisted on retaining Travers as lecturer. The result was that, for several months, Hooker preached at the morning service, and in the afternoon Travers, from the same pulpit, confuted what the master had said. The public (and good-humoured) debate continued until sometime in 1586, when Travers was silenced by archiepiscopal command.

Whitgift was able to silence this lecture because he had risen to the top of the ecclesiastical ladder by dislodging the previous archbishop,

Edmund Grindal. It was Grindal's fall from royal favour that had signalled most clearly the rejection of Puritanism and, specifically, the rejection of the Puritan preaching campaign. Grindal, one of the returning Marian exiles, had been at the centre of church life since the beginning of Elizabeth's reign. He was not among those who refused to soil their hands by accepting high office, and rose through the senior ranks of Bishop of London (1559), Archbishop of York (1570) and Archbishop of Canterbury (1575). In the northern province, Grindal had reposed considerable confidence in responsible lectures and exercises as means of improving the quality of the parochial clergy.

A campaign of accusation and innuendo began and became more determined when Grindal moved to Canterbury. At Southam, Warwickshire, the local exercise had fallen under the control of extreme Puritans who enjoyed the patronage of the Earl of Leicester (see below, pp. 120ff.). This brought together a united critical caucus of religious 'establishment men' and the earl's political rivals. The end result was that Elizabeth summoned Grindal to her presence and ordered the immediate suppression of all exercises. It was a case of irresistible force and immovable object. Instead of meekly submitting to his sovereign's diktat, the archbishop responded with a 6,000-word letter in which he not only declined to stop the tutorials but also took it on himself to assume the role of Her Majesty's spiritual director. Some brief extracts convey the tone of Grindal's response:

> I cannot marvel enough, how this strange opinion should once enter into your mind, that it should be good for the Church to have few preachers. Alas, Madam! Is the Scripture more plain in any one thing, than that the gospel of Christ should be plentifully preached; and that plenty of labourers should be sent into the Lord's harvest; which, being great and large, standeth in need, not of a few, but many workmen? . . .
>
> Ye have done many things well; but except ye persevere to the end, ye cannot be blessed. For if ye turn from God, then God will turn away his merciful countenance from you. And what remaineth then to be looked for, but only a terrible expectation of God's judgments, and an heaping up of wrath against the day of wrath? . . .

I am forced, with all humility, and yet plainly, to profess that I cannot with safe conscience and without the offence of the majesty of God give my assent to the suppressing of the said exercises; much less can I send out any injunction for the utter and universal subversion of the same. I say with St Paul, 'I have no power to destroy, but to only edify'; and with the same apostle, 'I can do nothing against the truth, but for the truth'. If it be your Majesty's pleasure, for this or any other cause, to remove me out of this place, I will with all humility yield thereunto and render again to your Majesty that I received of the same . . . Bear with me, I beseech you, Madam, if I choose rather to offend your earthly Majesty than to offend the heavenly majesty of God.[13]

It goes without saying that Elizabeth Tudor was not accustomed to being addressed in such terms. We might also observe that had she been every inch her father's daughter, Grindal would have paid for such effrontery with his head. Her first impulse was to sack him, but her councillors pointed out the difficulties – both constitutional and pragmatic – of such a course of action. The end result was a fudge: the archbishop was sequestered from carrying out any of his duties, which were to be performed by the Bishop of London, Richard Whitgift. The lectures and exercises did not all cease. Public sermons and preaching schools continued under various guises. But the writing was on the wall. As soon as Grindal died in July 1583, Whitgift formally took his place, and it is against this background that the Travers affair must be seen. It was only 18 months later that Queen Elizabeth summoned a meeting of senior clergy and subjected them to a long harangue on the relationship of Crown and Church. One of her chief complaints was:

You suffer many ministers to preach what they list, and to minister the sacraments according to their own fancies – some one way, some another – to the breach of unity; yea, and some of them so curious in searching matters above their capacity as they preach they wot not what . . . I wish such men to be brought to conformity and unity, that they minister the sacraments according to the order of this realm and preach all one truth . . . And we require you that

75

you do not favour such men being carried away with pity, hoping of their conformity . . . for they will be hanged before they will be reformed.[14]

It was almost 40 years (Christmas 1545) since her father had appealed to Parliament to stop the bitter divisions in a Church riven by quarrels between name-calling 'papists' and 'heretics'. Little, it seems, had changed – certainly among more active and dedicated English Christians. And, just as before, dissidents were driven underground. Lollards, Catholic recusants, Anabaptists – all were of the same ilk, determined to worship in secret and cling to the truths they held dear. And 1582 was the year that the first Brownists went into exile to preserve the purity of their faith.

Robert Browne came from a well-to-do family based at Tolethorpe in Rutland (part of the Midlands heartland that would produce many separatist groups, including the nucleus of the Pilgrim Fathers – see Chapter 8). Permanent evidence of the Brownes' wealth, munificence and influence is to be seen in the fine parish church of All Saints, which was funded entirely by members of the family. Like many people in the mercantile class of the period, their money came from wool and their leading figures were Merchants of the Staple. They took their appropriate places in county and municipal society. The name Browne appears on the lists of Stamford aldermen and Rutland sheriffs. They were, it almost goes without saying, related to other major families in the area – including the Cecils of Stamford Baron, some two miles from Tolethorpe. The Cecils and Brownes were kinsfolk and it was the Brownes who could boast the more ancient lineage. However, it was William Cecil, recently created Baron Burghley, who was the most important member of local society. The queen's first minister had, by 1571, rebuilt his family residence in the grandest current style to create the impressive Burghley House. The Brownes undoubtedly basked in the sunshine of their cousin's pre-eminence in the years when young Robert was emerging from childhood. He was a younger son of Anthony Browne of Tolethorpe and was born sometime in the 1550s. He completed his education at Cambridge University, achieving his bachelor's degree in 1572. He was thus present when the controversy over Thomas Cartwright (see above, pp. 57f.) came to a head. Robert was known to be 'forward in religion', something that created friction in his family. Anthony Browne was not alone among parents worried about the influence of radical religion on their sons. Laurence Chaderton at Christ's College received a firm message from his father:

> If you renounce the new sect which you have joined you may expect all the happiness which the care of an indulgent father can secure for you; otherwise I enclose in this letter a shilling to buy a wallet with 'Go and beg for your living.'[15]

Robert Browne may or may not have been 'cut off with a shilling', but he was removed from Cambridge and told to earn his own living. He spent the next few years teaching in London but was otherwise unchastened. When Browne senior discovered that his son was open-air preaching, he ordered him back to Tolethorpe. But the young rebel quit the family home again to go and live with an old family friend, Richard Greenham, rector of nearby Dry Drayton. Greenham, a moderate Puritan, recognized in Browne a talent for preaching and encouraged him to continue his ministry. The Bishop of Ely soon put a stop to this activity, whereupon, in 1580, Browne moved on to Norwich, where another old university friend, Robert Harrison, was Master of St Giles's Hospital. Both men were soon busily engaged preaching in the city and its environs.

Of Browne's oratorical skill there can be no doubt. His career well illustrates the old truth that if you proclaim extreme ideas loud enough, long enough and with frenzied conviction, and particularly if your message provokes a hostile response from those in power, you will attract a following. Browne and Harrison soon had a congregation.

But what were they proclaiming, how did it differ from mainstream Puritanism and why was it widely dismissed as foolishness? A platform of Christian protest at the state of the nation already existed and voices of complaint were rising to a crescendo in the 1580s. Even at the distance of over four centuries we can sense the widespread unease. England was a small Protestant nation in a Europe where the forces of Counter-Reformation were on the march. In France and the Netherlands, English co-religionists had their backs to the wall. Scotland, though Calvinist, was a nation in conflict; the four regents who had, in turn, ruled in the name of the infant James VI had all, between 1568 and 1581, died violent or suspicious deaths. The ex-queen of Scots was living in the Midlands, an unwilling guest of an unwilling hostess, and the focus of occasional Catholic plots. In Spain, it was known that Philip II was biding his time before launching his 'Enterprises of England'. Why, people asked, was the nation so insecure? Had God forsaken his people?

Puritans were not slow to point out that the godless English only had themselves to blame for their plight. In 1583, the gentleman and author Philip Stubbs became an overnight sensation when he published *The Anatomy of Abuses: containing a Discovery or Brief Summary of such Notable Vices and Imperfections as now reign in many Countries of the World but especially in a famous Island called Ailgna* [that is, Anglia] . . . *together with examples of God's Judgements.* In his encyclopaedic diatribe, Stubbs exposed the evils of gambling, drunkenness, whoring, extravagant dress and personal adornment, gluttony, cupidity, playgoing, usury, swearing, ribald music, violation of the Sabbath, bear-baiting, lewd books, and every other vice that he could cram into 200 pages of text. All such sinful behaviour, Stubbs pointed out:

> springeth from our ancient enemy the devil, the inveterate corruption of our nature and the [stubborn] malice of our own hearts, as [well] as from the efficient causes and stinking puddles of all uncleanness and filthiness whatsoever. But we are now new creatures, and the adopted children of God created in Christ Jesus to good works which God hath prepared for us to walk in, and therefore we ought to have no fellowship with the works of darkness . . .[16]

'No fellowship'? How was contamination to be avoided? The official answer was: by church teaching and civil law working hand in hand. It was at this point that Browne shouted 'No!'

> We hold all those preachers and teachers accursed which will not do the duties of pastors and teachers till the magistrates force them to . . . they give up the weapons of their warfare into the enemies' hands, and then say they cannot do anything because of this . . . These weapons they have given away, for they have not the keys

of the kingdom to bind and loose and to retain or pronounce 'remitted' the sins of men, seeing they grant there is much open wickedness incurable among them and also insist that it needs to be tolerated. Yes they have given up these keys to the government authorities or to the spiritual courts, and therefore have no right to call themselves the church of God or lawful pastors of it.[17]

So Browne wrote a little later (1582) in his self-defining tract, *A Treatise of Reformation without Tarrying for Any.* This angry young man was not just opposing Elizabeth's church settlement, in which crown courts and episcopal courts operated within their own spheres; he was taking on the Geneva pattern, worked out by Calvin and variously applied in those polities that drew their inspiration from it. This was not only heresy; it teetered on the brink of treason. The authorities could scarcely ignore an orator who scornfully declared that the only way to reform the national Church would be to hang non-preaching ministers from their own steeples, *pour encourager les autres.* The Bishop of Norwich had Browne arrested in 1581.

The young man was, obviously, a considerable embarrassment to his family. Whether they interceded for him or whether Bishop Freke, aware of the Brownes' connection, thought it as well to tread carefully is not clear, but certainly Lord Burghley was approached, and he suggested that the bishop should be lenient with a man moved by 'zeal rather than malice'. Browne was unchastened. As soon as he was released he returned to the sheep of his flock who, if anything, were emboldened by their leader's suffering. History immediately repeated itself – arrest, episcopal complaint, ministerial intervention, release. Now the Brownists sought safety in exodus. Cartwright and his close supporters had already moved to Middelburg, the capital of Zeeland, recently freed by Dutch rebels from Spanish control, and been accorded a warm welcome, but anyone who thought the two bands of exiles would combine was quite wrong. Just as an earlier generation of refugees in Mary's reign had taken their squabbles with them, so Cartwright's people and Browne's followers were soon at loggerheads. Cartwright was committed to reforming the English Church from within. Browne insisted – with hysterical invective – that it was irredeemable. The *only* true Church was the assembly of perfect disciples living in *total* obedience to Christ. Probably it was his argument with Cartwright that spurred him to set out his separatist ideology in *Reformation without Tarrying* and other pamphlets. Copies were sent to Browne's supporters in East Anglia – with dire consequences. Three of them were hanged for handling 'seditious' writings. We should not fail to grasp the significance of this event. As Professor Marshall has pointed out, it was 'the first official killing in England to target christologically orthodox fellow Protestants'.[18]

This manic control freak was now running out of friends. Few could live up to the 'perfection' he required – and which he, also, defined. By the end of 1583, he had parted company with Harrison and most other members of his little community. When he set off on his travels again it was with but four or five male disciples and their families. England was not safe for him, so he made for Scotland. Would the Knoxian regime suit him? It is no surprise whatsoever to discover that his unruly tongue and constant fault-finding once more landed him in trouble. Within weeks he was once more in prison and Burghley was obliged to make representations on his behalf through diplomatic channels.

The narrative continues, boringly repetitive. It has been calculated that Browne was imprisoned on 32 occasions. Three informative facts stand out about the career of this irritable and irritating man. The first and most obvious is his tenacity. He was not deterred by sufferings. Over and again he will have consoled and fortified himself with Jesus' prophecy to his disciples: 'If you belonged to the world, then the world would love you as its own. But I chose you from the world, and you do not belong to it; that is why the world hates you' (John 15.19). Perhaps what was even more testing of his resolve was failure. His powerful oratory won him many followers, but most of them forsook him in order to walk an easier path. The thick-skinned apostle of the true Church would have assured himself that such backsliders were not real members, but did his sturdy self-belief never falter? To withstand the insults, the punishments and the desertions took courage – or folly. Often the barrier between the two is porous.

The second aspect of Browne's story that cannot fail to surprise us is his survival. For that he had to thank his social class. Three men who hawked his books went to the gallows. But the author of those books lived into old age. Why? Because the colporteurs were simple tradesmen, while Browne came from gentry stock. The rigid stratification of Tudor society explains much that we would otherwise find puzzling. Browne attracted a following, not just because he was silver-tongued but because he was educated and a gentleman. He came from the stock of those born to lead. Others joined his band because they were born to follow. The same system protected him. Tailors and shoemakers, like the East Anglican martyrs, were expendable. The man whose families provided the officials who administered law and order in the shires had to be treated more circumspectly.

Third, it seems strange, on first consideration, that the most powerful man in the kingdom, the man who enjoyed the confidence of the queen throughout the greater part of her reign, the man daily shouldering the burden of multifarious affairs of state, should, over and again, have devoted his time and energy to rescuing a troublesome fellow who offered little thanks in return and showed no sign of learning from his mistakes. Family loyalty? Genuine affection? Possibly. However, Lord Burghley had other reasons for wanting to deal quietly and unobtrusively with Protestant extremists like Robert Browne. His own inclination was towards a progressive Protestantism, committed to further reform and based on an educated, preaching ministry. He strove long and hard to try to get the queen to see that the real enemy was not native Puritanism but international Catholicism. Though not drawn to Presbyterianism, he was in sympathy with critics of the episcopate. He opposed the rigidity of the Whitgift regime. Burghley, the astute politique, could see clearly what Whitgift, the blinkered authoritarian, could not: that forcing Puritans up against the wall was exacerbating that very reaction that Whitgift (and the queen) deplored. Defiant ministers were meeting together for mutual support, and some earnest lay people had given up on the Church of England altogether – hence Robert Browne. The trouble was that cases like Browne's provided fuel for the reactionary opposition. It was therefore in the best interests of the reformist cause for such problems to be dealt with as speedily and discreetly as possible.

But Browne never made it easy. After a family conference with Burghley, the zealot was ordered to take up lodging at Stamford, where his Cecil relatives could keep an eye on him. Two years later, however, the incorrigible preacher 'broke bail' and travelled the 40 or so miles to Northampton, to continue proselytizing. The authorities were, by now, very chary about dealing with this turbulent troublemaker with powerful connections. Instead of proceeding through the courts, the Bishop of Peterborough used his ultimate spiritual sanction. He excommunicated Browne. That did the trick. The ceremony of excommunication was public, impressive and humiliating. Usually it took place in three stages, with offenders being given at each one the opportunity to repent. If they remained obdurate they were cut off, not only from the rites of the Church, but also from communion with all 'good Christians'. At what point Browne buckled we do not know, but buckle he did. In 1589, he went back to live at Stamford, where he became the master of the grammar school. Two years later he was ordained and Lord Burghley instituted him as rector of a church in Northamptonshire, close to his birthplace at Tolethorpe. He was, by now, a 'conventional' Puritan and preached against separatism, something that involved him in occasional spats with former followers, who continued to call themselves 'Brownists'. Some of them showed their contempt for Elizabeth's Church by voting with their feet.

Few, if any, separatist-inclined Puritans wanted to go that far, psychologically or geographically. Most activists still hoped to change the Church from within, but there was increasing movement as the atmosphere became more hostile. Things were turning nasty. In July 1583, only days after the three Brownists were hanged in East Anglia for circulating seditious literature, Whitgift became Archbishop of Canterbury and wasted no time in turning the screws on religious dissenters. One of his first acts was to issue *Three Articles* to which all parish clergy must subscribe on pain of deprivation. Each minister had to agree:

1. That her Majesty, under God, hath, and ought to have, the sovereignty and rule over all manner of persons born within her realms . . . either ecclesiastical or temporal, soever they be.
2. That the Book of Common Prayer, and of ordering bishops, priests and deacons, containeth in it nothing contrary to the word of God . . . and that he himself will use the form of the said book prescribed in public prayer and administration of the sacraments, and none other.

3. That he alloweth the book of Articles, agreed upon by the archbishops and bishops of both provinces, and the whole clergy in
Convocation holden at London in the year of our Lord God 1562 . . .
and that he believeth all the Articles therein contained to be agreeable to the word of God.

The backlash was immediate, widespread and loud. William Cecil complained to the archbishop in person, telling him that his draconian
measures smacked of the Spanish Inquisition. There were protests in
Parliament. Petitions and deputations from the shires arrived at Lambeth
Palace and on the Council's table. Most remonstrances launched against
the new official policy foundered on the rock of Whitgift's obduracy. But
one aspect of church life that actually emerged stronger from the conflict
was preaching.

The protests came from people who did not want to be deprived of
a preaching ministry. Clergy unable in good conscience to sign up to
Whitgift's articles lost their jobs. The combination of these two facts
meant that lay individuals and corporations funded more lectureships.
It also meant that, in many areas, the brotherhood of Puritan ministers
became closer. Regular meetings of clergy, known as 'classes', already existed, but they now grew in number. Throughout the country hundreds
of clergy – beneficed and unbeneficed – gathered, usually monthly, for
prayer, mutual exhortation, and discussion of pastoral problems and
church politics. There was no uniformity about these conferences and,
since many were of a clandestine nature, they have left very little by
way of documentary evidence, but it is clear that they all had a distinct
aroma of Genevaism. For example, many exercised internal discipline
and enforced obedience to decisions arrived at through discussion. As
the reign drew towards its close, it began to appear that what was emerging was a Church within a Church.

6

Mission and money

While Elizabethan Anglicans, Puritans and separatists were fighting their domestic battles, English mariners were belatedly joining the race to explore and exploit the New World. By the 1530s, the mineral wealth of South and Central America was being plundered by Spain, and Portuguese mariners had overcome the vastness of the Atlantic and Pacific oceans to reveal that the western American seaboard could be reached by vessels sailing either eastward or westward from their home ports. However, it was 1580 before Francis Drake joined the honour roll of long-distance sea captains by his epic circumnavigation, and Thomas Cavendish's ill-fated attempts to replicate and build on Drake's achievement (1586–1592) showed how difficult it was for sailors based in the higher northern latitudes to exploit trade routes south of the equator. Cavendish died during his second attempted circumnavigation in 1592. English hopes of opening commercial links with the Orient and the western American seaboard, which could be policed by English governments, still rested on discovering a north-west passage. This dream remained unfulfilled, which is why, in the closing years of the sixteenth century, Queen Elizabeth I's subjects began to explore the eastern coastlands of North America. Before we begin to chronicle the development of New England where the *Mayflower* émigrés would eventually establish themselves, we must explore the motivation that lay behind European colonization. In particular, we need to understand the varied and sometimes conflicting imperatives that drove them to sing the Lord's song in strange lands.

Henry VIII did not 'found the British navy' with the aim of establishing a world-spanning empire. From early in his reign he began commissioning great ships – out of vanity, determined to position himself among the most splendid and powerful of contemporary monarchs. The 1,400-ton

Henry Grace à Dieu (commonly known as the *Great Harry*), modestly named after himself, was the biggest ship in Europe when it was launched in 1514. The vessel was a deliberate answer to the great caravels plying between Seville and Lisbon and the new Iberian trading settlements. More specifically, it was a response to the 1,000-ton *Michael* built by Henry's brother-in-law, James IV of Scotland. The *Great Harry*, like the *Mary Rose* that followed it, was made for fighting, with gun ports (an innovation) and 180 cannon. Later, as Henry deliberately entered the arms race with Spain and France, further vessels were added to the royal fleet and, by the end of the reign, when he had provoked potential invasion by his rivals, the royal navy had become a vital defensive shield.

The boost given to the shipbuilding industry by royal patronage led to rapid technical improvements. Merchant vessels became bigger and sturdier. They carried larger crews. They ventured further from their home shores. Mariners honed their skills. They grew more daring. And unscrupulous. Henry VIII's reign was a good time for opportunists.

The second Tudor was totally obsessed with gratifying his own desires. His first lord chancellor, Thomas Wolsey, succinctly identified the key to success in Henry's court: 'Give the king what he wants.' If the royal need was for money, Wolsey negotiated new taxation. If his master was intent on waging war, Wolsey took care of the logistics. If it was a matter of arranging the annulment of Henry's marriage to Catherine of Aragon, Wolsey was expedited to deliver. But he failed and, because he failed, he fell. His replacement was Thomas More, whose heart simply was not in the job. As the rift between the king and the pope widened, More tried to serve two masters and, because he could not give the king's policy 101 per cent support, he fell. The poisoned chalice was now delivered into the hands of Thomas Cromwell, the most talented politique of all Henry VIII's ministers. He was both principled and pragmatic. Principled because, as a convinced Evangelical, he wanted to steer England along the path of reform. Pragmatic because he understood well that the king would only embrace progressive religious policies if he believed them to be in his own personal interest. Cromwell, a man of prodigious industry and clear vision, successfully untangled Henry's matrimonial problem. This action was widely unpopular, but that did not matter as long as the minister had the monarch's backing.

Now it was necessary to dismantle the age-old structure that supported papal authority – the monastic system. Henry might well have baulked at that, had Cromwell not presented his master with an audacious plan that would enable him to indulge to the full his most extravagant ambitions. He showed the king how he could become the richest ruler in Christendom and permanently prevent a papal comeback. Thus began the biggest land grab in English history: the Dissolution of the Monasteries. Phenomenal wealth poured into the treasury as religious houses, their estates and their treasures came into royal hands. However, there was still opposition to the Dissolution, particularly from conservative members of the nobility. Again, Cromwell proved equal to the challenge. Lands newly acquired by the Crown were available for sale through the Court of Augmentations, a government agency specifically set up for this purpose. Whatever their own religious sensibilities, hundreds of major landowners rushed to take advantage of this once-in-a-lifetime opportunity to acquire estates and consolidate their holdings. They thus became complicit in royal policy and were extremely unlikely to make a stand on religious principle at the risk of losing their newly acquired assets. What was created in the 1520s was, thus, a culture of greed and power.

Merchants and mariners could scarcely avoid becoming part of this plunderocracy. There were other factors that impinged more directly on the lives of English seamen. They shared the ocean with rivals from other nations that were manifestly more successful. Spain and Portugal had established over several decades an unassailable lead in trade with the Orient for spices, gems, silks and other exotic luxuries, and a monopoly of the import of precious metals from South and Central America. The quandary facing enterprising English entrepreneurs was obvious: they could remain forever frozen out of lucrative trade or they could resort to piracy. There were plenty of homeward-bound vessels ripe for plunder. The Iberian argosies laden with their fabulous treasures were vulnerable to attack by maritime bandits on the long oceanic voyages to their home ports.

Piracy was a crime and recognized as such by the laws of all the major powers, but it could be, and was, legitimized by two factors: war and religion. In 1544, Henry VIII, getting ready for the invasion of France, ordered all shipowners and captains to 'prepare and equip to the sea such and so many ships and vessels furnished for war' and decreed that they might 'enjoy to his and their proper use, profit and commodity, all and singular such ships, vessels, munition, merchandise, ware, victuals and goods' as might come their way as the result of hostilities.[1] Within months, plundering on the high seas reached a new level when the Bristol captain Robert Reneger, acting with government connivance, captured the Spanish ship *San Salvador* en route from Hispaniola to Seville and appropriated bullion to the value (in modern terms) of £3 million. The *San Salvador*'s crew were subjects of the emperor Charles V (Spain now being part of the Habsburg Empire), with whom Henry was not at war. The imperial ambassador was therefore justifiably outraged when he discovered that Reneger had been lauded as a hero rather than punished as a criminal. Any pretence of maintaining the rule of law at sea now disappeared.

As the Reformation became firmly established, piracy even received divine sanction. Conflicts at sea were regarded as confrontations between truth and heresy (if you were Catholic) or truth and the delusions of Antichrist (if you were Protestant). When English sailors were captured, they found themselves in the prisons of the Inquisition or consigned to work on the galleys. Yet, even rulers ardent in matters of faith could become pragmatic where profit was concerned. When Catholic Mary Tudor was at war with Catholic France, she encouraged her nautical subjects to be vigilant against the foe and to thankfully receive the spoils of war that fell into their hands.

By the time her half-sister came to the throne, plunder from buccaneering made up a significant part of royal income. Elizabeth had two overmastering concerns: to make ends meet and to avoid involvement in the wars of religion engulfing England's Continental neighbours. For 17 years, she managed to remain aloof from the conflict between Philip II of Spain and his Protestant subjects in the Netherlands, despite the urgings of her Council and the provocation of Catholic plots. But her reluctance to encourage rebels in the Low Countries to take up arms against their divinely appointed sovereign did not preclude her sharing in the profits of piracy. She turned a blind eye to the growing attacks mounted by her subjects on the Spanish treasure fleets returning from the New World. When Francis Drake returned from his voyage of circumnavigation in

1580, he was to lay at the queen's feet an unprecedented bounty of gold, silver and jewels 'liberated' from the Spanish galleon *Nuestra Señora de la Concepción*. Her share of the expedition's profit paid all her governmental expenses for a whole year. Ironically, income from the New World colonies financed both sides in the religious war in the Netherlands.

However, England derived other long-term benefits from Drake's epic voyage and his other audacious maritime exploits. The route of the *Golden Hind* in the Pacific provided vital information for English map-makers. Having plundered his way northwards along the west-facing coast of South America, Drake had stirred up such a hornets' nest in the Spanish settlements that he could not return the way he had come. His solution to the problem was to continue along the American coast until he discovered the western end of the assumed North-West Passage. Other mariners, starting at the Atlantic end, had long sought this seaway, which would give their nations virtually private access to the oriental markets. Alas, it was not to be, as Drake's chaplain, Francis Fletcher, noted in his diary:

> we conjecture either that there is no passage at all through these northern coasts (which is most likely), or if there be, that yet it is unnavigable . . . though we searched the coast diligently, even unto 48 degrees, yet found we not the land to trend so much as one point toward the East, but rather running on continually North-West, as if it were directly to Asia.[2]

This negative conclusion confined English interest in the Americas to those areas of the eastern seaboard not colonized by Spain.

England's tutelage in matters maritime had been long, but by the end of the century the nation was almost top of the class. Its shipwrights were building sturdier vessels. Its mariners had mastered the latest navigational aids and techniques. Its merchants were beginning to stake out an important place in international commerce. The Muscovy Company was chartered during the reign of Mary Tudor by the elderly Sebastian Cabot and his protégé, Richard Chancellor. Their primary objective was the discovery of a north-east passage to the Orient. They never achieved it and Chancellor perished in the quest for it, but he and his colleagues did establish a sea route to Russia. When Drake handed Elizabeth I her share of the profits from his circumnavigation, she ploughed some of this windfall into the establishment of the Levant Company, which henceforth enjoyed trading rights with the Ottoman Empire.

Mercantile interest was therefore still focused on the East. Neither the government nor private investors had any interest in challenging Iberian commerce with the Americas or the Indian Ocean. The distances involved, and therefore the costs and risks, were too great. However, a new Protestant-tinged nationalism was emerging. The prevailing mood in the country was progressively anti-Catholic. That does not mean that it was pro-Protestant in any meaningful sense of such a term. Indeed, most of Elizabeth's subjects would have been hard put to explain the theological differences between Rome and Geneva, let alone the fine nuances of official Church of England doctrine. It was simply that the xenophobic prejudice of this island race, never far below the surface, had a new target: Roman Catholicism and, more specifically, its Spanish hellhounds. A new breed of loyalist propagandists emerged who made their appeal to populist sentiment to urge their fellow countrymen to look beyond fending off Philip II's invasion attempt of 1588 and attacking Spain's homeward-bound argosies. They raised people's sights to challenging Iberian colonial supremacy. Among the propagandists of expansionism were the two Richard Hakluyts (1530–1591 and 1552–1616), John Dee (1527–1608) and Thomas Harriot (1560–1621). They used geography, history, old legends and economics to stir their compatriots to bold overseas adventure. In effect, they invented a new mythology.

Dee was England's greatest Renaissance polymath – mathematician, geographer, alchemist, occultist and pursuer of universal knowledge. He became an adviser to the queen on all things maritime, and in 1577 published *The General and Rare Memorials pertaining to the Perfect Art of Navigation*. It was Dee who invented the concept of the 'British Empire', not only as a future aspiration, but as a historical reality that had divine blessing. Basing his argument on the twelfth-century *Historia Regum Britanniae* by Geoffrey of Monmouth, an agglomeration of fact and fantasy, Dee asserted that an ancient Welsh prince by the name of Medoc had not only crossed the Atlantic and discovered North America, but had actually settled there and established a colony – proof of England's prior claim and divine election to rule other lands and peoples. This attempt to provide historical justification for the assertion of national superiority was not unique in the history of civilization. Polybius in the second century BC regarded it as axiomatic that Romans were superior to Phoenicians in physical strength and courage. Hitler based his expansionism on the 'self-evident' transcendent worth of the Herrenvolk. Examples are legion of propagandists who have sought to undergird their policies with assumptions of moral superiority. In the case of the English proto-imperialists of the sixteenth century, religion lay at the root of their programme to challenge the colonial supremacy of Spain and Portugal – or did it?

Richard Hakluyt the elder, a lawyer and Member of Parliament, was fascinated by overseas adventure. He kept company with some of the pioneer explorers bent on finding routes to the East, trading with the Ottoman Empire, or venturing into Persia. He gathered information about the Spanish colonies. He helped the great Flemish cartographer Abraham Ortelius to make a new world-map. And in 1584, when Walter Raleigh was planning to establish a settlement in what is now North Carolina, Hakluyt wrote a pamphlet to sell the plan to potential investors. He listed 31 reasons in support of English New World colonization. The first was to glorify God by winning 'infidels' for Christ. The second was strengthening the position of the Protestant faith. However, after this pious opening there is no further mention of a Christianizing mission or how the gospel was to be proclaimed among the indigenous peoples. Although he itemized the skills that would be needed in the proposed settlement to ensure its rapid and secure establishment, there was no mention of preachers or pastors.

Hakluyt was responsible for the upbringing of his young cousin, also named Richard, and he imparted to the younger man his own passionate belief in transplanting English culture in other lands. Hakluyt junior became an ordained minister, a chaplain to Robert Cecil, secretary to Elizabeth I and James I, and also served on the diplomatic staff of the ambassador to France. He was acquainted with most of the pioneer venturers of the day and became the scribe of their exploits and of others, past and present. Cashing in on the euphoria roused by the defeat of the Spanish Armada, Hakluyt published, in 1589, *The Principal Navigation, Voyages and Discoveries of the English Nation*, a work that, when reprinted and enlarged (1600), ran to over 2,000 folio pages. This monumental work may be seen as a secular counterpart to that other encyclopaedic work of Elizabeth's reign, John Foxe's *Acts and Monuments*. Both writers used history as a source of anecdotal information to illustrate the progress of humanity (and particularly of the English nation) to its present position. Foxe demonstrated that Elizabethan Protestantism was the legitimate heir of Christian heroes and heroines who, over 1,500 years, had been the guardians of the pure gospel. Hakluyt's conviction was stated in the oft-quoted defence of imperialism:

> to posterity no greater glory or honour can be handed down than to subdue the barbarians, to recall the wild and the pagan to life in civil society, to lead the savage back within the orbit of reason, and to imbue the atheists and those alienated from God with reverence for divinity.[3]

Thomas Harriot thoroughly endorsed this principle. After leaving Oxford, he found himself a young man of means and able to indulge his interests in mathematics and navigation. He attracted the patronage of Sir Walter Raleigh, currently planning to establish a settlement on Roanoke Island (North Carolina). The back story of this project is worth outlining for the light it sheds on the convictions of the promoters and the means they employed to achieve their objectives.

Raleigh and his half-brother, Humphrey Gilbert, were Devonians raised among relatives and neighbours steeped in the traditions of the western seas. Gilbert, the elder, chose a military career and served in both the Netherlands and Ireland. He was ruthless, uncompromising and headstrong. His contempt for the Irish rebels is indicated by his custom of ringing his tent with the decapitated heads of his captives. Gilbert's bull-in-a-china-shop attitude to foreign policy is typified by a serious observation made in 1577:

> Her Majesty might annoy the King of Spain by fitting out a fleet of war ships under pretence of a voyage of discovery, and so fall upon the enemy's shipping, destroy his trade in Newfoundland and the West Indies, and possess both regions.[4]

And that was long before England and Spain were officially at war. Gilbert, however, did obtain a charter to found a colony in Newfoundland. The resultant expedition was a flop, and it was not until 1583 that he was able to make a second attempt with five ships, one of which was captained by Walter Raleigh and served by a crew recruited in part from English prisons. He landed at St John's Bay and claimed an extensive territory for the queen with himself as governor. It was a fiasco. Gilbert antagonized the English and French fishing communities already working in the sea off Newfoundland, and his settlers showed a distinct disinclination to settle. Gilbert now headed south, intending, it seems, to establish a colony in the temperate zone. Nothing came of this, and on the voyage home Gilbert's ship foundered, taking all the crew to the bottom. However, something of his gung-ho spirit survived and Raleigh was able to take over his half-brother's charter, with instructions to found a colony in eastern North America as a base for the exploration of the interior and as a haven from which to molest Spain's shipping lanes.

Raleigh never took part personally in the next settlement attempt. He was a royal favourite, enjoying the benefits of life at court while milking his extensive Irish estates. He sent exploratory expeditions, and this is where Thomas Harriot enters the story. He went, not as an aggressive imperialist, but as a scholar, intent on discovering all he could about the land and its people. He learned the local Algonquian language and extensively researched the local flora and fauna of the region Raleigh had named 'Virginia'. Harriot was the first visitor to North America to realize that the interior was very extensive, and the first to make a serious study of the natives, their beliefs and customs. In other words, he treated Virginia as a country with its own established society. His *A Brief and True Report of the New Found Land of Virginia* (1588) was the first scholarly attempt to provide a basis for possible future colonization. He urged respect for the local peoples but, if he appreciated their intelligence, it was because he considered them ripe for 'civility and the embracing of true religion'. Across the Atlantic, however, Raleigh's endeavours were faring no better than Gilbert's. His first Roanoke settlement was abandoned after a year. A second group of 117 men, women and children disappeared without trace.

A century after the European colonization of the Americas had begun,

Spain and Portugal had established flourishing multi-ethnic communities, boasting towns, cities and rural estates where many aspects of life in the Old World were flourishing. England had achieved nothing. There were several reasons for this discrepancy. The most obvious is England's geographical position. Until such time as English shipwrights were able to build vessels large enough and strong enough to sustain regular commerce with the Caribbean region (a voyage of some nine weeks, given favourable conditions), maritime activity was largely limited to piratical raids. Added to such considerations of practical seamanship was the shortage of cash. Tudor state budgets did not run to financing major colonial ventures. Pioneering projects were left to private enterprise, with, as we have seen, results that were far from encouraging. Those temporary settlements that were achieved were unable to report discoveries of mineral or other resources likely to excite backers. To Harriot it was reasonable to suppose that somewhere in the interior of Chesapeake Bay there lurked deposits of gold and silver such as the Spanish conquistadors had stumbled on further south. Harriot introduced his fellow countrymen to the habit of smoking tobacco, and Raleigh brought to his Irish estates a root vegetable that came from Peru, via Spain – the potato. Neither was calculated to excite the mercantile community.

Yet, for all that, voyages to strange lands and the hazards of seaborne voyages had taken root in the English imagination. We need look no further than Shakespeare for evidence of this. Tales of maritime adventure and misadventure featured in *The Merchant of Venice*, *Twelfth Night* and particularly *The Tempest*, the bard's last, undisputed solo play, inspired, it would seem, by the wreck of the *Sea Venture* on the coast of Bermuda, en route for Virginia (1609), and the survival of its complement of settlers (see below, pp. 186f.).

Theoretically, 'preaching the gospel to every creature',[5] and thus hastening the Second Coming, was still the official pious objective of colonization, but by the time the reformed nations of Europe joined in long-distance sea travel and the establishment of settlements in distant lands, motives had become much more mundane – not to say brutal – than in the days of Columbus. Yet, New Spain had been conquered by both soldiers *and* monks. From the earliest days, therefore, materialism was at war with spirituality or, to put it more crudely, greed and violence clashed with love and religious devotion. The Franciscans and Dominicans, who began their work in Mexico in 1524-1525, saw themselves as harbingers of the kingdom of God, servants of that gospel which had to be preached to all peoples before the end of the world could come. There was a strong dose of feudalism about the regimen established in Mexico. Spanish settlers were granted *encomienda*, estates comprising several native villages. The grantees – *encomenderos* – combined the functions of military protectors and judges, providing stability and security. In return, they had the right to levy taxes. Part of their responsibility was to facilitate the work of missionaries.

The first of these to arrive in 1524-1525 were Franciscan and Dominican friars. In order to establish an ecclesiastical superstructure, the Franciscan Juan de Zumárraga was nominated as bishop by the emperor Charles V, with the additional title 'Protector of the Indians'. Thus, from the beginning, the potential for conflict between conquerors and conquered was recognized, and the missionaries acted as a protective barrier. Many of the first friars were radicals, reared in the humanist tradition of Erasmus. They showed respect for indigenous traditions and sought to present the gospel in terms Mexican peasants could understand. Part of Zumárraga's vision was for the translation of the Bible into Amerindian dialect. The colonial situation, however, was not simply that of the relationship between local people, settlers and missionaries. The imperial government imposed a bureaucratic administration directly responsible to the Crown. All the elements of social, political and religious discord that were features of life in the Old World were thus transported to the New: central government versus nobles; nobles versus peasants; secular authority versus religious authority; radical Christianity versus tradition. Underneath the overlapping layers of authority that made up the power structure of Spanish colonial America were the original inhabitants. Exploitation was written into the system.

Further afield the situation was even worse. As Spanish rule spread into what are now Bolivia and Peru, economic development bore heavily on the natives. Wherever product demand appears, it sucks in investment in the form of capital and labour. Just as in England a ready export market for wool and woollen cloth led to the enclosure of common land and the conversion of arable land to pasture, so in the Spanish colonies demand for meat, hides, tallow and wool resulted in large-scale stock ranching, which destroyed communal farming and the village economy that rested on it. The mining of precious metals created a gold-rush mentality among hopeful settlers, who worked feverishly to register claims and dig shafts. Except that they did not, of course, do the hard graft themselves; not when there was on hand a ready task-force of natives who could be pressed into working long hours for low pay. Hard working conditions and the spread of disease resulted in a high death toll among the pick-and-shovel labourers.

How did all this square with the Christian mission and the hastening of the arrival of the kingdom of God? Inevitably, the answer depends on our theological standpoint. Roman Catholic leaders applauded the phenomenal victories of the Church Militant. Within a generation, the mission in Mexico claimed to have made over a million converts. It was said that, at the summit of his work there, the Franciscan Peter of Ghent held mass baptisms for as many as 14,000 people. Peter spent 40 years among the Mexicans, learned their language, and built churches, schools and hospitals. The landscape around Lake Titicaca, on the borders of Peru and Bolivia, was studded with large churches built under the direction of Dominican friars determined to make a visual statement that would challenge the impressive Inca temples that had hitherto dominated the region. Nothing on this scale in the Western Church had happened since the work of St Boniface and his colleagues in what is now Germany and the Netherlands. But there was a monumentally significant difference: the eighth-century Anglo-Saxon Benedictine monks did not have the backing of a technically superior army and a colonial government committed to establishing and maintaining control by any and every means. When, in 1572, the last Inca, Tupac Amaru, was captured and sentenced to death (despite the pleadings of the Spanish friars), he was kept in prison in order to receive religious instruction. According to one eyewitness, he made the following confession from the scaffold:

> Be it known to you that I am a Christian, they have baptised me and I wish to die under the law of God. And I do have to die. All that I and my ancestors the Incas have told you up to now – that you should worship the sun Punchao and the huacas, idols, stones,

rivers, mountains and vilcas [a species of tree] – is completely false. When we told you that we were entering [the temple] to speak to the sun, that it advised you to do what we told you, and that it spoke, this was false. It did not speak, we alone did: for it is an object of gold and cannot speak. My brother Titu Cusi told me that whenever I wished to tell the Indians to do something, I should enter alone to the idol Punchao . . . afterwards I should come out and tell all the Indians that it had spoken to me, and that it said whatever I wished to tell them.[6]

The sincerity of such conversions could be, and was, challenged from time to time. Similarly, some Catholic critics cast doubt on the purity of the Christian faith preferred by the Amerindian *conversos*. Images and places of worship hallowed by centuries of use before the conquest were often 'absorbed' to make it easier for people to make the transition to the faith of the white people.

How much English church leaders knew about the intricacies of life in the Iberian colonies is problematic. In principle they disapproved of 'Catholic barbarity'. But they also learned from it. The as yet unsubdued countries yielded not only mineral and vegetable resources but also the workforce to exploit them. Yet joining in the colonial race still lay in the future while England was absorbed in political and religious competition with its neighbours.

Writing in 1584, Richard Hakluyt senior sought to persuade Queen Elizabeth that 'western discovery will be greatly for the enlargement of the Gospel of Christ whereunto the princes of the Reformed religion are chiefly bound, amongst whom Her Majesty is principal'.[7] We may well wonder whether Hakluyt really believed that the conversion of 'primitive' peoples was a charge laid on the spiritual heirs of Luther and Calvin; that expansion into the New World would be to the eternal benefit of its peoples or that planting the gospel in the hearts of Amerindians was an important step towards the establishment of the kingdom of God. At an early date in the reign of the fifth Tudor a clear marker had been put down for those interested in weighing piety against pragmatism. In 1565, the queen had made a grant of arms to the Devon buccaneer Sir John Hawkins. Its crest was 'a demi-Moor in his proper colour, bound and captive, with annulets in his arms and ears'. This armorial device, prob-ably requested by Hawkins but certainly approved by the royal heralds, represented his most successful trading venture to date.

The queen had given her backing to a particularly audacious series of ventures – which strained diplomatic ties, exploited the febrile rela-tions between Philip II and his subjects in the distant Caribbean, and established clearly that, despite protests to the contrary, when it came to a contest between the greater good and profit, between mission and money, between God and mammon, the dice were heavily loaded. Hawkins' first voyage had taken place during the reign of Mary, when English vessels could, without hazard, operate in the colonial domain of the queen's husband, Philip II. Canny entrepreneur that he was, he had understood that the West Indian plantation owners and gold miners were desperate for a commodity in short supply: agricultural labour; disease and harsh working conditions having decimated the local population. The colonists had become dependent on slaves brought, principally by Portuguese ships, from West Africa. It was this trade Hawkins decided to break into. Between 1562 and 1569 he led three expeditions to the region of Sierra Leone where he acquired, by trade with coastal chiefs, direct raiding and, on one occasion, plundering a Portuguese ship, hundreds of slaves. These were taken to the islands and coastlands of the Caribbean where the unfortunate wretches who had survived the Atlantic crossing were exchanged for molasses, ginger, hides and other local produce to sell in England. The Spanish government resented this invasion of their monopoly, but the governor of the New World settlements was not dis-posed to adhere too nicely to directives from distant Seville if there were good deals to be done with 'heretical pirates'.

The 'triangular trade' delivered handsome profits to investors, including the queen. It established Hawkins' reputation and turned him into some-thing of a legend. No expostulations were heard from Protestant members of the Council, or Parliament, or the merchant community. No one seemed to be asking how violence and rapine were to be squared with the Bible. Hakluyt and other advocates of colonial expansion might talk about spreading the faith, but that was all so much window dressing. Evangelical many of Elizabeth's subjects might be. Evangelistic they were not.

7

Divided we stand

Policy I hate: I had as lief be a Brownist as a politician.

The witless Sir Andrew Aguecheek's scornful dismissal of Brownists will have drawn laughter from the audience of Shakespeare's *Twelfth Night* for the very reason that the name had, by this time (1601-1602), become a byword for stupidity.[1] Unlike 'Puritan' and 'papist' it was not so much a contemptuous insult as an expression of pity. Brownists were people so committed to literal biblicism and their determination to live by every jot and tittle of the written word of God that it became impossible for them to exist in normal human society. These were sad folk who could not cope with the cut and thrust of life in a broken world and so withdrew into their own perfectionist stockades. There was no need to be angry with Brownists because they did not comprise a threat to the existing order. They were not rebels seeking to *change* society. They simply withdrew. In avoiding the moral and theological corruption they saw in the sinful world around them, they *ipso facto* did not challenge that world to embrace their beliefs. By the end of the sixteenth century, the word 'Brownist' had become a common term for the increasing number of Christian separatists who were opting out of Elizabethan society. Even though Robert Browne himself had, as we have seen, made his peace with the establishment, the name stuck and was applied to a range of separatists who turned their back on the world at large.

By the 1580s, religious radicalism in Europe had split into several minor movements. It was, in fact, endemically fissiparous. Once the authority of the pope had been replaced by the authority of the word of God written in a language 'understanded of the people',[2] Christian belief and practice was in the hands of men who interpreted that word in different ways and persuaded bands of followers to accept and live by their interpretations. The logical end point of this process was individualism – every Bible student his or her own theologian. We all know that, by subtle dialectic and manipulation of proof texts, almost any religious proposition can be advanced and defended. Religious innovators have been doing this for the best part of 2,000 years. In so doing, they have challenged the prevailing concept of 'church', since, by definition, a Christian church is an assembly of people who agree on certain 'truths'. There was nothing new about what was happening in the spiritual hothouse of sixteenth-century Europe; it was just happening faster and more frenetically than ever before. Professor Marshall neatly captured the mood of those times in the title of his history of the English Reformation: *Heretics and Believers*.

While the majority of Queen Elizabeth's subjects were content with her religious settlement, the minority, on whom the historian must, of necessity, concentrate, were part of a confessional continuum, reaching back via the Marian exiles to the Lollards and earlier. The bulk of the Puritans hoped to change the English Church from within. Even the Presbyterians were not intent on breaking away from the establishment. When we explore the earliest Elizabethan 'separatists' that we can discern, it is not at all clear that they saw themselves as people who must withdraw from the Church by law established. In 1567, a hundred or so people gathered in London's Plumbers' Hall, supposedly to celebrate a wedding. In reality, they were taking part in an illegal act of worship. About 17 or 18 people were arrested and spent some months in prison. Bishop Grindal of London was convinced that he was dealing with a breakaway group, as he explained in a letter to Bullinger:

Some London citizens of the lowest order, together with four or five ministers, remarkable neither for their judgment nor learning, have openly separated from us; and sometimes in private houses, sometimes in the fields, and occasionally even in ships, they have held their meetings and administered the sacraments. Besides this, they have ordained ministers, elders, and deacons, after their own way, and have even excommunicated some who had seceded from their church. And because masters Laurence Humphrey, Sampson, Lever, and others who have suffered so much to obtain liberty in respect of things indifferent, will not unite with them, they now regard them as semi-papists, and will not allow their followers to attend their preaching. The number of this sect is about two hundred, but consisting of more women than men. The privy council have lately committed the heads of this faction to prison, and are using every means to put a timely stop to this sect.[3]

However, other contemporaries did not agree with the bishop's description of the Plumbers' Hall worshippers. Some identified that group as Presbyterians. There also seems to have been a measure of overlap with one of the 'stranger churches' (groups of foreign religious refugees allowed to follow their own practices and not under episcopal authority). Clearly, membership of the extremist fringe was extremely fluid. It was only as the establishment gradually got a stronger grip on the situation, over subsequent decades, that separatists were forced into self-identifying and self-justifying groups. What I think we can say is, first of all, that the extremists saw themselves as inheritors of a long tradition of dissent and, second, that they believed they were recipients of progressive revelation from God, who was revealing to them, exclusively and more fully, his plans for each succeeding generation.

Before we consider in detail the history of those separatist groups that would eventually include the travellers on the *Mayflower*, we ought to remind ourselves of the context within which their protests were launched. The whole English Church was not convulsed over such questions as 'Who belongs to the elect?' and 'Where is the visible Church?' At the end of the century

the rector of a parish in Kent found that of four hundred communicants, 'scarcely 40' had any knowledge about sin, Christ, death and the afterlife. It was said of men in south Yorkshire and Northumberland that they were totally ignorant of the Bible and did not know the Lord's Prayer. A Yorkshire boy, when quizzed by the minister, could not say 'how many gods there be, nor persons in the godhead, nor who made the world, nor anything about Jesus Christ, nor heaven or hell'. Otherwise he was 'a witty boy and could talk of any worldly things skilfully enough'. A Lancashire woman when asked about the Jesus Christ mentioned in the Creed, replied 'she could not tell, but by our dear Lady it is sure some good thing or it should never have been put in the Creed but what it is I cannot tell you'. An old man from Cartmel . . . a regular church attender . . . when Christ was mentioned . . . said, 'I think I heard of that man you spoke of, once in a play at Kendall, called Corpus Christi play, where there was a man on a tree, and blood ran down'.[4]

It was because play-goers did not see beneath the sober costume and the pious talk of *all* Puritans and could not distinguish Presbyterians from Brownists that they could laugh at Ben Jonson's portrayal of 'a sort of sober, scurvy, precise neighbours that scarce have smiled twice since the king came in'.[5]

Shakespeare's satire was more penetrating and all-embracing. In *Twelfth Night* (first performed in 1602), audiences were introduced to the noble Lady Olivia who, having forsworn marriage, rules her estate without the aid of a husband, and has in her household a good-for-nothing uncle, Sir Toby Belch, who takes advantage of her hospitality to indulge in drunken revelry. Despite his humorous antics, Belch is a nasty piece of work who preys on friend and foe alike (including his dim-witted companion, Sir Andrew Aguecheek). His particular bugbear is Olivia's steward, the holier-than-thou Malvolio. Belch and his accomplices play an elaborate trick on their quarry, which ends in his being locked up in a darkened room. Play-goers can hardly have missed the allusion to the queen, the bullying church establishment, and precisionist Puritans who were thrown into prison on the order of the Court of High Commission. What the play-goers were offered was a kind of double bluff. Malvolio was not the stock image of the Bible-bashing Puritan. Rather he was a lampoon of the image put out by Whitgift's propagandists. Similarly, Belch and Aguecheek were caricatures of the caricatures publicized by Puritan satirists. The 'message' of the play was that in Olivia's Illyria, just as in Elizabeth's England, self-righteous religious prigs were part of the problem – but so were their pitiless persecutors.

Considering the fact that Browne was eventually reconciled to the official Church of the nation (he served his parish faithfully for over 40 years), it is scarcely appropriate that his name came to be applied to all separatists and that he is still sometimes referred to as the father of

'Congregationalism'. Insofar as that word defines the principles of independency – that each congregation is a self-contained unit – it will serve to describe the breakaway assemblies of the sixteenth and seventeenth centuries, but it cannot be stretched to cover the many shades of doctrine and practice of all the separatist groups. What we can say is that most of them shared certain characteristics to do with exclusivity, authority and intolerance, and that it was these characteristics that invited hostile reaction.[6]

The reformed Church of England followed Calvin in distinguishing between the visible and the invisible Church:

> Holy Scripture speaks of the Church in two ways: sometimes it means by that word the Church which is such in very truth, no one being included excepting those who by the grace of adoption are children of God, and by the sanctification of his Spirit are true members of Jesus Christ . . . But often, by the name of the Church, it means the whole multitude of men who, scattered over various regions of the world, make the same profession of honouring God in Jesus Christ, have the same baptism as evidence of their faith, who by the partaking of the Supper claim to have unity in doctrine and in charity, who accept the word of God and seek to protect the preaching of it in obedience to the commandment of Jesus Christ. In this Church there are some hypocrites, mingled among the good, who have nothing of Jesus Christ but the title and the appearance . . . However, as it is necessary for us to believe that the Church is invisible to us and known to one God alone, so we are also commanded to hold the visible Church in honour and keep ourselves in communion with it.[7]

For Calvin, it followed logically from belief in a sovereign God who alone elected those who would be saved that the true Church was invisible to mortal eyes. Most separatists stood this assertion almost on its head: the visible Church was manifestly corrupt and theologically in error. Therefore it was not the Church. No matter how many righteous people might belong to it, it was not the Church. Because holy discipline was not applied to drive out all sin and all error, it was not the Church. Because it was not *perfect*, it was not the Church.

The true Church consisted of those communities of people in covenant with God who submitted to the discipline of God's word *as set forth by his chosen pastors*. What was at stake was a clash of authority – just as it had been when Lollards were dragged before the ecclesiastical courts; when Martin Luther defied Pope Leo; when Thomas Müntzer and Luther urged their opposing supporters to the bloodbath at Frankenhausen; when any cult or sect leader proclaimed: 'I speak in the name of God – follow me.'

Authority. Discipline. These were at the heart of the conflict between the leaders of the state church and those who elected to secede from the state church. Here was no issue of freedom of conscience. Both sides asserted the right and duty of ministers to impose what the laity should believe, and the duty of the laity to submit to their guidance.

Archbishop Whitgift was as forthright as Robert Browne about this. It is no coincidence that the conflict between ecclesiastical authority and the rival authority claimed by separatist leaders coincided, in 1583, with the death of Archbishop Grindal and the consecration of Whitgift. The new primate set out his manifesto quite clearly in a letter to Sir Francis Walsingham, the queen's secretary: 'I have taken upon me the defence of the religion and rites of the Church of England, to appease [that is, bring to order] the sects and schisms therein, to reduce all the ministers thereof to uniformity and due obedience.'[8]

One of Whitgift's first acts was to equip the church hierarchy with sharp teeth. He increased the powers of what had been a rather vaguely defined tribunal for settling a range of ecclesiastical disputes – the Court of High Commission – and employed it specifically as a weapon against Puritans. This body became a focus of the resentment not only of religious radicals but also of civil lawyers who saw it as a rival to the crown courts. This was only the beginning of the archiepiscopal witch hunt. Whitgift now issued a set of articles to which all clergy were instructed to subscribe. Among other points inimical to Puritans was the assertion that the Elizabethan Prayer Book 'containeth nothing contrary to the word of God' and that, therefore, all ministers must use it *in toto*. In the summer of 1584, at the very time that he was dealing with the latest instalment of his kinsman's turbulent career, Cecil told the archbishop to his face that his authoritarian stance was 'Romish' and that his attempts to straitjacket the beliefs and conduct of the clergy smacked of the Spanish Inquisition. Lord Burghley was not alone in complaining. Hundreds of clergy objected to the archbishop's high-handedness.

It was not only issues of church faith and practice that were giving rise to angry letters and unpleasant publications. The atmosphere in the public domain in the early part of this decade was toxic. The year 1584 saw the publication of a pamphlet with the innocuous title *The Copy of a Letter Written by a Master of Arts at Cambridge*. Better known as *Leicester's Commonwealth*, it was a vitriolic attack on Robert Dudley emanating from a Catholic press on the continent. Its catalogue of libellous accusations was wide-ranging and extreme, presumably based on the principle that if the authors threw enough mud some of it would stick. They claimed to be loyal subjects warning Elizabeth against conspirators close to the throne who drew their support from Calvinist groups that were poised ready to seize power when Dudley's plot to usurp power came to fruition.

Leicester's Commonwealth demonstrates that it was not just 'Brownists' who were attacking their enemies with any weapons that came to hand, and it indicates how acute the crisis of the 1580s was. Observers on both sides of the religious divide sensed that the years of cautious, tightrope diplomacy were coming to an end: the Protestant–Catholic Armageddon was almost upon them. The succession of conspiracies against Elizabeth's throne; the activities of defiant Puritan ministers and Catholic priests; the persistent rumours of Guise plots to invade Scotland; the severance of diplomatic relations with Spain; the assassination of William of Orange; the progress of the seemingly irresistible Parma in the Low Countries; the papal excommunication; the plans maturing in Madrid for an invasion of England; all were signs that the storm was about to break. It was now that Burghley, with strong parliamentary support, took an initiative which, as well as making practical provision for the worst possible scenario, was meant to identify for a queen still reluctant to face facts just who her real enemies were. The Bond of Association pledged the thousands of substantial Englishmen who signed it to wreak vengeance on anyone who assassinated the queen. Any claimant to the throne seeking to profit from so monstrous an act would be hunted down. The obvious target was Mary Queen of Scots and her Catholic backers. It was frustrating for the majority of Elizabeth's advisers that she persisted in considering Puritans to be just as treacherous as Catholic recusants. She dug her heels in over unfurling the Protestant banner in her foreign policy and in applying the final solution to the Mary Queen of Scots problem. Only at the end of 1585 did she consent to English troops going to the aid of the Dutch rebels, and it was a year after that that consent for Mary's death was wrung from her.

The next gauntlet thrown down to the church leaders – the Marprelate controversy – made the Browne affair look like a polite after-dinner discussion. The year 1588, of course, witnessed the Spanish Armada scare. The nation went on the alert to face the threat of invasion launched by Philip II, the erstwhile husband of Mary Tudor. Elizabeth's subjects feared – or hoped – that another reversal of the nation's religious identity was imminent, that the old queen would have her revenge from beyond the grave. Early in the year a false rumour that the invasion force was on its way sent hundreds of south coast residents fleeing inland. The government suppressed the publication of almanacs. Small wonder when the year produced two lunar eclipses, and a certain prophecy attributed to the fifteenth-century astrologer Regiomontanus was in circulation: 'Though in this remarkable eighty-eighth year the world will not melt away, yet in all parts of the world governments will fall and there will be mourning enough.'[9]

As great as the apprehension was the relief and rejoicing when (doubtless with divine intervention on behalf of the victors) the Armada was decisively defeated. Some of the bolder Puritan spirits decided that the moment was right to ride the wave of euphoria and anti-papal triumphalism. They directed popular attention away from the enemy without to the Rome-tinged enemy within. October 1588 to September 1589 was the year of the Marprelate controversy.

Within that brief timeframe, seven outrageously scurrilous tracts were published that harnessed a new and powerful force to ecclesiological debate: satire. This calumny of church leaders went way beyond the humorous exposés of Boccaccio and Brant. The queen was mightily offended. The bishops were outraged. And the people loved it. The anonymous 'Martin Marprelate' poked fun very specifically at the bishops and other senior clergy by name. Aylmer of London was too fond of the bottle and spent his Sundays bowling rather than worshipping. Whitgift was a vainglorious ass who loved pompous display. Cooper of Winchester was an inveterate gambler. Richard Bancroft, who had recently delivered a swingeing attack on Puritans in a sermon at St Paul's, was addicted to wrestling and little more than a thug. Marprelate mercilessly lampooned the cupidity of the clergy, their worldliness and their lack of learning. His fundamental message was, 'When you abandon the biblical pattern of church government, this is the sort of rubbish you end up with':

> Is it any marvel that we have so many swine, dumb-dogs, non-residents . . . so many lewd livers, as thieves, murderers, adulterers, drunkards, cormorants, rascals; so many ignorant and atheistical dolts, so many covetous Popish bishops, in our ministry; and so many and so monstrous corruptions in our Church?[10]

The arrows struck home, so painfully that the hierarchy launched a frenzied campaign to unmask and silence Martin Marprelate. In fact, he was probably more than one person – a team of writers and printers who moved their operation from safe house to safe house whenever the episcopal bloodhounds got too close. The paper trail led pursuers through those very Midland shires where the parents of later *Mayflower* voyagers were living (see below, pp. 123ff; 152ff.). Crown and Mitre rather belatedly resorted to answering Marprelate in his own terms. They recruited playwrights of the calibre of Robert Greene and Thomas Nashe to enter the fray by making fun of 'holy hypocrites'. The renegade press was located and silenced but not before it had stimulated a bitter public debate that now seriously worried the government. Most of those who enjoyed the public slanging match were not supporters of the Puritan cause, but it is significant that on 31 May 1593, when John Penry, one of the leading members of the Marprelate gang, was hanged at St Thomas-a-Watering, an execution site on the Old Kent Road, linking the capital to Canterbury, one chronicler recorded that it was done in a hurry with scant advertisement 'lest he should have raised some tumult either in going up or on the gallows'.[11]

In this same year, the government's campaign against the Puritans achieved its greatest victory. Gradually, parliamentary opposition to

Whitgift and the hard-line bishops had been worn down and legislation went through both houses with the no-nonsense title 'An Act to Retain the Queen's Subjects in Obedience'. That mesh was fine enough to catch both Catholic recusants and Puritan separatists. All who refused to attend their parish churches were identified as 'seditious sectaries and disloyal persons'. Shunning the queen's religion was, in future, to be accounted a felony, punishable by a prison sentence or banishment. Anyone charged under the Act could avoid the penalty only by making a public submission in words that unequivocally and explicitly excluded the Calvinist concept of 'church':

I, *A.B.*, do humbly confess and acknowledge, that I have grievously offended God in condemning her majesty's godly and lawful government and authority, by absenting myself from church, and from hearing divine service, contrary to the godly laws and statutes of this realm, and in using and frequenting disordered and unlawful conventicles and assemblies, under pretence and colour of exercise of religion: and I am heartily sorry for the same, and do acknowledge and testify in my conscience that no other person has or ought to have any power or authority over her majesty: and I do promise and protest, without any dissimulation, or any colour or means of any dispensation, that from henceforth I will from time to time obey and perform her majesty's laws and statutes, in repairing to the church and hearing divine service, and do my uttermost endeavour to maintain and defend the same.[12]

Elizabeth was urging her Puritan subjects to become Nicodemites. Her revenge against Calvin had been a long time coming. It was all the sweeter for that.

By this time there were so many dissident groups across the theological spectrum – from Catholic recusants to Anabaptists – it seemed that only such draconian action could safeguard the concept of the nation-church. As for those determined to reject the Elizabethan settlement, their harlequin beliefs all had one common factor – the visible Church. For example, John Smyth embraced Anabaptism and rejected the doctrine of original sin. Yet, like other separatists, he claimed that his church was the only one, based on the definition of the true Church as 'a visible communion of saints . . . joined together by covenant with themselves'. 'All religious societies except that of a visible church are unlawful,' he insisted. He made a direct correlation between the manifest evils of society and the concept of a national Church. Because England was, in his opinion, 'Babylon, the mother of all abominations, the habitation of devils and the [abode] of all foul spirits and a cage of every unclean and hateful bird', the official Church presided over by the secular head of state could only be a diabolical delusion.[13] The psychological attraction of this clear-cut, black-and-white teaching is obvious. Anyone who believed in the Calvinist doctrine of election needed some assurance that he or she was really among the chosen few. Membership of an exclusive, *visible* community, called out from the rest of humanity to be *holy* (a word that in biblical Hebrew – *qōdeš* – and Greek – *hagios* – has the connotation of sacredness, purity and also separateness), provided that guarantee. Problems, however, arose because such communities of zealots in pursuit of personal and corporate purity were prone to amoeba-like bifurcation. This is evidenced by the prehistory of those groups from which the *Mayflower* voyagers emerged.

The richest soil from which the separatist tree sprang was Cambridge University. It was here that the conflict between Thomas Cartwright and John Whitgift began in the 1560s. Cartwright, as we have seen, sojourned briefly in Middelburg, where he had his altercation with Robert Browne in 1582. Meanwhile, back in Cambridge, Presbyterianism was far from dead. It was here also that, 20 years later, two other students began their tortuous and troubled spiritual journeys. Francis and George Johnson were sons of a prosperous Yorkshire woollen draper, and both became radicalized during their university years. The unhappy relationship of the brothers provides a pointer to tendencies that bedevilled some separatist communities. Francis and George shared extremist religious views, but they also experienced a sibling rivalry that, in time, turned to hatred.

The first dramatic incident that propelled the Johnsons into the limelight of religious controversy occurred early in 1589. Francis, by now a fellow of Christ's College, decided to make himself the spokesman of the sizeable number of Cambridge malcontents who were at loggerheads with the establishment over the governance of the university and wider religious issues. In a sermon delivered in the university church of Great St Mary's, he deliberately doused with petrol the smouldering embers of protest. He declared that the organization of the English Church in general and the Cambridge system in particular had led to 'ignorance, atheism, idolatry, profanation of the sabbath and disobedience to superiors'.[14] This would have landed him in hot water at any time, but at the height of the Marprelate witch hunt the authorities were particularly sensitive to criticism. Archbishop Whitgift demanded stern reprisals. Students took to the streets in angry protest. Francis was dismissed from his fellowship and spent a spell in prison (it would be the first of many).

Once freed he betook himself, like Cartwright before him, to Middelburg, in Zeeland, the nearest Dutch city where religious refugees were welcomed. He was one of many migrants for whom this was an obvious staging post. The United Provinces were in the full flower of their golden age and attracting foreigners of all kinds: merchants, craftspeople, soldiers, and students, as well as religious exiles. It was there that Francis became acquainted with the writings of two other Cambridge alumni, John Greenwood and Henry Barrow. Both men had emerged from the university as convinced radicals. Greenwood, after a few years as an ordained minister, abandoned holy orders and became the leader of a separatist assembly in London. He spent several brief spells in prison. Henry Barrow, some ten years Greenwood's senior, joined him in what was by then known as the Southwark Independent Church. By 1586, he found himself also in prison. It was while confined that the two men wrote three pamphlets setting out their teaching. These were sent to the Low Countries for printing, which is how Johnson encountered them. He was won over to the belief in the visible Church, as a community of saints in which holiness was achieved through good teaching and firm discipline.

Francis Johnson returned to England in 1592 to take up leadership of the Southwark assembly because Greenwood and Barrow were still in prison. He was able to visit them in their confinement and encourage them to be steadfast in their sufferings. Seemingly, their courage needed no such bolstering. In various examinations by the Court of High Commission, they showed themselves to be steadfast, stubborn and arrogant. Not only were they an annoyance to their interrogators;

they were also an embarrassment. The bishops now had the power to proceed against dissidents by the 1593 Act to retain the queen's subjects in their due obedience. This provided the penalty of death or exile for offenders guilty of 'devising and circulating seditious books', and sedition included refusal to be reconciled to the queen's Church. The stubborn separatists had forced Whitgift and his associates into an uncomfortable corner. They genuinely did not want to be driven to the exigency of inflicting capital punishment. It smacked too much of the Inquisition. But Greenwood and Barrow refused to offer their opponents an escape route. Even after sentence had been passed, several attempts – ultimately futile – were made to talk the prisoners into recantation. Twice they were brought from their prison to the place of execution in the hope that this would frighten them into pleading for mercy. On a third occasion they were taken to the scaffold and the nooses were placed around their necks, only to be removed. On 6 April 1593 they were brought thither again. This time there was no reprieve.

By this time, both the Johnsons were also in prison. George had taken a teaching post in London after leaving Cambridge and was an active member of the separatist community, which sometimes met in his schoolhouse. It may well be that the election of Francis as leader of the group on his return from exile was the last straw added to the camel's back of their relationship. From this point they were rivals rather than associates.

By now the best solution for all parties seemed to be exile. The government could wash its hands of the troublemakers and they would be free to worship and believe according to their own insight. So migration across the North Sea continued. Francis Johnson, however, having had a taste of the fractious Netherlands assemblies, was reluctant to rejoin the company of believers in a foreign land. He petitioned the Crown for permission to seek a home for himself and his imprisoned friends in one of Her Majesty's overseas settlements where they could establish their own laws and customs. Once again Lord Burghley, now in his seventies, came to the rescue of religious extremists. It was almost certainly the minister who was the instigator of a scheme devised by Charles Leigh, a London merchant, a colonial enthusiast and a man with Brownist sympathies. England was currently involved in a spat with Breton and

Basque merchants over the use of the Magdalen Islands, in the Gulf of St Lawrence, as a base for fishing and seal hunting.

The English merchants believed the answer would be to set up a *permanent* colony, rather than the seasonal camps that had previously supported the fishermen. But could any hardy souls be found to go and live in this relatively inhospitable location? To Burghley it must have seemed that the bringing together of Johnson and Leigh was a marriage made in heaven. In 1597, the Johnson brothers and two companions travelled with Leigh on two ships, the *Chancewell*, commanded by Stephen van Harwick, and Leigh's own *Hopewell*, as an advance guard of separatist 'pilgrims' (a word they consciously used). They were to be followed the next year by other members of their fellowship. The result was a combination of just about all the calamities that were later to become commonplace in the New World religious settlements.

The trouble began before the ships had even left England. At Falmouth, George Johnson distributed among the crews religious material that was clearly (according to the Act) seditious. Francis managed to pacify the angry captain, but his zealous sibling continued his proselytizing once they were at sea. When the ships reached the Newfoundland coast they were separated in the fog. The *Chancewell* subsequently ran aground and was then attacked and stripped by Basque fishermen. Van Harwick was intent on reprisals, much to the dismay of George Johnson. The captain, who must by this time have been thoroughly sick of his pious and argumentative passenger, told him that he had three options: stay ashore and chance his luck with the natives, surrender to the Catholic Basques, or join in the planned attack. George was spared the choice by the reappearance of the *Hopewell*.

Meanwhile Leigh's ship had also hit trouble with the foreigners and became involved in running battles with both Breton and Basque vessels. By the time the two ships' complements were reunited, arguments were rife and all sense of common purpose had evaporated. Leigh had lost control to a group of mariners who were set on turning the voyage into a piratical spree. Francis Johnson's little company had fallen into rival theological camps and were arguing fiercely about abstruse doctrinal issues. As usual, George Johnson was at the centre of this discord. There was now no question of setting up a colony. The *Hopewell* set course for home.

By the time they reached Southampton, they had decided to head for the United Netherlands without drawing attention to themselves en route, something made difficult by the evangelizing activities of George Johnson, who did not know the meaning of the word 'discretion'. The Johnsons chose Amsterdam for their destination because other members of their London group had eventually relocated there after other towns had closed their doors to them. The little English community was in dire straits and worse problems were to come. The most obvious difficulty was poverty. The wanderers had spent all their money during their quest for a haven. They were given some succour by the local council, but this in turn created problems when members of the English group fell out among themselves over the fair distribution of relief funds. It may have been destitution rather than (or as well as) religious conviction that drove some of the separatists to join an Anabaptist group. Probably others had simply packed their bags and gone home (for by the time the Johnsons arrived, their church numbered only 40 souls).

The other problem was Henry Ainsworth. This amiable, scholarly Norfolk man was yet another Cambridge Puritan who had moved to the radical edge and sought refuge in Holland. He arrived in Amsterdam about 1595 and was welcomed as a teaching elder by the group that would later claim the name of the 'Ancient Brethren'. By the time the Johnsons rejoined the group in 1597, they found Ainsworth well ensconced and much loved as an effective teacher. For a few years, Henry and Francis worked well side by side, but the seeds of discord and jealousy had been sown.

Nor had the George problem gone away. Francis's younger brother had found a new *casus belli* – his sister-in-law. Thomasine Boyes was the widow of a wealthy haberdasher who was also a member of the London separatists. She and Francis were married while Francis was in prison. George was furious. Whatever deep-seated resentment may have influenced him we can only speculate, but he focused his intense and long-running campaign against Thomasine on her manner of dress. She was wealthy and she was used to the fashionable world of the English capital. She chose her clothes accordingly. In George's eyes, her attire was not becoming of a modest Puritan lady. He complained that it was colourful, showy and immodest. Francis staunchly backed his wife's right to dress as she pleased. Doubtless, he was motivated by love, but the fact that Thomasine brought to her marriage an income of £500 per annum must have strengthened their relationship.

For the best part of a decade, the English separatist community flourished. More groups arrived to join the Ancient Brethren. But there was to be no strength in numbers. Each party that came had its own leaders and theological emphases. For example, the followers of John Smyth, who insisted on believers' baptism, departed from the Ancient Brethren in 1609. At the same time, Johnson and Ainsworth were falling out over the issue of the powers of the eldership. Both sides were guilty of petty behaviour. It seems that, at one point, Francis led a breakaway group to Emden, far to the north in Friesland province. But that was another failure, and the 'Franciscan Brownists', as they were now known, were soon back in Amsterdam. At this point the 'Ainsworthian Brownists' moved out of their premises and opened a new church just two doors down the street (1610).

And George Johnson? In 1603, he had been expelled from the Amsterdam fellowship. He returned to England where his zealous tongue soon led to his rearrest. He died in prison in 1605. He left behind him a ticking time bomb in the shape of an exposé of the Ancient Brethren, and its sundering into fractious factions. His *Discourse on some troubles and excommunication in the banished English Church at Amsterdam Published for sundry causes declared in the preface to the pastor of the said Church* had been delivered to the printer before his departure from Amsterdam and was written in the white heat of fraternal enmity. George claimed to be offering his admonition to his brother to point out the troubles that would arise if Francis continued on his current course. In fact, what the *Discourse* revealed was the long-standing rivalry that had existed between the brothers. But, whatever were the deep motives behind George's prophecy of disaster, the sad fact is that it was to be fully realized.

This was the toxic atmosphere encountered in 1607–1608 by groups of fresh migrants who arrived from Scrooby in Nottinghamshire under the leadership of John Robinson and William Brewster. It is not to be wondered at that they did not stay long in Amsterdam.

8

The Midlands nursery

The 1620 Pilgrims were creatures of their environment, and products of their history. They were who they were because they lived in a certain place at a certain time. Their hopes, fears and beliefs; their understanding of themselves and their world and the Greater Reality beyond the cosmos were shaped by their family and community background. That is why we are taking time, in this study, to distil the experiences of the generations preceding them. In them were concentrated the disparate aspirations of their forebears – not just their parents and grandparents, but also their nearer spiritual ancestors. That is why we must now look closely at late sixteenth-century life in the East Midland counties of England. There a religious zeitgeist evolved that was the result of geography, patronage and education.

'The highways be cried out upon; every flood makes them impassable.'[1] So reported one of Thomas Cromwell's agents from Lincolnshire in 1539, and his words indicate the problems faced by travellers in sixteenth-century England. Most roads referred to by the writer as 'highways' we would probably describe as lanes. Municipal authorities were responsible for maintaining the roads and bridges in their immediate vicinity, but the long stretches between towns were not kept in good repair unless the merchants who used them regularly clubbed together to employ gangs of workmen. This basic fact of life has three implications for the spread of religious ideas and the establishment of communities of believers that is the subject of our story: (1) dwellers in the relatively isolated rural communities were hungry for news from the wider world; (2) market towns were not only the economic hubs but also the social centres of their regions; (3) rivers and man-made watercourses were the principal commercial arteries throughout much of England, connecting towns deep inland with coastal ports and harbours.

The 'bones' of the physical and social landscape of England's regions determined their character. Thus, it is no surprise that the conservative rebellion against the changes imposed by the Tudors in 1536–1537, 1549 and 1569 occurred in the far north and the far west, areas distant from government control and impervious to the rationale supporting innovation. Similarly, we can make sense of the concentration of clandestine Lollard groups in the Colchester–Bristol corridor when we understand the good roads and commercial links that enabled preachers and book-smugglers to connect unsophisticated but independent-minded artisans and mercantile communities. In the same way, we can see reasons why tensions might emerge in a region where people were loyal to the Crown but vulnerable to religious impulses that set them at odds with the kind of church the Crown was sponsoring. That region embraced much of the central English counties of Lincolnshire, Nottinghamshire, Rutland, Northamptonshire and Warwickshire. The major eastern ports of Kingston-upon-Hull and Boston were connected with towns deep inland, such as Doncaster, Gainsborough, Nottingham, Northampton and Lincoln by navigable waterways – the Don, Trent and Witham. The region was bisected by the Great North Road, along which traffic daily flowed to and from the capital. Also fairly close at hand was Cambridge University, which, as we have seen, was a brewhouse of religious radicalism. To the east lay the Fens, a barrier both physical and psychological, where the way of life could scarcely have been more different from that of the gentle hills and valleys further inland. Henry VIII had not only been expressing royal pique when he referred to the fenland folk as 'the rude commons of one shire, and that one of the most brute and beastly of the whole realm'.[2] They were as inhospitable as the watery terrain in which they lived, and very defensive of their traditions.

Just how early Protestantism penetrated the ruling elite of the East Midlands may be illustrated by the well-known story of Anne Askew (name originally spelled 'Ayscough'), the Lincolnshire martyr. She came from one of the leading gentry families in the region, with several estates, from Stallingborough in the north-east, which had an outlet to the Humber estuary, to Basford and Nuthall, near Nottingham. She had three brothers, one of whom studied at Cambridge, while the others achieved places at the royal court. Anne was therefore open to influences

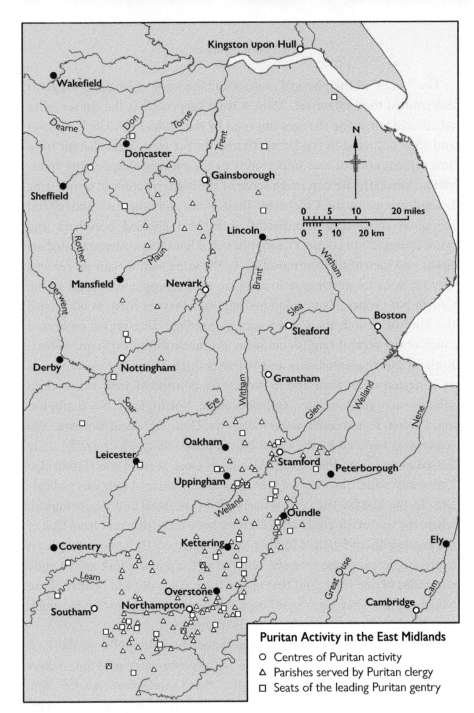

Puritan Activity in the East Midlands

○ Centres of Puritan activity
△ Parishes served by Puritan clergy
□ Seats of the leading Puritan gentry

Geography played a major role in framing the social and religious life of the area. The Great North Road, running SE–NW from Stamford to Wakefield via Grantham, Newark and Doncaster divided the uplands region, with its numerous gentry estates, from the more sparsely populated fenland in the east. The riverain network conveyed Continental influences deep into the interior. (Map by Lovell Johns, © SPCK.)

from various sources. Merchants trading across the North Sea brought a variety of goods into Kingston upon Hull (now known as Hull) and Boston, transferred them on to smaller vessels and conveyed them to markets far inland. Some of them brought with them Tyndale's New Testament and Lutheran tracts. Francis Askew, Anne's eldest brother, when home from the university, could explain how some of the leading academics were interpreting the word of God. Christopher and Edward, her courtier siblings, would have been able to report on the Evangelical groups springing up in the capital and reveal how even members of the royal household were being won over to the reformed faith. But there were others among the gentry families she knew who were also embracing the Reformation. Just a few miles from the Askew Nottinghamshire estates was Aslockton, the home village of Archbishop Thomas Cranmer. It was Cranmer who had trained Edward in the arts of the courtier and recommended him for the king's privy chamber staff. Another neighbouring Nottinghamshire family were the Lascelles of Sturton-le-Steeple. One commentator in Anne's later story asserted that John Lascelles (a colleague of Christopher's in the royal privy chamber) was Anne's mentor in things heretical. It is clear that both of them were anti the prevailing ecclesiastical establishment, opposed priestcraft, and believed that Henry's break with Rome had not gone far enough; specifically, they rejected the sacramental doctrine of the real presence. When put on trial for her faith, Anne called the Lord's Supper 'a most necessary remembrance of [Christ's] glorious suffering and death'[3] and not a repeated sacrifice.

This sounds very much like Zwinglian belief and is certainly not Lutheran. Or did it derive simply from a common-sense reading of the English Bible? When pressed to explain how she understood the words of institution 'This is my body . . . This is my blood', Anne asserted that they were spoken metaphorically, as when Jesus was referred to elsewhere in the Gospels as a vine, a lamb, a rock, a gate, and so on.[4] Anne was an assiduous Bible student and could quote it extensively by heart. She was accused of being a 'gospeller' – someone who read and expounded the vernacular text to her illiterate servants and neighbours. On religious grounds, she left her husband in 1544 and travelled to London, where she joined a group of like-minded Evangelicals in which John Lascelles was already well known. There were several such gatherings, some attached to city churches under the leadership of unorthodox clergy, others meeting more clandestinely, but all drawing sustenance from the vernacular Bible and books written by anticlerical authors. For zealous Evangelicals, London in the 1540s was an exhilarating place to be. Their faith and enthusiasm were strengthened by fellowship and ardent preaching, and they enjoyed the added frisson of being hunted by the bishop and his agents. Many of the 'brethren' were examined by the episcopal and municipal courts. Most of them buckled under pressure and recanted. Not so Anne and her friend John Lascelles. They perished in the fires of Smithfield in July 1546.

It is difficult for us to imagine the impact of this event on the families and friends of Anne and John back in the shires. The death of two of their own was more than a personal tragedy. Within months a detailed account of Anne's interrogations (including the use of torture) had been published abroad and smuggled into England, where it rapidly became a bestseller. The message it carried to the leaders of local society was that no one was immune to prosecution for unorthodox religious views. Hitherto, heresy prosecutions had largely involved (apart from renegade priests and monks) members of the lower orders of society. Noble and gentry families had usually been exempt from examination because the Crown relied on them for maintaining order in the provinces. The unspoken rule that magistrates, major landowners and even senior municipal authorities should not be challenged about their religious beliefs was a constant frustration to diocesan bishops, who not infrequently grumbled to the Council about the spread of heresy among the educated laity, and the patronage extended to radical clergy, domestic chaplains and itinerant preachers. It would be a serious matter indeed for the 'top brass' in the East Midlands if their freedom of religious belief was about to be curtailed. In the event, any such anxiety was short-lived. Six months after the fiery ordeal of Anne Askew and John Lascelles, Henry VIII died. The new regime of the young Edward VI placed real power in the hands of reformist ministers, and attendants and tutors in the entourage of the boy king. When Protector Somerset and, subsequently, the Duke of Northumberland, in collaboration with Archbishop Cranmer and his supporters on the episcopal bench, pressed on with the work of Reformation, they drew on widespread support in those southern counties where religious radicalism had a long history. Now, however, Protestantism was extending its power base into the Midland shires.

During the Marian persecution, at least 50 men and women from the region sought refuge in Continental centres of reform. For many, exile was the forge on which their theology was hammered out. From Geneva, Zurich, Frankfurt and other breeding grounds of dissent we can trace many Puritan connections to preachers, patrons, families and parishes in the years that followed. As various parties fought for the soul of the Church of England during the early decades of Elizabeth's reign, lay patronage was a vital factor. Nowhere was that patronage more vital or more earnestly sought than in the East Midlands. In 1560, a list was drawn up for the benefit of Robert Dudley, Earl of Leicester. It consisted of 28 'godly preachers which have utterly forsaken Antichrist and his Romish rags'. Of those thus named, 21 were returnees from the continent.[5] Leicester and his associates found jobs for most of those on the list.

One of them was Anthony Gilby (c. 1510-1585), a native of Lincolnshire, who had studied at Cambridge. His years of exile ended in Geneva, where he associated with John Knox and assisted William Whittingham, an accomplished scholar who was in the process of supervising the production of the Geneva Bible. On his return, Gilby was appointed by Henry Hastings, Earl of Huntingdon (Leicester's brother-in-law), to the incumbency of Ashby-de-la-Zouch, Leicestershire (Huntingdon's principal residence). He became, in effect, the leader of Leicestershire Puritanism and was instrumental in establishing several preaching 'exercises'. At the same time, he engaged in a literary war against upholders of the 'unreformed' English Church. Despite his notoriety, he was never seriously molested or interrogated, a fact that says much for the protection provided by his powerful patron.

We have already noted that the local boy William Cecil was an influential friend of the Puritans. From his political beginnings as MP for Stamford (from 1543) and secretary to the Duke of Somerset, Lord Protector of the realm, until his death as Baron Burghley (1598), he was almost continuously at the centre of influence. He spent much of his years in power extending his family home at Stamford into one of the most impressive mansions in the country, and it became a physical declaration of his pro-Puritan local influence. Another great house currently a-building nearby was Exton Hall, home of Sir James Harington, to whom progressive Protestants also looked for political support. Between them Cecil and Harington controlled over a third of the livings in Rutland, and they did not hesitate to use them to further the careers of Puritan clergy.

However, it was Robert Dudley who, *par excellence*, was the aristocratic mainstay of the Puritans. He and his brother Ambrose, Earl of Warwick, had their principal seats at Kenilworth Castle and Warwick Castle respectively. Some 20 miles to the east of their home territory lay the market town of Southam, and 20 miles further on again was Northampton. Puritan activity in both these places would soon embroil the Dudleys in serious controversy (see below, pp. 133ff.). The lengths they were prepared to go to in defence of their protégés were remarkable. No one knew Elizabeth better than Robert Dudley. He realized that her concern for stability and unity in Church and State went deeper than consideration of practical politics. Her attachment to established rituals, beautiful music, chaste ornamentation, discipline and decorum had deep emotional and aesthetic roots. Yet he often went behind her back in supporting ministers of whom she disapproved, and sometimes he argued with her face to face.

The career of Thomas Lever (1521-1577) provides a notable example of Leicester's patronage from very early in the reign. Lever had enjoyed Dudley clientage back in the reign of Edward VI. When he went into exile in 1553 it was with the definite intention of setting up an English Protestant action group, for he took with him a band of young men from both universities who eventually settled at Aarau, Switzerland. We might be justified in seeing here a precursor of the migrant churches, such as the *Mayflower* group, whose members left England 50 years later with a doctrinal and liturgical package ready for use in a new land. Mary's early death meant that the group could return ready to contribute their insights to the continued reform of the Church of England. Lever looked to his old supporters, the Dudleys, for his further advancement, and he did not look in vain. He became rector and archdeacon of Coventry and coupled his duties there with a peripatetic preaching ministry. He was also granted a canonry at Durham.

That was where the trouble started. Lever was impatient. The pattern of church he found in Scripture – a pattern that the reformed ecclesiae he had so recently encountered claimed to be following – was not being established by Elizabeth's cautious settlement. Lever knew what the Church was and wanted her to see it established *now*. He refused to wear a surplice and campaigned vigorously against such 'popish' abuses. This lost him the Durham canonry but, closer to 'home', he was secure and filled the parishes in his archdeaconry with men of his own persuasion. The lengths to which Leicester was prepared to go were quite remarkable. Lever was stating no less than the truth when he wrote to his patron shortly before his death in 1577: 'I and many others have by your means shed quietness, liberty and comfort to preach the gospel of Christ.'[6] Yet the survival of radical Evangelicalism in the central shires did not depend only on sympathetic aristocrats and ministers of the Crown who were influential in high places. Local affairs were in the hands of gentry families to a greater extent than in areas, such as the north and the west, where feudalism had been slower to fade and ancient families like the Nevilles, Percys and Courtenays still commanded widespread allegiance. Middle England was the domain of families like the Askews, Lascelles, Knightleys, Markhams, Disneys and many others who, through ancient lineage or recent enrichment at the expense of the fallen monasteries, or both, controlled vast acreages and the people who lived in them. These families made up the county class, which provided magistrates, sheriffs, MPs and other officials, and kept the cogs of local politics well oiled. They were the principal employers and landlords. Their wealth came not only from husbandry but also from the rural and urban industries based on it. The gentlefolk who commanded wide acres of grassland (the sort of people Thomas More castigated for commandeering common land and turning arable to pasture) raised sheep and cattle for the burgeoning cloth and hide industries. Some turned old conventual buildings into the first English textile factories. Often in conjunction with their urban, mercantile neighbours (with whose families they frequently intermarried), they turned towns such as Stamford, Leicester and Northampton into the most productive centres outside London for the manufacture of shoes and leather goods. Their commercial success was proclaimed in the fine manor houses that, in growing number, graced the Midland landscape (and provided employment for masons, carpenters, glaziers, tilers and other construction workers).

The Venetian navigator John Cabot (*c.* 1450–*c.*1500) was
the first to sail from England and explore the coast of North
America. In 1762 his exploits were celebrated in this mural
in the Doge's Palace in Venice by Giustino Menescardi.
(Copyright: akg-images/Science Source.)

The Dutch humanist Desiderius Erasmus set academic dovecotes fluttering with his *Novum Instrumentum Omne* (1516), a Greek New Testament with a new Latin translation that called into question aspects of the Vulgate. (*Novum Testamentum Omne*, 1522 (second edition of above title) shown. Reproduced by kind permission of the President and Fellows of Queens' College, Cambridge)

The order and manner of the burning of *Anne Askew, John Lacels, John Adams, Nicholas Belenian,* with certaine of the Councell sitting in Smithfield.

In 1546, the burning of the 'Lincolnshire Gospeller' Anne Askew and others caught the public imagination and its impact was perpetuated by John Foxe in his *Acts and Monuments*, first published in 1563. (From *London in the Time of Tudors*, by Sir Walter Besant, Adam & Charles Black, 1904.)

TO THE MEMORY OF ROBERT BROWNE, A
FOUNDER OF THE BROWNISTS, OR INDEPENDENTS
RECTOR OF THORPE ACHURCH, 1591-1631
WHO WAS BURIED IN THIS CHURCHYARD 8ᵀᴴ OCT. 1633
A TRIBUTE TO A LIFE WHEREIN, AMONG MANY
THINGS OBSCURE, ONE THING SHONE BRIGHTLY, THAT
CHRIST WAS BY HIM EXALTED AS HEAD ABOVE ALL.

ERECTED BY CONGREGATIONALISTS IN CONNECTION
WITH THE VISIT TO NORTHAMPTON, OCT. 1923, OF THE
CONGREGATIONAL UNION OF ENGLAND AND WALES.

This memorial plaque to Robert Browne (1550–1631), the first
English separatist, was placed in the grounds of St Giles's
Church in Northampton in 1923. Although Browne died
in the local jail, his exact burial site is unknown.
(Copyright: David Humphreys/Alamy Stock Photo.)

Tomb of Thomas and Faith St Paul (or St Poll) in St Lawrence's
Church, Snarford, Lincolnshire. Sir Thomas (d. 1582) belonged to
a long-established Puritan family. In the carving, he holds a sword
in one hand and a book (presumably a Bible) in the other.
(Copyright: Richard Croft.)

What little was left by the nineteenth century of the impressive episcopal residence of Scrooby Manor, where William Brewster's congregation met, survived only as part of a later farmhouse.

(Copyright: Pictures Now/Alamy Stock Photo.)

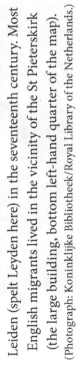

This plaque on the wall of the St Peterskirk in Leiden commemorates the English migrants who lived and died in the city between 1609 and 1630.

(Copyright: Maurice Savage/Alamy Stock Photo.)

Leiden (spelt Leyden here) in the seventeenth century. Most English migrants lived in the vicinity of the St Pieterskirk (the large building, bottom left-hand quarter of the map).

(Photograph: Koninklijke Bibliotheek/Royal Library of the Netherlands.)

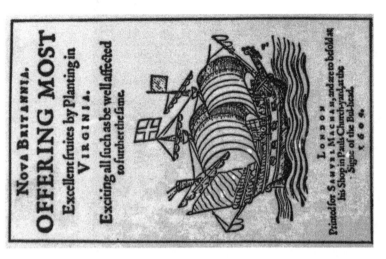

Sir Edwin Sandys, Treasurer of the Virginia Company, and one of the pamphlets he had published to encourage settlement in the colony.

(Copyright: portrait: akg-images/De Agostini Picture Library; advertisement: Bettmann/Getty Images.)

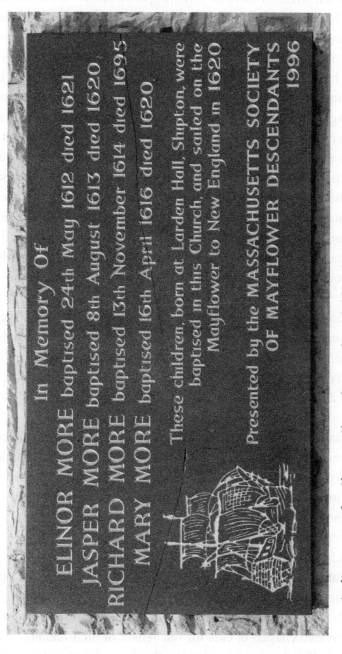

In Memory Of

ELINOR MORE baptised 24th May 1612 died 1621
JASPER MORE baptised 8th August 1613 died 1620
RICHARD MORE baptised 13th November 1614 died 1695
MARY MORE baptised 16th April 1616 died 1620

These children, born at Larden Hall, Shipton, were
baptised in this Church, and sailed on the
Mayflower to New England in 1620

Presented by the MASSACHUSETTS SOCIETY
OF MAYFLOWER DESCENDANTS
1996

A plaque erected at Shipton, Shropshire, to four children born to Catherine More but disowned by her husband, Samuel, and shipped on the Mayflower as indentured servants.
(Copyright: John Hayward/Alamy Stock Photo.)

These innovators and entrepreneurs were not people who compart-mentalized their lives, serious and thrusting in business but conservative and passive in terms of religion. It should not surprise us that, for many, unquestioning submission to Crown and Mitre did not sit easily with them. They were individuals of conviction. It would be no exaggeration to say that many of them saw themselves as warriors engaged in a conflict against popery, superstition and immorality. Relations between neighbouring landowners were sometimes coloured by ancient feuds and rivalries. Territorial competition, old grievances and frustrated ambition often rose to the surface. Religious differences added another *casus belli* to the situation. Prominent families known to be recusants or firm sup-porters of the half-reformed Elizabethan Church were, alike, anathema to their Puritan neighbours. In 1572, George Carleton of Overstone, near Northampton, complained to Lord Burghley of all such, and called on the government to 'tread the bad underfoot'. He assured the minister that godly counsels would have the support of

a great people, daily increasing, which are professors of the gospel towards sincerity. And as they hate all heresies and popery, so they cannot be persuaded to bear liking of the queen's proceedings in religion, by reason that our Church here is not reformed. This people consist of all degrees, from the nobility to the lowest.[7]

It was the very existence in their midst of landowners and magistrates who were 'enemies of the gospel' that spurred on Puritan gentry to lead the necessary work of creating a godly commonwealth. They had the social position and the material resources to choose incumbents for the livings within their gift and to oversee the message proclaimed by those incumbents.

The parochial system actually encouraged zealous landowners, much to the frustration of the bishops. Many parishes were too poor to support a resident incumbent. Some, indeed, still lacked their own church. The gaps could be filled by preachers approved by the manorial lords, some of whom provided chapels of ease for the benefit of their tenants, which would be staffed by clergy supporting the theology of their patrons. They paid the pipers and were determined to call the tune. Let us consider some of these powerful lay people who were consciously shaping the religious life of the region.

Sir Richard Knightley of Fawsley, Northamptonshire, had a history as patron and campaigner in the Puritan cause extending over 50 years. In 1567, the Earl of Leicester, determined to ensure that Puritan ministers were not hampered by either episcopal restraint or poverty, established an incorporated body to provide for 'the preachers of the gospel in the county of Warwick'. Among the wealthy local gentlemen who endowed the institution with lands and who were nominated as trustees was Sir Richard Knightley. Clearly, the support of Knightley and his colleagues turned the Warwickshire–Leicestershire borderlands into an Evangelical hotbed, so much so that their enemies complained directly to the queen. This was the situation that set off the chain of events that ended in Archbishop Grindal's sequestration (see above, pp. 74f.). Knightley was not a whit chastened by royal displeasure. Twenty years later we find him involved in the notorious Marprelate affair (see above, pp. 105f.). In the autumn of 1588, the secret transportable press on which the anti-episcopal tracts were printed was temporarily lodged at Fawsley and subsequently moved thence to a hiding place in another of his houses, Norton, in Sherwood Forest. With Whitgift's bloodhounds getting closer it was relocated again at Wolston, near Coventry. Its discovery there led to Knightley being arraigned in the court of Star Chamber (a court used increasingly by the Tudors to deal with opponents of royal policy) for 'maintaining seditious persons, books and libels'. He was fortunate to escape with a swingeing £2,000 fine.

This did not put an end to his principled stand in support of Puritan ministers. In 1604, the new king, James I, tried to follow his predecessor in inaugurating and enforcing his own brand of religious settlement. He could no more impose unity than could Elizabeth. When he ordered the sacking of all beneficed clergy who refused to subscribe to a new set of ecclesiastical canons passed by Convocation, protests from the Midland counties were immediate. Among the names that appeared on a petition raised in Northamptonshire was not only that of the 72-year-old Sir Richard Knightley, but also of his son, Valentine. This brought Richard another Star Chamber fine – £10,000 this time. By the time of Sir Richard's death (1615), the family's allegiance to radical reform was well entrenched. The head of the family from 1618 to 1639 – another Richard – was a close supporter of the parliamentary leaders John Pym, John Eliot and John Hampden, and in 1630 was, with other Puritans, among the founders of the Providence Island colony. Yet another Richard Knightley of Fawsley was an MP for Northampton and one of the prominent opponents of King Charles I in the 1640s.

It is not surprising to discover confessional connections linking leading families and establishing kindred alliances spanning several generations. Estate-building and other economic considerations continued to dominate gentry marriage negotiations, but among those 'earnest in religion' doctrinal allegiance was obviously also important. Jane Askew, younger sister of the Lincolnshire martyr, married George St Poll of Snarford whose will, drawn up during Mary Tudor's reign, leaves no doubt about his Calvinist convictions:

> I bequeath my soul unto God, trusting by the merits of his only Son, our alone Lord and Saviour, to have forgiveness of all my sins and to be in the number of those whom he, by his Holy Spirit, hath sanctified to everlasting life.[8]

The St Polls' Puritan commitment continued down the generations. George's grandson (another George) was particularly noted for supporting Evangelical students at Cambridge. The oration at his funeral (1613) made mention of at least six prominent preachers who were beholden to St Poll for his support. Even more ardent in the cause was his wife, Frances Wray, whom he married in 1580. She was the sister of Sir William Wray, MP for Grimsby and one of the wealthiest landowners in Lincolnshire. John Smyth, of Sturton-le-Steeple (home of the Lascelles), who separated from the Church of England to become a founding father of the Baptists, called him 'a principal professor and protector of religion in these quarters (for what a multitude of faithful ministers are debtors to you in the flesh) . . . I, among the rest, have rested under your shadow.'[9] Frances's benefactions were as generous as her husband's. She provided three fellowships and six scholarships for 'suitable' candidates at Magdalen College, Cambridge. One of her protégés, Richard Bernard, was closely involved in the separatist controversy early in the seventeenth century. Finding himself pulled in different directions, he resigned his living at Worksop, Nottinghamshire, and established his own independent church. Returning later to the Anglican fold, he set out his reasons in *Christian Advertisements and Counsels of Peace Also Disuasions from the Separatists' Schism, Commonly called Brownism.* He dedicated the work to Frances.

After St Poll's death Jane married another Lincolnshire worthy, Richard Disney. Much of the couple's time was spent at the Disney estate at Greasley, north-west of Nottingham. The religious inclination of Jane's second husband is suggested by the names of six of the stepchildren she now inherited – Daniel, Zachary, Sirach, Sarah, Judith and Susan. When husband and wife were eventually buried back at Norton Disney church, just across the Trent Valley near Newark, a pious memorial brass affirmed 'the steadfast faith which they had in and through the mercy and merits of Christ our Saviour', and the inscription went on, 'These truths are set forth that in all ages God may be thankfully praised for these and such like his gracious benefits.'

By 1603, the White family of Sturton-le-Steeple (where the Lascelles still held the manor) had made the 37-mile journey to relocate at Greasley, the Disney manor. It may be that Bridget, the 24-year-old daughter of this family, was already engaged, for her fiancé also came from Sturton and they were married on 15 February 1603. The newlyweds moved to Norwich where Bridget's husband had gained a position as associate pastor at St Andrew's Church. However, they were soon on the move again. Rather than accept the Prayer Book in all its details the young minister and his wife headed back to the area where they knew they would be accepted, and set up home at Scrooby, near Sturton-le-Steeple, from where he preached in several of the local churches. His name was John Robinson, destined to be famous in the story of the Pilgrim Fathers.

Hopefully, enough has been said to indicate the interaction and inter-relatedness of influential lay families in the swathe of country between the valleys of the Don and the Great Ouse. Whatever policies might be decreed at Whitehall and however much professional churchmen might resent interference in diocesan affairs, on a day-to-day and year-to-year basis it was the leaders of rural and urban society who set the tone of life in the East Midlands. Several of them were working closely with Puritan clergy to reform the standard rituals and to superimpose on parish life extracurricular preaching activities. Some were ready to go even further. The letter George Carleton wrote to Cecil in 1572 contained what reads almost like a threat. Referring to the more zealous of his colleagues, he observed:

> so hot is the desire of God's truth in them that they will not [re]frain themselves to favour any the laws or ordinances set forth by the queen in God's matters, but such as are void of all offence, and reformed according to sincerity. This people, as they do not like the course of our Church, so they do and will practice assemblies of brethren in all part of this realm, and have their own churches in companies . . .[10]

From quite early in the reign the shocking possibility was lurking in the shadows that, from within the Anglican ranks, there might rise up men who would found a Church within the Church or a Church *without* the Church – alternatives equally repellent to the queen and the ecclesiastical establishment. What innovations were some Midland clergy and their backers actually introducing? To find answers to this question, we must look more closely at the prophesying, exercises and lectureships that were set up in the Midland counties.

Those committed to the establishment of a regular preaching ministry were very conscious of a need to educate the public. By 1580, the turmoil of the preceding half-century had had profound effects on the national psyche. The dearth of preaching in the early years and the non-availability of vernacular Bibles had given many people a thirst for the New Learning. There had been a considerable boost to education and a noticeable rise in literacy. But the excitement of discovering 'new' truth had, inevitably, diminished with the passing of the years when the English Bible was no longer a novelty and the bitter experience of religious conflict had blunted the enthusiasm of many ordinary folk. In 1582, one Essex Puritan complained:

> But let the Preacher speak never so plain, although they sit and look him in the face, yet if ye enquire of them so soon as they be out at the

church doors, ye shall easily perceive that (as the common saying is) it went in at the one ear, and out at the other. They will say peradventure, after this manner, It was a good sermon. I wold we could follow it, he said very well: here is a perfect ready man in the pulpit. But ask, what doctrine did he handle? Then are they at a pause, and set at a dead lift.[11]

It was this ignorance/apathy that activists were striving against just as vigorously as papistical error and ecclesiastical compromise over ritual and clerical dress. Another factor with which radical churchmen had to contend was the increase in the number of educated clergy. The Puritan movement was, to some extent, the victim of its own success. Although the educational standard of the parochial clergy still left a great deal to be desired, there was a steady increase in the number of ministers who could, and did, preach. And they were not all Puritans. Fewer and fewer of them had experienced the Marian baptism of fire and the exhilarating fellowships of Geneva, Zurich, Frankfurt and Strasbourg. More and more of them were 'middle-of-the-road Anglicans' with one eye on preferment. These were the main bastions against which those seeking to revivify the Church of England had to direct their fire. And their most effective cannons were the lectureships. We have already seen something of their origins and, as they developed, they took on different aspects from time to time and place to place. However, in the area we are concerned with, they had certain common characteristics. They were regular courses of public sermons. They were based on Calvinistic interpretations of the biblical text. They were delivered (for the most part) by unbeneficed clergy, and these had the active support of magistrates and municipal authorities who paid their stipends and controlled their hiring and firing. However, in Northampton and the surrounding area something more ambitious was essayed – nothing less than a replication of the civic–ecclesiastical polity of Geneva: the building of a new Jerusalem in England's green and pleasant land.

The impetus for this politico-religious innovation came from an impressive alliance of landowners and civic dignitaries. At the top of the list we find the name of the Earl of Leicester. Then came Sir Richard Knightley and George Carleton MP, the aggressive Presbyterian, both of whom would later be involved in the Marprelate controversy. Among the Northampton mercantile elite were the mercers Edward Morley and William Coldwell, and William Raynsford, a baker, all of whom served as mayor at various times during Elizabeth's reign.

As for the clergy, we gain tantalizing glimpses of extramural activity going on throughout the region. Puritan clergy gathered in groups, sometimes referred to as 'exercises' but also known as 'classes', for prayer, study and mutual encouragement. There can be no doubt that they discussed the shortcomings of the Elizabethan settlement and the need for further reformation. For conscientious and caring bishops, such activity presented a dilemma. How could they encourage better education and deeper spirituality among the clergy while, at the same time, keeping a wary eye on potentially seditious assemblies? Exercises, or whatever the participants chose to call them, were fine as long as they made their members better at their jobs, but for some, allegiance to the Puritan cause got in the way of proper performance of pastoral responsibilities. In 1570, for example, the people of Maxey, near Stamford, complained that their incumbent, Richard Liveley, was neglecting them to attend meetings and preach elsewhere. Such examples reveal the tension existing between membership of the Anglican establishment and commitment to the Puritan 'ginger group'. What the authorities were up against was not just the conduct of individual ministers or even local 'covens'; Puritan clergy were part of a wider – indeed a national – community. Enter the mysterious William Fludd. One vicar of All Saints, Northampton, recalled later how this itinerant overseer travelled from exercise to exercise, 'like an apostle or patriarch or he knows not what, always taking upon him to be a chief director'.[12]

While we concentrate on local events in the East Midlands, it is important not to lose sight of what was happening in the wider Christian world. The 1560s and 1570s witnessed a ratcheting-up of religious tension in Europe that led to political convulsions and the loss of thousands of lives. Calvinism was on the rampage in France and the Low Countries. Government attempts to resist it led to armed conflict. In 1567, Philip II of Spain despatched the Duke of Alva and an army of 12,000 men to crush Protestant rebellion in the Spanish Netherlands. In 1570, Pope Pius V excommunicated Elizabeth I and relieved her subjects of their loyalty to the 'heretic queen'. In 1572, the notorious St Bartholomew's Day Massacre cost the lives of some 10,000 Huguenots (Calvinists) throughout France. England's Continental neighbours were now locked in vicious religious warfare, and one result was the migration of hundreds of Protestant refugees across the Channel and the North Sea. Another arrival was the Catholic Mary Queen of Scots, who had fled from the Calvinist regime across the border and, from 1569, was lodged in Tutbury Castle, a mere 30 miles across the Trent Valley from Nottingham. Because the exile had a claim to the English Crown, she was the white hope of Catholic activists and the focus of plots. These events could not fail to be major talking points that roused suspicions and reinforced convictions.

The overheated atmosphere of religious partisan confrontation revealed itself in the expansion of the lectureships movement. In London churches there were ten regular lectureships in 1572. A decade later there were 30. It is not surprising, given this activity in the capital, that Matthew Parker and his supporters were worried about the spread of radicalism. The archbishop warned hysterically that the Puritans were bent on establishing Anabaptist communes similar to that of Thomas Münster, who had led his frenzied supporters into battle in the Peasants' War 50 years earlier. For their part, the champions of Calvinist doctrine and ecclesiology who had close connections with London were eager to replicate in the provinces the advances made at the centre. One way to achieve this was to provide local havens for preachers who had been ousted from their positions in London because of their extremist views.

Thus it was that the famous (or notorious) Percival Wiburn came to Northampton. Both a scholar and a zealot, he was one of those returning exiles who sought to apply his talents in the establishment of a thoroughly depapalized English Church. He achieved the advancement his undoubted gifts merited, but his opinions, which he expressed in a manuscript treatise for the benefit of Heinrich Bullinger and friends abroad, soon plunged him into hot water, and Archbishop Parker deprived him of his London benefice. However, such was the confused state of affairs in the early years of the reign that he was able to retain some of his ecclesiastical offices and he was not inhibited from public preaching. Wiburn did not lack for influential patrons, prominent among whom was the Earl of Leicester. Supported by Knightley, Carleton and the leading aldermanic families of Northampton, he invited the talented renegade to 'come over into Macedonia and help us'.[13] Eagerly followed by the leaders of society and allowed free rein to establish his version of the godly community, Wiburn devised the 'order' of Northampton in 1571.

It was important, not for its longevity (its life was cut very short) but for its audacity in seeking to install a full-blown Geneva-style polity. A civic and ecclesiastical partnership was established to ensure not only the faithful, regular preaching of the word of God but also its bearing fruit in the lives of the townsfolk. To achieve this, each of the parish churches hosted, in turn, weekday sermons in addition to the Sunday proclamation and regular catechizing classes. Attendance by the citizens was compulsory, and enforced by the civic officers and the bishop's representatives acting in concert. To ensure that these leaders remained theologically and morally 'sound', they were required to attend a weekly meeting with the preachers. The ministers themselves of the towns and the vicinity also gathered once a week for mutual exhortation and enlightenment on the pattern of the old prophesyings. On top of this, all the clergy of the county were to attend quarterly meetings, so that the teaching and practices fostered in Northampton would act as leaven in the rurality.

This was clearly a foreign Reformed-style polity bolted onto the English diocesan system, and it put the bishop in a quandary. Initially, Edmund Scambler of Peterborough gave the pious enterprise his blessing. He could scarcely do otherwise since it had the backing of the queen's favourite and so many notables of town and shire. Yet he had strong reservations. Scambler was one of those churchmen of whom Elizabeth heartily approved. He had been a 'Laodicean' during the Marian years, and his reward in the new reign was rapid promotion. He knew well what side his bread was buttered on. But in his diocese he faced someone who exercised almost royal power and who had the backing of a significant number of his own clergy. The bishop tried a tactful approach with Leicester:

[Wiburn] is, as it seemeth to me, studious of innovations. For although your lordship doth like the substance of his doctrine, or the most part thereof, even as do I, yet know you not . . . as I do, the contention and discord that is in Northampton ... about matters, ceremonies and things indifferent, about which he showeth as much zeal as about the principal grounds of religion.[14]

Tension increased between temporal and spiritual authorities in the shires, and Leicester came to see himself as the defender of Puritans against episcopal bullying. 'The care of this world truly hath choked you all,' he once wrote in blanket condemnation of the bishops.[15]

A major reason for Dudley's anger was the treatment of his protégé, Percival Wiburn. In the summer of 1573, Wiburn was among a group of ministers summoned before the Council and forbidden to preach. Later in the year the queen herself intervened, issuing a proclamation demanding conformity to the Prayer Book and the official dress code prescribed for clergy. Yet even this was not a victory for the reactionaries because the rules were enforced in different dioceses with varying degrees of severity and consistency. Whatever directives came from the top, bishops had to be sensitive to local feeling.

In Northampton and its environs, the removal of Wiburn and others provoked varied reactions. There were protest demonstrations on behalf of the dispossessed and, as he went on visitations, Bishop Scambler can have been left in no doubt that significant numbers of townspeople and villagers resented not only being forced to use the Prayer Book but also having non-preaching clergy foisted on them. Many people voted with their feet, forsaking their parish churches for others where the ministry was more to their taste. In Northampton, the ambitious 'new Geneva' ceased to function, but the exercise was by no means at an end, and various aspects of the civic and ecclesiastical reform continued into the 1580s and beyond. As for Wiburn, he removed to nearby Whiston, whither many 'disciples' resorted to hear him preach.

The situation could easily have degenerated into a multitude of personality cults with each minister attracting his own following. This was to a large extent obviated by the strong sense of collegiality among the Puritan clergy. An example of how the exercise system in Northampton and the surrounding countryside worked is illustrated by the case of John Sibthorpe, rector of Ashton. In the summer of 1574, he preached an exercise sermon in All Saints Northampton in which he argued that 'the word of God and the laws made by the prince do not agree touching the wearing of the surplice'. When hauled before the bishop's court he produced evidence that the three other ministers attending the exercise had approved his message. According to extant records no action seems to have been taken against Sibthorpe.[16] Further north, in Lincolnshire, the 'cathedral' of Puritanism was Grimsthorpe, between Grantham and Stamford. This was the seat of Catherine Willoughby, Dowager Duchess of Suffolk (1519-1580), venerable champion of the reformed faith ever since the reign of Henry VIII. This trenchant Evangelical noblewoman had been the most senior of the Marian exiles. With her second husband, Richard Bertie, and a large entourage she had toured several centres of Continental reform. On her return she spent most of her time on her Lincolnshire estates. As the leading lay patron in the county she presented incumbents to 22 parishes and never failed to install 'sound' Bible-based men who could, and did, preach.

The overall picture of Midlands church life in the early Elizabethan years is, unavoidably, confused. There were parishes where few sermons were ever heard, and parishes that were linked with others by exercise networks. There were lay folk (undoubtedly the majority) who dutifully attended Sunday services whether or not sermons were delivered, and lay folk who went 'gadabout' to godly expositions. There were pockets of exercise activity within a religious landscape of quiet conformity. Inevitably, it was the centres of vigorous Puritan activity that were most talked about and that inscribed indelible marks on society.

History is made by minorities, and what happened in England's middle shires was just one example of what was disturbing the peace of Europe. Perhaps, in the 1570s, a measure of compromise could have been found. It might have proved possible for a range of theological opinions to be held within the Church of England. It seemed at one point, when strictures against Puritans were not rigidly enforced, that Elizabeth's subjects might find themselves members of a broad Church. In fact, it would be 300 years before such a state of affairs emerged. To governments of all kinds it seemed axiomatic that political and religious stability were inextricably tied together. In 1582, this principle was succinctly enunciated by a Continental jurist: *cuius regio, eius religio*, 'the ruler's religion is the religion of the people'. It was scarcely three years later that Elizabeth invoked this principle in the harangue to Convocation we have already quoted (see above, p. 75). Obedience was the chain binding her subjects to her. For the queen, this was more than a principle: it was a passion. She famously declared that she had no desire to open windows into people's souls. As long as there was outward conformity she would not press matters. What she could not or would not understand was that many of her subjects were not prepared to separate inward and outward religion. This was something that touched her more deeply than most other *affaires d'état*. Her loathing of Puritan activists was something that both disturbed and bewildered some of her closest advisers. Sir Francis Knollys spoke for them when he observed:

> It grieves my heart to see . . . the zealous preachers of the gospel, sound in doctrine . . . to be persecuted and put to silence as though there were no enemies to her Majesty and to the state but them.[17]

It is no wonder that the queen was frustrated. Her church policy was being undermined by certain 'noblemen and gentlemen' to whom she felt entitled to look for support in the localities. There can be no doubt who she had principally in mind. After eight years the affair at Southam still rankled. This town, just over the diocesan border in Coventry and Lichfield diocese, was much influenced by developments in Northampton. The vicar there, John Oxenbridge, set up an exercise and brought in an overseer, Eusebius Paget, a deprived Northamptonshire minister. It was an instant success and drew in supporters from as far afield as Daventry, some 10 miles distant. It also had the support of the leading noblemen in the region, Robert and Ambrose Dudley. There is no evidence that the local bishops raised any objection to the proceedings at Southam (as we have seen, many within the ecclesiastical establishment were in favour of anything that encouraged the ministry of the pulpit). But Paget was certainly tarred with the Presbyterian brush, and someone gave the queen a lurid (and probably exaggerated) report on events at Southam. Elizabeth chose to make an issue of it, telling Leicester to take a firmer grip on church affairs in his territory and ordering Archbishop Grindal to put an end to all exercises. He refused, and the queen, as we have seen, vented all her fury on him. Dudley was too dependent on royal favour to disobey a straight command and the Southam exercise was suppressed, much to the anger of Puritan leaders, who were shocked at the earl's desertion. Replying to one of them, Leicester tried to explain his position:

> generally for the exercises which I have known and heard of in many places, there was never thing used in the Church that I have thought and do think more profitable both for people and ministers, or that I have more spoken for or more labored in defence of, even from the beginning, especially where they are used with quietness to the conservation and unity of the doctrine established already and to the increase of the learned ministry . . . I fear the over busy dealing of some hath done so much hurt in striving to make better . . . that which is . . . good enough already that we shall neither have it in Southam nor any other where else . . . And this have I feared long ago would prove the fruit of our dissension for trifles first and since for other matters.[18]

The dilemma expressed by Dudley goes to the heart of the problem. It was essentially a clash of authority. Elizabeth took her stand on *cuius regio, eius religio*. The Puritan leadership looked to a different imperative, as Grindal observed: 'obedience proceedeth of conscience; conscience is grounded upon the word of God'.[19] The two sides were like tug-of-war teams. The harder they pulled, the more intransigent they became. Beliefs and practices that might have been modified by charitable debate became immovable principles. Elizabeth had won over Southam but, when she reflected on that victory in 1585, she had to acknowledge that very little had changed.[20]

9

New king, old problem

We do now with patience expect the consummation of our gracious
king's coronation, after which we hope he will hearken him to our
motions in behalf of the Church.[1]

So wrote Stephen Egerton, a London clergyman, in 1603. Egerton had
good personal reasons to hope for a settlement of the divisive issues that
had created deep rifts in English religious life during the reign of Queen
Elizabeth. Although the incumbent of St Anne's Blackfriars, he had earlier spent three years in prison for getting too close to Henry Barrow and
John Greenwood. He was far from being alone in the hope that the new
monarch would restore religious unity to the English Church. But, of
course, all parties concerned had their own interpretations of the word
'unity' and no one knew exactly what their new sovereign meant by it.

This was a crisis moment in the life of the nation. Few English men and
women could remember life before Elizabeth's reign. They faced a novel
future with curiosity and, in many cases, with some anxiety. Several of
the new king's subjects, driven by personal ambition or representing interest groups, hastened to meet their sovereign as he made his leisurely
way southwards during the summer. A handful of dissidents indulged
in a hare-brained plot to replace James with his cousin, Arabella Stuart
(small wonder the king took to wearing a reinforced, assassin-proof
doublet). Less desperate, though equally concerned, were those seeking a
resolution of the disordered state of ecclesiastical affairs.

People closely in touch with church leaders in Scotland might well
have been confused because religious life north of the border seemed
to present an amalgam of contradictions. For decades, pro-Catholic,
pro-French elements had maintained a strong position among the noble
clans, particularly in the Highlands. The Reformation involved civil war

in the 1560s, and what emerged was a national Kirk that involved new growth grafted on to old stock. The state church, as in England, was still episcopalian, but superimposed on it was a Reformed, Presbyterian polity on the Genevan pattern. Unlike in England, this fusion actually worked. Vestments, altars, images and saints' days all disappeared. Preaching took centre stage in worship, and the Book of Common Order enshrined a much simpler liturgy than the English Book of Common Prayer. Firm discipline was maintained by councils of ministers and elders within parishes and by regional, ministerial presbyteries. English Puritans hoped (and in some cases expected) to see such a godly regime established in their own land.

Several jumped the gun and approached the king during his progress. The most famous of the representations made at this time was the Millenary Petition, so called because its sponsors claimed to be acting on behalf of a thousand of their brethren. They politely asked the king to allow a debate on a long list of practices they had always found objectionable – confirmation, private baptism, priestly absolution, signs and symbols such as the cross in baptism and the ring in marriage, special dress for clergy – in other words, all those elements Puritans had, over more than a generation, been complaining about.

They received a strong clue to the king's attitude even before the royal cavalcade reached London, when a new book hit the bookstalls. James's *Basilikon Doron* had been written in 1599 as a private treatise for his elder son on the art of kingship. In 1603, it went on general sale and thousands rushed to buy it. Some would have been alarmed to read James advising his heir to 'hate no man more than a proud Puritan'.[2] The 37-year-old monarch might have been well advised to emulate his predecessor's reticence. Elizabeth had turned keeping her own counsel into an art form. James, by contrast, was a man being carried along on a wave of euphoria. All his life he had been taught, preached at and lectured by Calvinist theologians who had impressed on him that, while he enjoyed supreme authority in the state, in the Church he was merely a layman, bound to accept the guidance and direction of Kirk ministers. Now he had emerged from this theologically overcast clime into the radiance of divine-right autocracy. Bands of sycophantic Englishmen welcomed him all the way from Tweed to Thames. There was no one at his side, now, to question his own self-evaluation. He was free to give his subjects the benefits of his many talents. Among those talents he numbered his skills as an author, a theologian and an arbitrator. All this he declared frankly in the speech he delivered to church leaders in the following January when he opened at Hampton Court the conference he had convened in response to the requests for church reform:

blessed be God's gracious goodness, who hath brought me into the promised Land, where religion is purely professed, where I sit amongst grave, learned and reverend men, not as before, elsewhere, a king without state, without honour, without order, where beard-less boys would brave us to the face . . . Our purpose therefore is, like a good physician, to examine and try the complaints, and fully to remove the occasions thereof, if scandalous; cure them, if danger-ous; and take knowledge of them, if frivolous . . .[3]

Later in the conference James made his attitude towards radical Puritans even clearer, and we can detect the years of frustration that lay behind the words:

If you aim at a Scottish Presbytery, it agreeth as well with Monarchy as God and the Devil . . . [Without episcopacy] I know what would become of my Supremacy, for NO BISHOP, NO KING . . . If this is all your party have to say, I will make them conform themselves, or else I will harry them out of the land, or else do worse.[4]

A direct, *post hoc ergo propter hoc* connection has often been made between the king's exuberant language and the flight of Puritans to the Netherlands and, ultimately, to the New World. This is to misunderstand both James's personality and the policy pursued by his government. The king was prone to overstating and underacting. His mouth and pen were unrestrained when he was condemning things he disapproved of – namely witchcraft, tobacco and the Geneva Bible – but, like many orators, he lacked the skill and the industriousness to build legislative edifices on the shifting sands of prejudice. Particularly, his desire to be seen as the universal peacemaker often softened his attitude when he was faced with the hard work of framing laws or negotiating treaties. In terms of day-to-day religious politics, the king adopted the pragmatic approach of his predecessor. As long as the mechanism existed to deal with trouble-makers, the government rarely took the initiative in persecuting Puritans. Professor Peter Clark, writing of the religious life of one county, Kent, observed that the promotion of an arch-conservative archbishop did not lead inevitably to serious upheaval at the grass-roots level:

> In Canterbury diocese [Richard] Bancroft, who succeeded Whitgift in 1604, deprived only half a dozen radical ministers, and for Rochester there is no evidence that anyone was deprived at all. At the same time, there was an important concession to Puritan sentiment in the county with the apparent suspension of the diocesan High Commission at Canterbury; and for all his bluster Bancroft made little attempt to convert the ordinary diocesan courts into engines for any kind of religious reaction.[5]

How, then, to explain the increasingly embittered clash between the hard-liners on both sides that led, among other results, to a fresh wave of religious migration? Responsibility certainly lies in part with the men at the top.

Within weeks of the Hampton Court Conference, Archbishop Whitgift died. Bancroft, who had been well groomed by Whitgift, took his place and held the primacy for the next crucial six years. Bancroft had cut his teeth in the conflicts with Cartwright and the Presbyterian fringe during his Cambridge days and he now girded on his sword for a show-down combat with the Puritans. Within weeks he had replaced Whitgift's general subscription to Prayer Book doctrine with an 'ex animo' form of assent. It was no longer sufficient for clergy to confirm their acceptance of the standard beliefs enshrined in the Church's worship manual; they had to state that they embraced them from the bottom of their hearts. Bancroft's net had a fine mesh. It is difficult to say how many were caught in it, but the number certainly ran to three figures. For a few, such as John Robinson, this was the last straw and they left the country. But the new broom did not reach into every nook and cranny of the national Church. Thanks to lay patronage, the majority of displaced clergy continued to function as private chaplains or town preachers. For their part, Puritan sympathizers in Parliament weighed in with legislation aimed at countering Bancroft's intransigence, much to the archbishop's fury, but in any case his reign was mercifully short and he was succeeded by the more amenable George Abbot (1611).

Yet, in the final analysis, major responsibility for a persecution that drove separatists from English shores lies neither with the king nor the archbishop. The fault lay with what we would today call the 'media'. Preachers, pamphleteers, balladeers and playwrights both responded to and stirred up popular prejudice. At the academic level traditionalists entered into serious debate on issues such as church order. Hitherto, defenders of the status quo had declined to challenge Presbyterian claims that rule by diocesan bishops was unscriptural. The party line had been that the New Testament specified no form of church government as mandatory for all time. Now, they met the radicals on their own ground by producing scriptural proofs in support of episcopal government. Historians have sometimes placed this documentary evidence centre stage when explaining the drama of these years, but it was not scholarly argument that created the mood of popular discourse. It was the Marprelate Tracts and the responses to them that had taken the debate downmarket.

All communities, at all times, have a tendency to scapegoat minorities. We oversimplify our complex problems in order to justify applying simple solutions. When things go wrong the easiest response is to blame 'them'. It matters not who the 'them' is – the Jews, the socialists, the immigrants or whatever group is currently unpopular. At the turn of the seventeenth century, witches and Puritans shared top billing on many people's hate lists:

> the invention of Puritanism . . . as the brand name for a certain kind of Protestant religiosity, social conduct and politics was indeed a defining moment in English culture, crystallizing and making concrete in the public mind something, like all stigmatic stereotypes, partly imagined, bearing only a grossly oversimplified and distorted resemblance to the teeming chaos of reality.[6]

Thus Professor Collinson pointed out how 'Puritan' became not just a term of abuse but a common intellectual shortcut for people who could not or would not grapple with the complexities of the religious situation.

The originators of the Marprelate controversy bear a large share of responsibility for creating the blame and counter-blame culture. By invoking satire as a weapon, they opened the way for professional humourists to enter the fray – and to do so very effectively. It was Bancroft who urged that the Martinists should be 'answered after their own vain writings',[7] and this opened the Pandora's box from which objects of abusive satire dribbled for much of the next century. Anti-Puritanism became part of the stock-in-trade of leading dramatists. Thomas Middleton's *The Puritan* probably made its London debut in 1606 and, amid much slapstick, relied for part of its humorous impact on the popular perception of Puritans as gluttonous, money-grubbing hypocrites. *The Family of Love*, staged about the same time, supposedly made fun of the sexual adventures and misadventures of the Familists, a Dutch sect with an English offshoot that was already dying out. Few people would have understood (or cared about) the distinction between such fringe groups, and their differences from Brownism or other unorthodox Protestant bodies. Audiences would have lumped them all together under the label of 'Puritan' and have welcomed *The Family of Love* and other plays offering similar fare as condemning, through the medium of humour, all religious groups claiming to live by a more rigorous creed. These exposés reassured play-goers that, for all their claims to piety, these religious extremists were 'no better than us':

> The processes of accentuation or caricature were in part a function of the projection onto the polemically defined other of those aspects of the observer's own position and situation that he or she least wanted to face or own.[8]

And for some English people, dislike of Puritans ran really deep; the behaviour of these precisionists was no laughing matter. John Manningham, while a student at the Middle Temple, wrote a diary covering the months between Elizabeth's last days and the arrival of the new king. In the private pages of this unpublished document, he commented bitterly that a

Puritan could be defined as 'one as loves God with all his soul, but hates his neighbour with all his heart'.[9] The majority, however, were content to allow public entertainers to speak their scorn for them – the wittier the better.

Within a few years Ben Jonson was treading similar ground and winning public acclaim for his more pungent satires, *The Alchemist*, *Bartholomew Fair* and *The Devil Is an Ass*. Witty ridicule (the more daring the better) was now the height of fashion, and Jonson, one of the popular 'celebs' of the day, was at his peak in the first half of James's reign, a welcome visitor to the royal court, for which he wrote several masques. In his plays, social stereotypes were more firmly embedded than in Middleton's. In *Bartholomew Fair* (first performed in 1614), the stock Puritan, Zeal-of-the-land Busy, makes his appearance, casuistically debating whether it is permissible for Christians to attend the iniquitous fair and there to eat roast pork (the flesh of an unclean animal):

> Verily, for the disease of longing, it is a disease, a carnal disease, or appetite, incident to women; and as it is carnal and incident, it is nat-ural, very natural: now pig, it is a meat, and a meat that is nourishing and may be longed for, and so consequently eaten; it may be eaten; very exceeding well eaten; but in the Fair, and as a Bartholomew pig, it cannot be eaten; for the very calling it a Bartholomew pig, and to eat it so, is a spice of idolatry, and you make the Fair no better than one of the high-places [that is, pagan shrines].[10]

Thus Jonson parodies the tortuous exegesis of the precisionist Bible students. However, the Puritans were not the only victims of Jonson's pen. All sorts and conditions of human beings were caricatured in the play. In fact, the *dramatis personae* extended to over 40 characters. The dramatist's fire power was wide. He was not setting up the religious hypocrite as his sole target. And that is significant. The cavalcade of actors who passed across the stage of the Hope Theatre represented an array of well-recognized 'types': 'no one equalled him in presenting the class-types of a highly organised or decadent society, with all their elab-orate vesture of custom, manner and phrase.'[11] So, when Jonson presented a stage Puritan, he was offering the members of his audience a caricature they had already decided on.

What was high fashion in London was not slow to be taken up in the provinces. Strolling players included in their entertainments what had become a conventional representation of those earnest in religion. Puritans became the victims of bawdy tavern songs such as 'A Satire to the Chief Rulers in the Synagogue of Stratford':

> Stratford's a town that doth make a great show,
> But yet it is governed but yet by a few
> O Jesus Christ of Heaven,
> I think they are but seven;
> Puritans without doubt.[12]

As this particular example suggests, ribaldry sometimes arose from resentment at the prominence Puritans often achieved in local affairs. Since they tended to be sober, hard-working citizens, not given to spending their time in frivolous pursuits, they prospered, became councillors, made profitable marriages and set the tone of local society. In other words, they were precisely the sort of people the Toby Belches of this world wanted to see 'taken down a peg or two'. The market stall-holders who regaled their customers with sniggering tales about their holier-than-thou neighbours, the balladeers who entertained frequenters of the inns with scurrilous songs, the ragtag hooligans who pelted sober-clad, Bible-carrying, church-bound families on the street were the behavioural descendants of the mid-Tudor malcontents who had broken into churches to tear down 'papistical' images.

Indeed, Catholics also were victims of ridicule and abuse in the reign of James I. Oliver Ormerod, a Somerset clergyman, was generous in his distribution of popular polemic. In 1605 and 1606, he published two substantial exposés. First came *The Picture of a Puritan; or a Relation of the Opinions, Qualities and Practices of the Anabaptists in Germany and the Puritans in England – Wherein is firmly proved that the Puritans do resemble the Anabaptists in about fourscore several Things*. This was followed by *The Picture of a Papist: or a Relation of the damnable Heresies, detestable Qualities, and diabolical Practices of sundry Heretics in former Ages, and of the Papists in this Age*. While theologians and politicians tried to steer the English Church between the Scylla and Charybdis of Rome and Geneva, the amateurs in towns and villages were much more interested in the comical lampoons or indignant rants of amateur protagonists.

The sin most regularly laid at the door of all Puritans was hypocrisy. It was an easy taunt because the godly set themselves high moral standards and, either overtly or covertly, represented themselves as more virtuous than their neighbours. It was thus almost inevitable that those neighbours would try to detect chinks in the armour of holiness or invent flaws they could not discover. Many Puritans brought enmity on themselves by campaigning against what they saw as loose morals and profane customs. It was part of their mission to reform society – and society, by and large, did not take kindly to being reformed. Conflict inevitably intensified when pietists found themselves in the position of being able to impose their holiness regimes. In 1607, the constable of Wells tried to stop the May Day games and was attacked by protestors, who set him on a donkey and led him round the town festooned in deriding placards. The Exeter merchant Ignatius Jordan was typical of this breed of zealots determined to save society from itself. This citizen of very humble origins became, by industry and frugality, one of the city's leaders. A long-serving council member and Justice of the Peace, he was mayor in 1617 and four times elected as MP. In each of these capacities, he fought against traditional Sunday sports and games, swearing, adultery and drunkenness. Enraged citizens threatened to take him to court on more than one occasion.

Yet, the fact that Jordan held prominent public office for most of his life indicates that he enjoyed widespread support. This warns us again not to present the religious friction of these years in stark black and white. Not all Puritans were separatists. Not all Puritans were ostracized by their neighbours. Not all Puritans saw the American colonies as havens for zealots escaping from a repressive English Church. The enterprise of the Reverend John White offers us but one of many alternative angles on the establishment of religious colonies in New England. He served as a rector in Dorchester for more than 43 years, where he exercised an unapologetic Puritan ministry that was well received by his parishioners. As well as Sunday services, he delivered lectures three times a week and saw to it that his congregation was well grounded in the Bible. He took seriously his responsibility to oversee the reformation of morals and did not shrink from advocating floggings, fines and other punishments for drunkenness, swearing and similar breaches of the biblical code of conduct. This did not conflict with his work as a dedicated pastor much given to charitable works, particularly among the more vulnerable members of Dorchester society.

What marks John White out as different from other Puritan clergy was that he could see the bigger picture. He followed closely the early colonizing endeavours in America, and there is no doubt that he was aware of the trials and tribulations suffered by the hopefuls en route from Leiden to New England. One of his own parishioners, Richard Bushrod, was a wealthy merchant who had a considerable stake in transatlantic trade. Every year he despatched a fleet to fish for cod and to trade for furs with the Amerindians. When news reached White of the difficulties experienced by the Plymouth settlement, he had a business proposition to put to Bushrod – one that would kill two birds with one stone.

To tell this story we must slightly overstep the bounds set for the present book, but it is important to see what other concerned parties were thinking before we become involved in the details of the exiles' move from Holland, via England, to America. White could see an opportunity that, potentially, could make Bushrod's business more efficient. He also saw a way of helping the first New England settlers, who were in a state of disarray. White was no friend of separatists. He believed that a godly community could be set up within the parameters of the Church of England – in Dorchester he was doing just that. It was obvious from tales coming back across the ocean that things were not working out for the settlers and that one reason was religious dissent: some people objected to the hard line being taken on aspects of doctrine and discipline by the Plymouth leaders. His solution was to turn Bushrod's purely commercial enterprise into a colonizing venture and to establish a New England settlement to which disgruntled Plymouthians could move. Bushrod's business was labour intensive because every ship he had to despatch carried, in addition to crew, the men needed for fishing and relations with the local people. White's plans were to leave these supernumeraries in New England to live off the land between voyages. These would then form the nucleus of a new colony that would have a sound commercial base and also remain in regular contact with England.

The scheme, one of many produced at this time of interest in and enthusiasm for American adventure, attracted widespread support, and a committee was formed under the chairmanship of Dorset landowner and member of the Virginia Company, Sir Walter Earle. Thus was created the Dorchester Company, which, having surveyed the coast for a suitable site, sent its first contingent of settlers in 1623. Like other projects of this era, the company's Cape Ann colony failed. Its 50 or so survivors moved to Salem, Massachusetts, founded by Roger Conant, one of the disillusioned Plymouth settlers who hankered after English mainstream-style Puritanism.

If the King of Scots ever applied his undoubtedly acute mind to a study of the spectrum of English religious life he had inherited in 1603, he would have found it more than just politically inconvenient. He would, surely, have been bewildered. It was more complex than anything he had hitherto experienced in his native land. For us, looking back over 400 years that have presented their own challenges to the way we understand and express our faith, the task is even greater. The more intently we peer beyond the mud-slinging and the lampoons, the prejudice and the misunderstanding, the more clearly we see, not only that English Protestantism was a Joseph's coat of many colours, but that most English Protestants were sincere men and women earnestly seeking to serve and worship their God. But who was this God? And what did he demand of his devotees? The answers they gave themselves were shaped by their cultural perceptions and their varied levels of education as much as, if not more than, their study of the Bible or their waiting on the revelations vouchsafed them by the inner voice of the Holy Spirit (even though they called on both to validate the content of the faith they projected to the world).

Take, for example, personal and corporate prayer. The Whitgift school advocated the use of the Church's set liturgy for private as well as regular worship. The prayers, they argued, were dignified in the language they addressed to the Almighty and they had an educational function, teaching lay people of all degrees how to approach God and what to say to him.

This was anathema to separatists because it interposed a cultural barrier between the intercessor and his or her heavenly Father. The celebrated writer and preacher Elnathan Parr urged his readers that feeling was more important than eloquence. That was all very well, but members of separatist assemblies could also be 'trapped' into employing language and mannerisms learned from their mentors. The playwright Thomas Daker described one of his characters casting eyes up to heaven 'like a Puritan', and another contemporary drama presented a character praying with a nasal whine, as though his tongue was in his nose. The manifest oddities of the extremists made them easy targets. Long gone were the days of the Lollards and the Marian Nicodemites who kept a low profile in order to avoid persecution. Protestant extremists in James I's reign wanted to be seen and, by being identified, to be a challenge to society.

Or, at least, the bolder radicals did. In the fragmented world of religious extremism, there were some who accepted, even courted, the suffering attendant on being 'different'. Continental Anabaptists of various hues embraced *Gelassenheit* (surrender of the self; willingness to embrace martyrdom). There was a stern logic in their position. Jesus had told his first disciples, 'I have chosen you out of the world. That is why the world hates you . . . If they persecuted me, they will persecute you also' (John 15.19–20 NIV). Believers who ventured deep into the thickets of unorthodoxy accepted their resultant sufferings as proof of their faithfulness to Christ. Some saw their punishment as the outworking of the divine plan, prophesied in Scripture. Had not St Paul boasted, 'By means of my physical sufferings I am helping to complete what still remains of Christ's sufferings on behalf of his body, the church' (Colossians 1.24)? At the turn of the seventeenth century there were few such Anabaptists in England, but there were leaders with individualistic versions of Christianity and some were prepared to be faithful unto death. A few, a very few, followed the trail blazed by Barrow and Greenwood in the previous reign.

The year 1612 witnessed the last two burnings for heresy in England. Bartholomew Legate went to the stake at Smithfield, and Edward Wightman was executed in Lichfield. Their heresies were such as would have earned them the ultimate penalty in most European states. Both men were anti-Trinitarian. Both condemned Catholicism and mainline Protestantism as diabolical deceptions. Both men based apocalyptic prophecies on their own individualistic readings of the Bible. The significance of their fate in the wider story of the growth of separatism is not their idiosyncratic beliefs but their handling by the authorities – and, more specifically, by the personal interest of the king in their cases. Church and state leaders in Protestant England had never been enthusiastic about burning heretics. It smacked too much of the Inquisition and it was difficult to justify theologically without the doctrine of purgatory. If final divine judgement followed immediately on death; if there was no intermediate state for the soul to be cleansed of every vestige of sin, then despatching unrepentant heretics into the presence of a just God was bound to make mortal magistrates uncomfortable. Every effort was made to dissuade Legate and Wightman from their errors. James followed both cases and actually argued directly with Legate.

The king took very seriously his role of Defender of the Faith. He published various spiritual treatises and sermonettes for the guidance of his people, of which these words from his reflections on Revelation 20 offer a taster:

Our actions then conformed to our estate are these: First, to call for help at God's hands: next, to assure us of the same, seeing we have a sufficient warrant – his constant promise expressed in his word. Thirdly, since with good conscience we may, being in the tents of the Saints, & beloved City, stand in our defence, encourage one another to use lawful resistance, and concur or join one with another as warriors in one Camp, and citizens of one beloved City, for maintenance of the good cause God hath clad us with, and in defence of our liberty, country, and lives: For since we see God hath promised not only in the world to come, but also in this world, to give us victory over [the forces of evil], let us in assurance hereof strongly trust in our God, cease to mistrust his promise, and fall through incredulity or unbelief: For then are we worthy of double punishment: For the stronger they wax, and the nearer they come to their light, the faster approacheth their wreck, and the day of our delivery: For kind, and loving, true and constant, careful, and watchful, mighty, and revenging is he that promiseth it: to Whom be praise and glory for ever.[13]

Most of James's theological polemic was directed against the upholders of Catholicism, but he did not hesitate to venture into the fray against Protestant heretics – even interfering in the internal religious affairs of other countries. In 1612, he gave the university of Leiden the benefit of his opinion concerning the ongoing debate between Calvinism and Arminianism. Professor Conrad Vorstius was the head of the party that challenged the orthodox Reformed position on predestination. The English king, as he explained to his ambassador at The Hague, felt constrained to offer his theological and philosophical insights:

> If the subject of Vorstius' heresies had not been grounded upon questions of a higher quality than the number and nature of the Sacraments, or the points of Justification, of Merits, or Purgatory, or the visible head of the Church, or any such matters, as are in controversy at this day betwixt the Papists and us; Nay more, if he had meddled only with the nature and works of GOD *ad extra* (as the Schoolmen speak). If he had soared [to] no higher pitch; we do freely profess, that in that case we should never have troubled ourselves with the business in such fashion, and with that fervency as hitherto we have done. But this Vorstius . . . [being] in the head a sworn enemy not only to Divinity, but even to all Philosophy . . . Let the world then judge whether we had no occasion hereupon, to be moved . . . as a Christian at large; yea, even as a *Theist*, or a man that acknowledgeth a GOD, or as a *Platonic* Philosopher.[14]

In matters doctrinal as well as political, James considered himself to be not only endowed with the intellectual and spiritual gifts that qualified him to be a universal moderator and peacemaker but also called, as an anointed king, to exercise the offices of Christian pastor and preacher. In 1618, it is recorded that, throughout a whole Sunday dinner in the royal privy chamber, the entire conversation was devoted to the latest *cause célèbre*, the trial of John Traske.

This saga, which was still making the 'headlines' at the very time that the New World-bound 'Pilgrims' were gathering in England for their epic voyage, provides further evidence of the ever-widening nature of the phenomenon we call 'separatism'. It also casts more light on how the authorities tried to deal with this growing problem. When James VI of Scotland became James I of England, John Traske was a young schoolmaster in Somerset, but his intense religious fervour drove him to seek a more prominent role and he took to an itinerant preaching career. By 1611, he had persuaded the Bishop of Bath and Wells to ordain him, but he failed to find a parish and continued his public speaking ministry. Lacking the time restraints of pastoral responsibility, he became very accomplished at this and frequently moved his hearers to tears. He soon had a following and was accompanied by assistant preachers. Their success and their unorthodox teaching had landed them in jail by 1617. Their message had taken on a very Old Testament complexion. They celebrated a seventh-day Sabbath, embraced the dietary laws of the old covenant, and abandoned Christian festivals in favour of Passover, Hanukkah and other Jewish festivals. Despite appealing directly to the king, Traske was brought into the court of Star Chamber, where he was found guilty of diverting His Majesty's subjects from their true obedience. How was this fellow to be silenced permanently if death by burning was ruled out? The answer was a life prison sentence – after he had been whipped through London, suffered a spell in the pillory, nailed by one ear, and had the letter 'J' (for Judaizer) branded on his forehead. From this point Traske's career bears similarity to John Brown's; he recanted his erroneous beliefs and was released in 1620. He continued preaching and, presumably, in orthodox vein since he does not feature in any extant court records. At some point, however, he joined a Baptist church.

To round off this Jacobean separatist miscellany we will consider the career of Henry Jacob. In contrast to Traske, Jacob might almost be described as a 'normal separatist' – if such animals existed. He spent most of his adult life grappling with the issue that, as we have seen, was at the centre of Protestant ecclesiology – authority. If it was not vested in the pope or the king or the episcopal bench, where was it located? Jacob found it impossible to accept the Presbyterian church-within-a-church solution, since it involved creating organizational subdivisions that were no more likely to be free of error than dioceses. The only assembly that could be identified as a true church was a visible, gathered congregation of saints who agreed to come together and govern themselves. In the 1590s, Jacob was a Brownist and one of the first separatists to flee to Holland. Yet he was temperamentally at odds with the tendency to ongoing fragmentation such as he witnessed at first hand in the English congregations in Amsterdam (Jacob was one of the many people who fell out with Francis Johnson). Nor could he in all conscience write off all English parish churches as in thrall to diabolical error. In 1603, he was one of the organizers of the Millenary Petition arguing for a tolerant ecclesiastical policy that would allow independent (Congregationalist) churches to exist side by side with established churches. Such 'semi-separatism' was an idea for which the time had not yet come – and would not come for another 150 years. When, in 1616, Jacob set up a church embodying his tolerant principles, a few individuals were prepared to cross denomination boundaries. But his south London assembly was snubbed by separatist leaders and parish clergy alike. And King James could only view it with suspicion.

10

John Robinson and Co.

Over the previous chapters we have steadily narrowed both our geographical and our theological focus. We have noticed that, while separatism was an impulse experienced by earnest Puritans in various parts of England, it was particularly virulent in the East Midlands, and we have suggested various contributory factors such as the Continental origins of unconventional beliefs, their easy spread via London and east-coast ports along the Great North Road and the riverain network, the intellectual support they received from radical theologians at Cambridge University, and the essential political backing provided by political leaders at court and in the shires. Now we can go further. We can place under our magnifying glass an area on the map measuring scarcely more than 75 square miles and we can identify a handful of devout believers who exercised spiritual leadership in that area.

But first a word of caution. We shall fail to understand these people if we are tempted to do our history 'backwards'; if we are concerned to identify them as the pioneers of a great nation. Even if we avoid clothing the members of this group in the patriotic and heroic garb of 'founding fathers', we may yet misread their characters, their situations and their actions by taking them out of context and focusing exclusively on this one group of people as though it was unique. It was not. But neither was it representative of a wider movement. We will be tracing the travels and adventures of a nucleus of separatist Puritans originating in a tract of land on the borders of Lincolnshire and Nottinghamshire bisected by the River Trent. In the course of no more than a dozen years, its members crossed the sea to Holland and then crossed the wider sea to North America. During that time the composition of the group changed as people joined, left or died. It slowly increased in numbers (perhaps to around 300 at its height), but only

151

35 eventually settled in America. The group was just one among many migrating communities (some 25 such existed in the Dutch Republic) and it could not be precisely identified by adherence to a closely defined set of Christian beliefs.

The area where the story of this particular community began is contained within a quadrilateral linking the towns of Gainsborough, Bawtry, Worksop and East Retford. The men whose dynamic interrelationship we will explore are William Brewster, Richard Clifton, John Robinson, John Smyth and John Helwys.

In the top left-hand corner of the area we have marked out is the quiet village of Scrooby. Current population is not much above 300 and it may have been less at the turn of the seventeenth century. If so, this belied its importance. Here stood a palace and an estate belonging to Archbishop Sandys of York. Scrooby was, at that time, on the Great North Road. Not only that; it was also one of the staging offices of the royal postal service. The keeper of that office had a busy and important job to do. He had to keep a stable of horses to ensure the rapid and secure delivery of mail passing between the court and the northern shires, and he had to cater to the needs of important travellers who were about the monarch's business. The man who oversaw the workings of this hub of the communications network was, thus, a trusted and influential figure, with friends in high places and a well-informed understanding of national affairs. In fact, few provincial officials could boast of more influential connections than the Scrooby postmaster. The position had become hereditary by the late sixteenth century and thus it was that, in the 1590s, William Brewster took over from his father the offices of both archiepiscopal bailiff and royal postmaster.

It seems that originally Brewster entertained even higher ambitions. On going down from Cambridge around 1584, he had joined the diplomatic corps as secretary to William Davison, Queen Elizabeth's ambassador to the United Province, currently fighting a war of liberation from Philip II of Spain. Davison was an outspoken Scot with strong Presbyterian sympathies. It may well have been his religious radicalism and his lack of discretion that contributed to his fall from royal favour – a fall that took Brewster too. By 1586, Davison had advanced to the position of the queen's principal secretary (in succession to Sir Francis

Walsingham). The regular contact with Elizabeth inevitably drew attention to their religious differences. This ardent Puritan was not the sort of man to back down over a point of principle – even when he was confronted by the queen. On one occasion, believing himself wronged by his royal mistress, instead of making a courtly apology he declared that he would withdraw and pray for her change of mind because nothing could save her from divine judgement if she continued obstinately on her present course. Elizabeth, who had demoted an archbishop for such insolence, was not about to be lectured by her secretary. A bigger crisis came in February 1587 when Elizabeth was faced with endorsing the 'final solution' regarding Mary Queen of Scots. Only with extreme reluctance could she bring herself to sign the death warrant. Then, after the deed was done, she tried to blame Davison, claiming that he had delivered the warrant without her permission. This was the end of Davison's political career. He retired from public life.

So did his friend, William Brewster. After a very brief career above the snowline of national politics, he contented himself with a life of public service on the lower slopes. Did he retire gracefully? He would have been less than human if he had not been disillusioned – even disgusted – with the way his friend had been scapegoated. His experience of politics at the top level can only have reinforced his conviction that the ordering of national affairs in Church and State was on a downward path if not firmly grounded in the plain word of God. But his diplomatic and political activity had brought him experience and contacts that would later prove invaluable. He had seen for himself the situation in the Low Countries. He had numerous contacts at court. He had probably met Edwin Sandys (the archbishop's son who later became a leading figure in the colonization of Virginia) and he certainly knew other major players in the politico-religious life of the nation. One such was Thomas West, who in 1602 became Baron De La Warr and a privy councillor. We later find Edward Brewster, one of William's sons, in the retinue of De La Warr, and it is reasonable to suppose that his advancement was due to the family connection. William had observed at close quarters how theological differences informed and shaped political action. At a time when Martin Marprelate and other raucous Puritans were challenging the leadership of the national Church, Brewster devoted himself to the support and encouragement of local religious radicals. As a landholder of some social standing he used his influence to secure appointments to some of the local churches and he brought in gifted preachers. But he also oversaw worship in his own house at Scrooby or in the chapel of ease there.

There were many such irregular gatherings of radical Protestants contemporaneous with the Scrooby assembly. In 1584, Giles Wigginton (or Wiggenton), sometime vicar of Sedburgh (and yet another product of Cambridge and East Midlands Calvinism), lampooned the current state of the English Church in a mock episcopal visitation of radical gatherings, and drew attention to the variety of flourishing 'conferences, disputations, reasonings, prayers, singing of psalms, preachings, readings, prophesying, fastings and feastings and such like holy exercises'.[1] Furthermore, it comes as no surprise that the men and women who met together under Brewster's roof were not united behind a body of doctrines on which they were all agreed. The disparate group of people who found their way to Scrooby Manor were united only in their dissatisfaction with the Church as established by Elizabeth and Whitgift and maintained even more rigidly by James I and Richard Bancroft, the new archbishop.

A dire picture was painted by William Bradford who, as a teenager, had belonged to the Scrooby fellowship; he later chose the path of exile, was a voyager on the *Mayflower*, and became Governor of the Plymouth settlement and wrote its first authoritative history. According to his narrative, official policy was embraced, at the local level, by many who hated Puritans in general and separatists in particular (insofar as they were able or willing to distinguish between the two). Bradford recalled how his friends and co-religionists

were scoffed and scorned by the prophane multitude, and ye ministers urged with ye yoke of subscription or else must be silenced; and ye poor people were so vexed with apparators and pursuivants, and ye commissary courts as truly their affliction was not small ... they could not long continue in any peaceable condition, but were hunted and persecuted on every side, so as their former afflictions were but as flea-bitings in comparison of these which now came

154

upon them. For some were taken and clapped up in prison, others had their houses beset and watched night and day . . . and most were fain to fly and leave their houses and habitations, and the means of their livelihood.[2]

It does not detract from this narrative of suffering to point out that Bradford's assessment was one-sided and coloured by his own early experiences of persecution. There was nothing new about the suspicion and aggression 'Brownists' attracted. It was the sort of reaction that had been experienced by Lollards, Protestant subjects of Mary Tudor and Catholic recusants. As with these other examples of religious intolerance, active hostility was sporadic and localized and coloured by other social factors. And, like Marian Protestants and Elizabethan Catholics, only minorities were forced into exile. Like the Nicodemites of the 1550s, the majority of separatists were only separatists at heart, conforming outwardly in order to live an easy life.

What marked out the Scrooby believers was their unwillingness to compromise in this way. To a large degree they exiled themselves. They had adjudged the culture of England to be pagan and anti-Christian and were fearful of remaining – *for their souls' health*. There was very much a sense of shaking off the dust from their shoes against the abode of Satan. Specifically, they feared for the salvation of their children and children's children if they were brought up in a defiled and defiling environment.

What is remarkable about the Scrooby fellowship is the coterie of original thinkers and staunch believers who were attracted to it by Brewster's engaging character and ardent belief, and also by the teaching of Richard Clifton. He was already ensconced as the rector of nearby Babworth before Brewster's return to the area, but Brewster was impressed with his preaching and attracted censure from the ecclesiastical authorities for forsaking his own parish church to attend services in Babworth. There is no surviving evidence of Clifton's getting into trouble. He was not inclined to separatism and kept his more outspoken criticisms of the establishment for the gatherings of the 'faithful' at Scrooby Manor. The numbers attending Brewster's meetings gradually increased, but there was no suggestion of separating. Nor did the bishop's officers initiate proceedings against such a prominent and well-connected man as the archbishop's bailiff. It seems that Brewster, who kept himself well abreast of national events, was content to watch proceedings and pray for change. Queen Elizabeth and Archbishop Whitgift were both old. While some religious progressives were impatient for change, others were prepared to wait on events. Brewster and his friends were in the latter category.

The determination of England's new king to bring all Puritans to heel changed the personnel and the mood of our East Midlands quadrilateral. If Scrooby was the progressive capital of this enclave it was largely because of the social standing of William Brewster and the inspired preachers he introduced to the meetings in his house and helped to establish in neighbouring parishes. Radicals in the region looked to Scrooby for leadership. In practical, day-to-day terms, this tended to mean that Brewster and his friends exercised something of a restraining influence over their more zealous and impatient neighbours. After 1605 that changed.

This was the year a cleric with a troubled career behind him arrived in nearby Gainsborough and, inevitably, made contact with the Scrooby group. John Smyth's clashes with authority began in his student days at Cambridge, where he was a contemporary of John Robinson (see below). When he moved to Lincoln he was suspended from his position as lecturer and preacher for his trenchant criticisms of church worship and practices. In 1605, he resigned his orders and moved to Gainsborough. This must be seen against the background of the backlash, provoked by the Gunpowder Plot, against 'schismatics' of all stripes who refused to conform themselves to the ordinaries of the Church established by royal authority. It is not surprising that it was Puritan ministers of the Lincoln diocese who called for a debate on the thorny issues of wearing the surplice, making the sign of the cross in baptism and kneeling to receive Communion. The framers of this appeal protested that they were among those 'who freely and willingly perform to the King and state all obedience . . . and have been always ready to conform themselves to any order of the church authorised by him not contrary to the word of God'.[3] By this time Smyth had already burned his boats and was calling for others of like mind to join with him in refusing fellowship with those who had, in his opinion, bowed the knee to Baal.

Smyth's relationship with the Scrooby believers at this point is not clear – and perhaps it was not clear then. There was undoubtedly a fellow feeling, an agreement on basic Puritan principles and a unity born of shared suffering, but there were certainly differences of opinion. Clifton, for example, rejected some of the doctrines on which Smyth based his call to separatism. There were also the beginnings of a rift between Smyth and one of his own disciples, Thomas Helwys. Helwys came from a well-to-do Midlands family whose main seat was at Bilborough, near Nottingham. After some years spent at the Inns of Court in London during the 1590s, he returned to Bilborough and turned his home into a radical haven similar to Scrooby. Then, around the turn of the century, Helwys and his family moved to Gainsborough. They had become devotees of Smyth's brand of Puritanism and joined the band of 60 or so dedicated separatists who gathered for teaching and worship at Gainsborough Old Hall, thanks to the patronage of the owner, Sir William Hickman. But Helwys's spiritual pilgrimage had not ended. It probably did not end until he came under the influence of Anabaptists in the Dutch Republic but, since his final position cut to the heart of Calvinist orthodoxy, it seems likely that he was already experiencing serious doubts by the time he arrived at Gainsborough around 1605. Helwys came to embrace Arminianism, the doctrine that salvation is on offer to all and capable of being received by anyone – not just those predestined by God to be numbered among the elect.

The last significant arrival in the Scrooby quadrilateral was someone we have already met briefly. John Robinson of Sturton-le-Steeple was another Puritan who had imbibed his faith at Cambridge. He resigned his fellowship at Corpus Christi College on his marriage and went to Norwich to take up the cure of souls in one of the city churches, but his conscience would not allow him to remain there long. As he later explained:

> We are bold upon the warrant of [Christ's] Word and Testament [to] proclaim to all the world separation from whatsoever riseth up re-belliously against the sceptre of his kingdom, as we are undoubtedly persuaded the communion, government, ministry and worship of the Church of England do.[4]

Robinson returned to his home territory in 1607 and joined the Scrooby fellowship. Indeed, he seems to have been the 'new blood' that fellowship was unconsciously looking for. He was in his prime, and had excellent academic credentials and obvious leadership qualities. Richard Clifton readily embraced him as assistant minister to what had, in effect, become the gathered church at Scrooby. But Robinson's sojourn was not destined to be long. Faced with growing local persecution, several of the brethren were getting itchy feet. And they were not alone.

The earnest souls who met for mutual encouragement and edification in Scrooby Manor formed just one of many such groups throughout the country whose members were trying to understand and respond to the religious upheaval England was going through. As papal authority gave way to royal authority, and royal authority gave way to the authority of the written word of God, so 'authority' came to mean, in effect, the control exercised by popular pastors and charismatic preachers. Those pastors and preachers were not always agreed among themselves; there was no doctrinal consistency within the wide ranks of Puritanism. Nor was the division between separatist and conformist always clear-cut: 'Separatists and non-separatists were at one in their belief that within the parishes of the Church of England were many thousands of elect and converted Christians.'[5] There were many partial separatists: men and women who kept a foot in both camps, worshipping with their neighbours and 'gadding about' to hear godly preachers (in that regard little had changed since the days of Lollard persecution). The pull of kith and kin, of employment, of loyalty to king and country was, in the majority of cases, stronger than the attraction of doctrinal precision. Of that tiny minority who decamped to the colonies in the first half of the seventeenth century an even smaller minority did so for purely religious reasons. Those who emigrated and those who remained behind clung to their conflicting convictions, and it is not insignificant that, of the five Scrooby leaders we have identified, only one ended up in New England.

It was the uncompromising stance of James I at the Hampton Court Conference and his well-publicized vow to 'harry from the land' all nonconformists that proved to be the tipping point for several of the Scrooby folk. They had endured the general opprobrium associated with the nickname 'Puritans' and the sporadic attacks instigated by Elizabeth's bishops, but now their hopes were dashed and their patience was at an end. In 1605-1606, there were various signs that the religious crisis was about to break. Not only did all the king's concessions to the Puritan faction fail to materialize, but the Gunpowder Plot did not provoke the official clampdown on Catholics that might have been expected. James, aware of the foreign policy implication of his attitude towards Catholics and intent on maintaining peace with all the courts of Europe, soft-pedalled his reaction. Indeed, it could be argued that it was the Puritans who came off worst. The new laws enforcing liturgical conformity and attendance at parish churches, though not enforced rigorously and consistently, put many pastors and lay people under heavier pressure.

At the same time, leaders of the Puritan gentry in the Midlands took an initiative of their own that has often failed to attract from historians the attention it deserves. We have encountered Sir William Wray and Sir George St Poll as advocates of the Puritan cause in Parliament (see above, pp. 124f.). They belonged to that interconnected group of Protestant county gentry which always undergirded the religious radicalism of middle England. Sir William was a patron of several Puritan clergy, including the extremist John Smyth. Wray had two sisters. Frances was married to his friend, George St Poll. The other, Isabel, was married to Sir William Bowes of Streatham, County Durham, and yielded nothing to her brother in terms of religious zeal. The Earl of Shrewsbury thought it necessary to warn Bowes against the influence Puritan preachers had on such 'simple women'. However, Sir William was completely in agreement over the move they jointly made in 1606. This was to summon a conference of prominent Puritan clergy to their house at Coventry to give earnest consideration to the question of separation from the official Church. No account of the discussion has survived and it is not completely clear who was in attendance (doubtless, discretion made it necessary for any documentary evidence of the meeting to be kept to an absolute minimum). However, it is generally understood that Robinson, Smyth and Helwys were among the attendees from the Scrooby and Gainsborough fellowships. If Brewster was there, he would have been able to share his personal experience of the Netherlands, for the practicalities of settling across the North Sea must have been discussed. It is doubtful whether, at that stage, anyone was thinking seriously about relocating to

North America. The fate of previous colonists was not very encouraging. The United Provinces was the only option. But migration to a friendly Protestant state was not without its problems. The exiles were escaping their conflict with royal authority but only to exchange that conflict for others. Some they encountered in their new home. Others were endemic; they took them with them.

The first to make a move were Smyth, Helwys and their followers in Gainsborough. Since their doctrinal stance was more extreme, they were more out of kilter with the state church in England and more at risk if they were put on trial. Yet, they might have thought twice about emigrating had they fully understood the religious complexity that would face them in the Republic of the Seven United Provinces, as the northern Netherlands now called themselves. After half a century of freedom-fighting against Spanish control, the republican north had established not only political and religious independence but also a re-markable degree of economic prosperity, known ever since as the Dutch Golden Age. Symbolic of this was the establishment in 1602 of the Dutch East India Company, which, floated on an issue of public shares, became the world's first publicly owned joint-stock company. (The English East India Company, though founded two years earlier, was an enterprise capitalized by a syndicate of wealthy merchants. Widening the investment base was a major step forward in global commerce.) But success came at a price. Winning territory, maintaining an effect-ive army and navy, and establishing and garrisoning border defences were cripplingly expensive. The only saving grace was that the war had bankrupted Spain. Both belligerents in the Netherlands were exhausted. They were longing for peace but unwilling to relinquish the principle they had been fighting over for almost two generations. But, in 1607, long and bitter negotiations were heading towards cessation of hostilities. A ceasefire was agreed, to enable extensive peace talks to begin. Eventually, this led, in 1609, to what was called the Twelve Years' Truce.

It was this change of climate that prompted fresh immigration to the republic. The Puritan settlement experiments in the Dutch Republic coincided almost precisely with the Twelve Years' Truce (1609-1622). As well as religious toleration, the United Provinces offered economic prosperity. Economic migrants bringing technical skills were welcomed by the government of the republic. The timing seemed propitious, the opportunities good and the risks minimal for any families prepared to work hard and make their contribution to the life of their chosen nation. English migrants were not the only ones to see the advantage of making a new life in the country that seemed to be chosen by God as the standard-bearer of Protestant Christianity. People were arriving from France, Germany, Scandinavia and even further afield to seek their fortunes in the chosen land. And that, for some of the English newcomers, was the problem.

We have seen something of the feuding that was undermining the existing English church in Amsterdam and we will return to it presently, but it was the influence of other religious groups that posed problems for the Smyth–Helwys migrants. The major debate occupying the minds of Dutch theologians was that between traditional Calvinists and those who followed the current professor of theology at Leiden University, Jacobus Arminius. The dispute – often ill-tempered – was at its height between 1603 and 1608 (Arminius died the following year). Arminius's aim was to refine the teaching of Calvin, particularly the understanding of prevenient grace. Whereas Calvinists held that this was granted only to the predestined elect, Arminius proposed that it was a gift to all humanity. In effect, this meant that everyone was able to decide whether or not to accept the salvation offered through the death and resurrection of Christ. God fore*knows* those who will accept this gift, but he does not fore*ordain* their acceptance or rejection. The controversy continued after Arminius's death, and in 1618 the Synod of Dort was convened for the specific purpose of condemning Arminius and all his works.

John Smyth, arriving in Amsterdam where Arminius had spent several years as a much loved pastor and preacher, took little time to come round to the popular, prevailing teaching. This, in itself, was sufficient to isolate him from most of the other English exiles, but he now fell under a more dangerous Dutch influence. Menno Simons (c. 1496-1561) had been one leader of the hydra-headed Anabaptist movement whose pacifist spirituality with its emphasis on discipline and high ethical standards proved popular in north Germany and the Netherlands. Smyth soaked up these new influences like blotting paper and struggled to reconcile them. Never a man to do things by halves, he warmly embraced

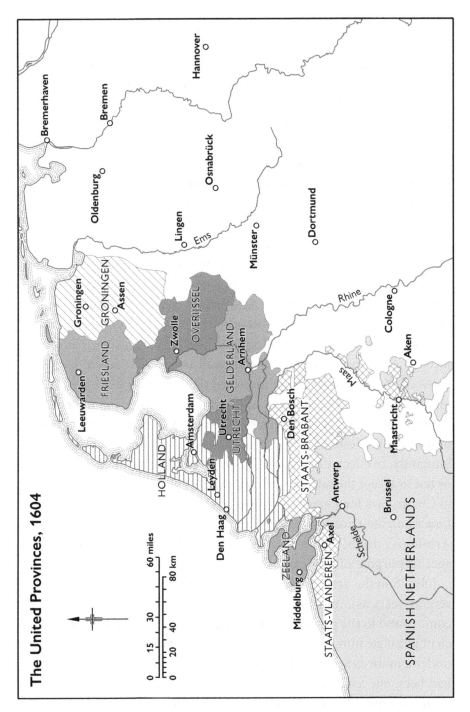

The United Provinces, 1604

By 1604, the Seven Provinces of Holland, Utrecht, Zeeland, Gelderland, Overijssel, Triesland and Groningen had gained their independence from Spain. The fate of Brabant was not finally decided until the end of the Eighty Years War (1568–1648), when Northern Brabant (Staats-Brabant) was finally ceded to the Republic. (Map by Lovell Johns, © SPCK.)

the Anabaptist principle of believers' baptism, and during the winter of 1608-1609 he solemnly baptized himself and went on to administer the rite to about 40 of his group. Still he had not reached the end of his somewhat serpentine spiritual journey and was constantly revising his doctrine in response to fresh 'revelations'. It is not surprising that the leaders of the English community lost patience with him and excommunicated him and his adherents. Having unsuccessfully sought admission to the Mennonite community, Smyth and his flock established their own church in the back premises of a bakery. But Smyth's inner discourse – now querulously searching, now aggressively asserting – was almost at an end. He died of tuberculosis in 1612.

By this time Thomas Helwys, who had originally taken on Smyth's mantle, had left Amsterdam. Before doing so, he had brought his lawyer's mind to bear on the theological challenges facing him and his fellow countrymen in the Netherlands. The results bore fruit in a number of treatises covering Arminianism and religious liberty, and critiques of Catholicism, Puritanism and the Mennonites. He also wrote *A Declaration of Faith of English People Remaining in Amsterdam*, which, in the fullness of time, became the doctrinal heart of the Baptist statement of teaching. His passionate quest for truth led him to the conclusion that the move to the Dutch Republic had been wrong. Christ's people, he insisted, should not flee from suffering. They should, like their Master, set their faces towards Jerusalem. Accordingly, he and some of his followers returned to London and set up in Spitalfields what would come to be regarded as the first General Baptist church. If Helwys aspired to persecution, King James readily obliged him. He was thrown into Newgate jail where, by 1616, he had died.

One of the fiercest critics of Smyth and Helwys among the English community in Amsterdam was Richard Clifton. This veteran of the Scrooby congregation made his North Sea crossing in August 1608, leaving John Robinson in charge of the remaining members of the fellowship, joined the Ancient Brethren, and was welcomed for his long years of pastoral experience and his theological understanding. Henry Ainsworth referred to him as a 'worthy soldier of Christ',[6] and endorsed his teaching and preaching ministry. However, when, within months, the split occurred between Ainsworth and Francis Johnson, Clifton remained with the Johnsonian majority. In Amsterdam, where he re-sided for the rest of his life, Clifton saw several of his old friends and colleagues come and go. He continued to minister to their spiritual needs in preaching and writing. William Bradford, a teenage orphan who had been taken in by Clifton, described him as the exiles' 'principal scribe', which suggests that he was kept busy providing the members of his little flock with devotional and doctrinal material. Determined to maintain them in the truth, he could not avoid being drawn into the dispute tearing the Ancient Brethren apart. His trenchant riposte against John Smyth's rejection of infant baptism was published in 1611. The next year this was followed up by a more wide-ranging defence of his theological position: *An Advertisement concerning a book lately published by Christopher Lawne and others against the exiled English Church at Amsterdam.*

The warfare between Ainsworth and Johnson was then at its hottest. It was partly a personality clash, but the partisans of the two leaders had provided themselves with biblical *raisons d'être*. The central issue, as with so many conflicts in the post-Reformation Church, was authority. In this instance, what was disputed was the authority of the eldership. The Johnson camp insisted that final authority in major disputes lay with the minister and elders. Ainsworth held that some issues were of such moment that they could only be resolved by vote of the entire fel-lowship. The clash was implicit in the whole separatist movement: having denied the power of the king and the bishops in all matters spiritual, where were the faithful to turn for guidance in all matters of Christian truth? Partisan sermons gave way to violent verbal abuse; token words were superseded by unseemly pamphlet warfare; disputes were taken to the secular courts. In December 1610, the members of Ainsworth's minority group were obliged to vacate the church premises (see above, p. 113), but they refused to let the matter rest, pursued it through the courts and regained possession in 1613.

This was the same year that Christopher Lawne wrote the lurid and sensationalist exposé to which Clifton found it necessary to respond: *The prophane schism of the Brownists or Separatists with the impiety, dissensions, lewd, and abominable vices of that impure sect: Discovered by Christopher Lawne, John Fowler, Clement Saunders, Robert Bulward; lately returned from the Company of Master Johnson, that wicked Brother, into the bosom of the Church of England, their true Mother* was a smear that verged on the pornographic and was followed up by more 'revelations' in the same vein: *Brownism turned the inside outward: Being a Parallel between the Profession and the Practice of the Brownists' religion.* Lawne was a Puritan merchant. On his conversion to separatism he had made his own way to Amsterdam, and became an elder in Ainsworth's church. Subsequently he fell out with the leader, was excommunicated, and returned to London. The stories told by the turncoat about his former brethren were of power-crazed and licentious hypocrites who misused their authority to carry out lascivious acts with servant girls and other young women, as well as imposing harsh and humiliating punishments to enforce discipline. One leader of the fellowship, Lawne averred, had well earned his popular nickname of 'Mansfield the Stripper'. Doubtless, such 'revelations' were designed to play to popular prejudice in Jacobean England. It was also a piece of propaganda; Lawne wrote to deter other Puritans from leaving the national Church. How much truth there is in this exposé is impossible now to determine. The allusions to sexual misconduct probably had their origins in the questionable behaviour of one of Francis Johnson's colleagues – behaviour that Johnson was complicit in covering up. As we have seen, this was not the only scandal that plagued the Ancient Brethren. After Johnson's death in 1618 many of his followers were reunited with Ainsworth's congregation. In 1621-1622, some attempted to settle in Virginia. Although a few reached the New World, most perished during an atrocious Atlantic crossing. However, Christopher Lawne, the whistle-blower, was more fortunate – slightly. He too set out for Virginia, and established one of the first Puritan plantations in 1618. He survived there for 18 months.

For the sake of clarity, it has been necessary to relate the biographies of the individual leaders whose lives were interconnected, rather than follow a strict chronological schema. So we come to the man whose name stands at the heading of this chapter and who was destined, with Brewster, to be the major link between Scrooby and the New England colony. By the time John Robinson joined Brewster's assembly, the decision to follow Smyth's example had already been taken and it is reasonable to assume that is why he and his wife joined. As to what happened next, we have very little evidence. Was there a planned operation or a piecemeal evacuation with small groups making their way to the coast as and when they were able? How was this emigration viewed by the government? Answers to these interconnected questions can only be tentative, or, rather, the facts used to support answers can be made to point in different directions.

Before we attempt any synthesis we must remember that, at this stage of religious migration, we are dealing with minute, almost infinitesimal, numbers. That, of course, does not make the experiences of those venturing abroad in search of a better life any less impressive, or inspiring or poignant, but it does mean that it has a different significance in the context of religious separation in England. Our only source relating to this aspect of the migration from Scrooby is *The History of Plymouth Plantation* written by William Bradford, who was Governor of Plymouth at a time when the initial hardships of the colony had been heroically overcome. The author's main concern was to impress on his readers the price their forebears had paid to secure their independence. Bradford gave a dramatic account of the difficulties various groups encountered in their endeavour to escape from England.

He tells the story of a 'large company' of people who, presumably having crossed Lincolnshire on foot (though he does not specifically say so), arrived at Boston in the autumn of 1607 and hired a ship 'wholly to themselves'. This suggests a well-concocted and intelligent plan, for Boston was, after London, the major port for all merchants dealing with the Low Countries. However, everything went wrong when the captain they had contracted to give them passage, having stowed their luggage aboard:

Took them and put them into open boats and there rifled and ransacked them, searching them to their shirts for money, yea even ye women, further than became modesty and then carried them back into ye town and made them a spectacle and wonder to ye multitude which came flocking on all sides to behold them . . .[7]

The would-be exiles were thrown into the local jail (still shown to tourists fascinated by the Pilgrim Fathers' story).

In the following spring, another attempt was made to get a group away in a Dutch boat (presumably organized by members of the Scrooby fellowship already safely arrived in the Republic). This time the rendezvous was a quiet spot on the coast of the Humber estuary near Immingham. The women and children were conveyed thither by boat while their husbands and fathers travelled overland. This time it was the shallow nature of the channel that thwarted their plans. The Dutch ship could not come close in shore and the travellers had to be brought aboard in boats. This fatally slowed down the escape plan. A posse of local people came to investigate, and the ship's captain, to avoid trouble, sailed away carrying on board those who had managed to get to the ship. Those left behind were hauled before the magistrates, who were clearly embarrassed by the situation. Eventually, Bradford reports, the authorities 'were glad to be rid of them upon any terms'.[8] Unfortunately, the author failed to specify what those 'terms' were. The menfolk who had escaped by ship found themselves in a worse situation when their vessel ran into a North Sea gale. In an heroic narrative reminiscent of St Paul's shipwreck off Malta (Acts 27), Bradford recorded how the mariners cried out despairingly, 'We sink. We sink', but their devout passengers prayed even more loudly:

'Yet, Lord, thou cans't save'. Miraculously the wind and waves subsided. When the ship reached port people came flocking, admiring their deliverance, the storm having been so long and sore, in which much hurt had been done, as the master's friends related unto him.[9]

These are the only incidents Bradford recounts in detail, though he assures us, 'I might relate many other notable passages and trouble which they endured.' He goes on to draw the moral that some good came of all these misfortunes:

their cause became famous and occasioned many to look into the same; and their godly carriage and Christian behaviour was such as left a deep impression in the minds of many. And though some few shrank at these first conflicts and sharp beginnings (as it was no marvel), yet many more came on with fresh courage and greatly animated others. And in the end, notwithstanding all these storms of opposition, they all got over at length, some at one time and some at another, and some in one place and some in another, and met together again according to their desires, with no small rejoicing.[10]

These tales had entered the folklore of the settlers by the time Bradford set them down, and we have no means of telling to what extent they had become embellished in the oral tradition. However, what Bradford does not say or hints at is revealing. His description of the attitude of the authorities is compelling. The indignities imposed on the travellers were not the works of officials but of greedy individuals such as the Boston captain and others ready to enrich themselves by preying on the vulnerable. Bradford offers a glimpse of local agents of mob law exercising their fear and hatred of people they did not understand (such as witches, foreigners and religious extremists). The agents of royal justice had no instructions as to how to deal with separatists trying to leave the country, as was clear in the Immingham story. In the case of the people incarcerated at Boston, Bradford was at pains to recount that the local magistrates treated them courteously and appealed to the Council in London for instructions. The result was that most of the prisoners were quietly released. William Brewster was among the handful detained to the next assize, but there is no record of his having been convicted of any offence.

There was no royally inspired witch hunt. James had threatened to harry nonconformists from the land and was quite happy to see them go. Champions of the 'Pilgrims', then and since, have claimed that migration was forced on them by persecution, and stories such as those just mentioned are deployed to demonstrate that repression of the separatists was savage and relentless; but hard cases make bad law, and religious conflict in early seventeenth-century England can never be accurately painted in stark black and white. The majority of men and women sincerely committed to radical Christian doctrines found ways to worship in their own country. Some went 'underground', holding their meetings in secret. Some enjoyed the patronage and protection of powerful individuals. Some, by proving themselves valuable and agreeable members of their communities, were popular with their neighbours and thus avoided the prying eyes and wagging tongues that could lead to unwelcome investigation. And then there were the semi-separatists, Christians who struggled to square their narrow biblicism with membership of the national Church.

Henry Jacob, whom we have already met, provides evidence of an eirenic stratum among the separatists. This Oxford-trained theologian was another leader who gathered a following of disciples whom he led to the Netherlands. His church was set up at Middelburg, in about 1600, but he spent quite a lot of time travelling back and forth between the Low Countries and England and visiting the other exiled communities. Thus, in 1610, we find him striking up a close friendship with John Robinson. His relationship with Francis Johnson was less cordial. Jacob was yet another person who fell out with that prickly autocrat. The reason was Jacob's passion for tolerance and moderation. He wrote an appeal to James I asking the king to allow Christian congregations a greater degree of freedom in worship. By 1616, he was back in London, seeking to realize his version of a church that was radical yet more open. At his congregational church in Southwark, Jacob welcomed members of the parish church and encouraged his own flock to attend sermons delivered by Anglican clergy. Grappling with the central issue of authority, Jacob argued for the autonomy of the local congregation in which democracy was expressed by the people choosing their ministers, to whose leadership they then submitted. He was prepared to recognize the office of bishop but only in the sense of someone acting as moderator in each region, a *primus inter pares* among the local church leaders. The presence of people like Jacob among the dissenters is proof that there were bands of several colours at the radical end of the English church spectrum. They were rejected and/or misunderstood by the rival upholders of those whose banners proclaimed 'No Bishop, No King' and 'We Are the Chosen Few – All Others are Damned', but they did exist and the story of these years is not complete without them. They formed what Professor Collinson called a 'variegated religious underground', in which 'the groundwork of future denominations was being laid: congregationalist, more than one kind of Baptist, and the Seekers and other progenitors of the Quakers'.[11]

John Robinson and William Brewster were among the last of the Scrooby faithful to make the journey to Amsterdam. Brewster's early exodus had been aborted and it seems that Robinson stayed as long as possible to minister to the remnant of those unable to up-sticks easily or whose earlier attempts at migration had been frustrated. Brewster finally took passage in the autumn of 1608, and the Robinson family followed within a few months. By this time they must have received reports back from Amsterdam about the disastrous faction-fighting within the English church there. As the prime movers of the Scrooby migration, they would have felt it incumbent on themselves to redeem the situation. By February 1609, they had applied for residency to the authorities in Leiden. Why Leiden? Almost certainly because, in the first instance, Brewster and Robinson had strong links with people in the city. Brewster, as we have seen, had spent time in the Netherlands during his years in the diplomatic service. Robinson had never been there (as far as we know), but he had had close connections with several people now living in Leiden, thanks to the fluid pattern of Protestant migration between England and the Dutch Republic. Before returning to Scrooby, he had been the pastor of St Andrew's Church in Norwich, where there was a sizeable congregation of immigrants from the Spanish Netherlands. Several of these found their way back across the North Sea to settle in the Protestant northern territory once it had broken free from Spanish control. For example, we know that in 1596 a group of such peripatetic believers travelled from St Andrew's Church to Leiden. They are unlikely to have been unique, for the Dutch authorities welcomed with open arms textile workers who had mastered the technique of creating the fashionable lightweight cloth for which East Anglia was famous.

Equally importantly, Leiden was the intellectual hub of the Dutch Republic. Its university, though young (it was founded in 1575), was the only major learning centre in the Republic. It attracted students and teachers from across Europe and had a unique reputation for toleration and the encouragement of free speech. It welcomed scholars of all shades of Protestant belief, and its current head, Justus Lapsius, was actually a Catholic. Here the major theological issue of the day – that between Calvinism and Arminianism – was being fearlessly and openly debated. Just as Wittenberg and Geneva had been the focal points of religious debate in their day, so Leiden was now. Both Robinson and Brewster had hopes of finding employment in the university, and other members of their fellowship looked to the educational establishment and the thriving economy of this boom town to obtain jobs.

A contemporary map of Leiden shows a compact city contained within a wall and moat, surrounded by low-lying, partially waterlogged land. The streets are crammed with houses and there are very few green spaces. Inevitably, the population growth that resulted from and contributed to economic prosperity created health and hygiene problems. Although there were cesspits, much sewage found its way into the canals. The newcomers had to find living quarters wherever they could and were in no position to obtain property in the less insalubrious districts. After a couple of years Robinson and his flock scraped together enough money to buy a building in the south-west area of Leiden near the Pieterskerk. They made of it a dwelling and a meeting hall. Behind it they erected a row of single cottages for their poorer members. It is very revealing that this street was dubbed by the locals 'Stink Alley'. Here, over the next nine years, the English community lived, brought up children, worked and died, their numbers increasing to around 300. Fortunes fluctuated from household to household. The more industrious, many of whom were textile workers, made a reasonable living. Others struggled.

Assimilation always brings problems – some associated with failure and others with success. On the one hand, the members of Robinson's congregation found it difficult to fit in. They had to learn the language and adjust to the local customs. They had to endure the taunts of neighbours, ever ready to blame the strangers in their midst for any misfortunes. On the other hand, the immigrants resisted rapid integration because they feared the loss of their own identity. Some of the barriers the newcomers encountered were of a religious nature. Just as they could not accept some customs practised by the English Church, so now they viewed certain Dutch attitudes as not to their taste. The refugees found it hard to reciprocate the toleration extended by their hosts in welcoming them. Dutch observance of Sabbath restrictions seemed very lax to the English settlers and, what was even worse, the Leiden authorities turned a blind eye to the existence in the city of a small Catholic community. Robinson's church members wanted to be on the receiving end of toleration but were not prepared to be on the giving end. As the years passed, this became a burning issue. Parents determined to bring up their children in 'the fear and nurture of the Lord' saw those children forming friendships with local boys and girls, even – horror of horrors – wanting to marry outside the faith.

In seeking to prevent the dilution of Christian truth they believed themselves called to uphold, the separatist leaders adopted both positive and negative techniques. They went on the offensive with their gospel, trying to persuade their neighbours to see things their way. They tried to force their younger members into marriage within their community. As we might imagine, this did not go down well with the locals. The authorities banned the separatists from carrying out their own marriage ceremonies. For good reasons, they forbade them to organize public charitable collections for the relief of their own poorer members. To many of the English community it must have seemed that the persecution they were experiencing was just as bad as the persecution they had fled.

But there were other even more profoundly unsettling factors. The end of the Twelve Years' Truce was fast approaching. Since 1609 the Spanish and republican authorities had used the cessation of hostilities to strengthen their borders and replenish their war chests. There seemed to be a growing possibility that hostilities would resume in 1622.

But the population of the Republic was not only plagued by fear of the future; deep-seated and violent discord was tearing their own communities apart. In September 1617, the municipal authorities of Leiden cordoned off the city centre and sent troops to man the barriers. This provoked a riot led by stone-throwing mobs in which many people were injured. The breakdown of public order was widespread, but Leiden was the worst affected place. It was the victim of its own success. Economic prosperity had produced exponential population growth. The open-door policy of the university had brought teachers and students from many parts of Europe: men who represented a wide range of theological viewpoints – Catholic, Calvinist and Arminian. The nationalist and religious mix was unstable. Add to this disputes and power struggles within the political leadership of the seven states and it is easy to see why many members of the English community were becoming anxious about the future. Unity was weakened as some came to believe that God was calling on them to uproot themselves once again in the interests of the purity of the faith.

As well as catering for the immediate needs of the English flock at Leiden, Robinson was active in the defence and explanation of separatism at an academic level. This involved him in attempting to unravel the theological issues dividing various separatist factions and also to establish his own position. He was consulted on these matters by Henry Jacob, as we have seen, and also by his exact Cambridge contemporary, William Ames, who was at that stage ministering to English residents in The Hague. Ames subsequently assisted Christopher Lawne in the compilation of *The prophane schism of the Brownists* by providing copies of his correspondence with Ainsworth and Johnson. This was yet another contribution to the public debate about separatism, aimed at demonstrating the reasonableness of religious dissent and exposing the faults of those who had made a shambles of the Ancient Brethren. Christopher Lawne, once a follower of Francis Johnson, had become disillusioned and returned to England.[12] Robinson was very busy wielding the pen on his own account, and his collected works run to three thick volumes. In 1613, Robinson confronted one of the leading Arminians in a three-day disputation. From his writings it is clear that, with the passage of time, Robinson moved towards a less exclusionist position not dissimilar to that of Henry Jacob.

Brewster also made his contribution to separatist literature, but as a publisher rather than a writer. Soon after his arrival in Leiden he set up a printing press. His first texts were grammars for teaching English to German and Danish students at the university. But soon he was dabbling in more dangerous waters. There was a ready market among Puritans in England for theological books that could not be published in James I's kingdom. Brewster commissioned a number of works in Latin, English and Dutch. Some were written pseudonymously by Robinson and smuggled across the sea. But the output of what came to be called the Pilgrim Press included more dangerous material. Brewster had taken as a partner and financial backer Thomas Brewer, one of the wealthier English exiles. Together they produced, between 1617 and 1619, a series of tracts in English and Latin, designed to be smuggled across the North Sea for Puritan readers back in their home country where strict censorship was in force. Brewer was the partner more possessed of a passionate mission. His not inconsiderable fortune was put at the disposal of separatists in Kent as well as in the Netherlands. To the end of his days in 1640 he was a fiery religious and political activist, and the English ambassador was scandalized that the activity of a man of such obvious standing and means should carry weight with his humbler fellow countrymen. The first contentious text published by the Pilgrim Press was a reprint of a 1606 work by Thomas Whetenhall (1525-1607). Little is known of this author, but Brewer and Brewster obviously identified with his evaluation of the importance of print as a tool of religious propaganda. Whetenhall boldly stated:

> This divine and miraculous art of printing was given of God as an undoubted preparation to make the way for the flying of his Gospel over all nations . . . As in the Apostles' time, by the gift of tongues their voices went out into the end of the world . . . in continuance of time, doubtless by *preaching and printing*, the sincerity of the Gospel shall so prevail that the great whore of Babell shall have her fall.[13]

The Brewster-Brewer press produced about 20 books, mostly pseudonymous, covering many of the familiar separatist shibboleths – episcopacy, kneeling for Communion, and 'popish' ceremonies. They also entered the Calvinist-Arminian debate. However, the works that were most contentious on the other side of the North Sea related to the Scottish Church and were by the Scottish divine David Calderwood. By 1618, James I believed himself strong enough to bring to heel the Presbyterian elements in his northern kingdom. He dragooned the church assembly into enacting the 'Five Articles of Perth' designed to bring Scotland into line with English practice. Several clergy, of whom Calderwood was one, protested. James was incensed, summoned Calderwood to his presence, and made him kneel while he subjected the minister to a long theological discourse. When Calderwood declined to receive royal correction or yield the names of all the protestors, he was thrown into prison and subsequently banished from the realm. It was thus that he ended up in Leiden, where in short order he published, via the Pilgrim Press, his refutation of the Five Articles.

Brewster had now, well and truly, burned his boats. Permanent return to England was out of the question. But life was also difficult in Leiden.

The authorities were embarrassed by the activities of the press at a time when they needed England's friendship. Good diplomatic relations were not helped when King James ordered his ambassador, Sir Dudley Carleton, to trace the source of such subversive literature and close it down.

To Brewster and several of his old friends the idea of another exodus began to appear attractive for a variety of reasons.

11
America 1600–1620

James I . . . had a very logical and tidy mind and one of the first things he did was to have Sir Walter Raleigh executed for being left over from the previous reign.[1]

Sellar and Yeatman's outlandish take on national history, *1066 and All That*, does, at some points, make fleeting contact with reality, and this is one of those statements that may not be a million miles from the truth. Raleigh, by 1617, had become something of an anachronism. Within months of James's accession he found himself in the Tower of London, having been pronounced guilty of plotting against the new king. He was the victim of court rivalries, exacerbated by his own foolishness and arrogance, which are of no relevance to this narrative. What *is* important is that during his 14 years of relatively comfortable confinement he continued to indulge in dreams of fresh colonial adventures. Except that they were not really 'fresh': they harked back to the dazzling legends that had gripped people's imagination ever since Cortes and Pizarro had discovered the mineral wealth of Latin America. The belief of new discoveries still to be made was kept alive by Richard Hakluyt junior, who in 1584 had assured his readers:

All that part of America eastward from Cumana unto the river of St Augustine in Brazil containeth in length along the sea side 2,100 miles. In which compass and tract there is neither Spaniard, Portingales nor any Christian man but only Caribs, Indians and savages. In which place is great plenty of gold, pearl and precious stones.[2]

Ten years later, Raleigh acquired some Spanish documents that, supposedly, described a kingdom deep in the forests of Guyana which was yet more fabulous than those of the Aztecs and the Incas. At its heart, on the shores of Lake Parime, stood the magnificent city of Manõa. Here lived El Dorado, the Golden One, a king who ruled a nation of sun worshippers. On ceremonial occasions the people cast golden votive offerings into the holy lake and El Dorado himself entered the water, naked except for a head-to-toe covering of gold dust. This fabulous land was the ultimate prize, just waiting to be grasped by the conqueror with the vision and the hardihood to risk all in order to seize it. In 1595, Raleigh decided that he would be that conqueror.

He was not alone. Another expedition was fitted out at the same time by Robert Dudley, the young illegitimate son of the Earl of Leicester. It was Dudley who was ready first. He reached Trinidad and claimed it in the name of Queen Elizabeth. Eager to explore the mainland, he quizzed the natives about El Dorado and the mineral resources supposedly located deep in the interior. They told him what he wanted to hear:

> he not only learned that those rich mines of gold were delivered (i.e. reported) of a truth but [he] descried (i.e. discovered) how the savages there hanged rich pieces of gold about their necks in the stead of breastplates, and a most common thing usually used among them. We have had at divers times at the least an hundred Indians come aboard us, and there was not one but by signs confirmed the richness of this mine.
>
> Wherefore when our worthy General had to the uttermost learned what they might inform him, finding [them] by all their demonstrations to agree in this for the admired riches of the place, he generally purposed the sending of his boat thither and withal much desired that some attempt should be made for the true discovery thereof, whereby he might the better satisfy either her Majesty or such at home as are meet to be advertised of such designs.[3]

The account written by one of Dudley's captains described in heroic detail the longboat voyage up the Orinoco, a hot battle with a Spanish man-o'-war and various other adventures that befell the expedition. But, needless to say, the record could not include the discovery of the Golden Ore.

Raleigh arrived in the same location days later and replicated much of what Dudley had done. He did penetrate further inland but, as far as gold was concerned, he too came home empty-handed. When he returned he was piqued to discover that a mere novice, a johnny-come-lately, had stolen his thunder. He complained to Robert Cecil, leader of the Privy Council, about mere adventurers interested only in plunder, in contrast to loyal subjects like himself who sought to enhance the wealth and prestige of England. He enlarged on his vision in a racy treatise entitled *The discovery of the rich and beautiful Empire of Guiana* . . ., a narrative that exaggerated his own exploits and the settler potential of the territory. The book proved popular at home and abroad, particularly in Holland, where three editions had appeared by 1617.

Several interesting facts emerge from this flurry of activity. The most interesting is that, three generations after the discovery of gold and silver in the New World, the possibility of fortunes to be made there still captured the popular imagination. Risk capital was readily available for captains like Raleigh and Dudley. The hazards of oceanic travel and the reported dangers from hostile environments and savages was not a deterrent to bold spirits. Furthermore, as long as England was at war with Spain and Portugal, challenging the superiority of the established colonial powers was almost a patriotic duty.

However, that last factor ceased to apply after James's accession. The new king, who saw himself as a universal peacemaker, was anxious to end the long-running war, and hostilities formally came to end when terms were agreed in the Treaty of London of 1604. By 1614, the king was negotiating a marriage between his son, Charles, and the daughter of Philip III. Any ambitious plans involving trespass in Spain's colonial territory were out of the question. Raleigh, however, never abandoned his dream, and in 1616 he managed to persuade a cash-strapped government to sanction one more Central American adventure. He assured James that he could pour untold treasure at his feet. This Guiana voyage was, literally, his get-out-of-jail card and the only card he had to play.

It may be that Raleigh really did believe his own publicity but, more likely, that he had come to realize that some of the El Dorado legends were mere fantasy. Certainly he had a plan B – the old privateering option. Should he not find native gold, there was still the possibility of obtaining Spanish gold by intercepting a treasure fleet. He was under strict instructions from James to avoid hostility with Spain but may well have calculated that, if he laid a fortune at the king's feet, no close enquiry would be made as to how he had come by it. However, Raleigh also took out insurance in the form of an arrangement with the King of France, who was prepared to employ him as a privateer. Thus, Sir Walter, the old courtier, sea captain, soldier and pioneer colonialist, sank every last penny of his own and whatever he could raise from friends and relatives to fit out his grand expedition, and in June 1617 he set out from Plymouth with an impressive flotilla of 14 ships, en route for the mouth of the Orinoco.

Unfortunately, in the end all his scheming and dreaming came to naught. He was too ill to lead the party up the river and it got into a fight with a Spanish garrison. To make matters worse, his son was killed in the engagement. Raleigh returned to face his king's displeasure. When it came to the point, he declined to activate his planned escape to France. At 70 he was too old to start a new life. On 29 October 1618, he was beheaded. The news travelled swiftly through Europe and was received with interest by some English exiles in the Netherlands who were, by now, considering the possibility of moving on to America. Many religious émigrés were making the painful discovery that life in the hospitable United Provinces did not offer answers to all their problems. In fact, the separatist communities were experiencing new difficulties – alienation from their foreign hosts and divisions among themselves. Spiritual fervour and ruthless logic combined to suggest that the time had come to move on.

A new century, a new reign and a new foreign policy inevitably had an impact on the process of American colonization. The major underlying factor was the decline of Spanish power. The Treaty of London (1604) and the Twelve Years' Truce (1609) in the Netherlands (see above, p. 160) provided the sixteenth-century superpower a much needed breathing space. Income derived from the worldwide empire was more than offset by administrative costs. The protracted wars with England and the Dutch were a major drain on resources and forced the Crown heavily into debt. Losses to English, Dutch and French privateers were more than a minor irritation. To make matters worse, serious outbreaks of plague between

1596 and 1602 carried off perhaps as many as a third of a million Spanish people. The nation's antiquated bureaucracy was not equipped to cope with all these crises. One result of friction between the government and the mercantile community that especially affected the situation in the Atlantic was the decline of Spain's naval potential. In the mid-sixteenth century, Spain could boast the biggest and best royal and merchant fleets in the world. By 1600, this was no longer the case. Shipbuilding had gone into a steep decline and the emerging maritime powers, England and the United Netherlands, had become the leaders in ship design.

The international situation might have changed, but the mindset of those in government and mercantile circles was slow to catch up. So far, colonial settlement on the North American littoral had proved hazardous and costly. Queen Elizabeth was not disposed to develop (and finance) an official colonial policy, and her successor was equally nig- gardly. James I's treatment of Raleigh indicates, among other things, that planting English settlements on virgin territory was not high on his list of priorities. Interestingly, England also lost another colonial enthusi- ast in the shape of Robert Dudley, Raleigh's rival. As a result of shabby treatment at the new king's court, he took himself into voluntary exile in Tuscany, where his considerable talents (including the designing of ships and the writing of a comprehensive maritime encyclopaedia, *Dell'Arcano del Mare*) were placed at the disposal of the Medici dukes. The establish- ment of new colonies thus continued to be left in the hands of merchant companies and private investors.

Such free enterprise might have provided a stable platform for colonial endeavour were it not for the fact that promoters were pulled in different directions. The majority saw settlements primarily as ports from which their ships could sail forth on that most lucrative activity of all – priva- teering. This activity, which agreeably linked patriotism, profit and (for some at least) Protestant zeal, attracted everyone involved, from inves- tors to crewmen, all of whom shared the profits of a successful encounter. Sites like Roanoke had been established specifically with maritime marauding in mind. By 1600, as many as 200 ships a year were sailing from England in search of victims laden with valuable cargoes on the high seas.

Only slightly less attractive to captains and investors looking for a fast buck were the natural resources of coastal America that came most easily to hand. Primarily that meant fish. Though the Newfoundland fisheries were shared with the sailors of France, the Netherlands and Portugal, there was plenty of fish (primarily cod) for all. Humphrey Gilbert had claimed the St Lawrence estuary regions for England, but the crews that came thither only set up seasonal camps. Attempts to establish permanent settlements (including that involving Francis Johnson and his little group of separatists – see above, pp. 110ff.) failed largely as a result of international rivalry. But business was booming. By the beginning of James I's reign, around 150 ships a year were leaving England for the fisheries and trading their cargoes to France, Spain and Italy – Catholic lands where there was an insatiable demand for fish. There was no need for permanent settlements.

All this, taken together with the dismal record of earlier attempts to establish North American settlements, had a dampening effect on new colonizing initiatives. However, the situation did have its plus side. Lessons learned during the war years prepared the mercantile community to take advantage of the era of peace that followed. England emerged stronger at sea than ever before. While Spain's shipbuilding programme failed to keep up with losses due to storms and enemy action, the output from English shipyards increased. The men who sailed enlarged their knowledge of the ocean and the American seaboard. The moneymen, also, were beginning to reassess the potential of settlements in the unexplored, unexploited western continent. To these quantifiable changes of perception we must add the development in the common mind of impressions fed by the written reports of travellers like Thomas Hariot, whose *A brief and true report of the new found land of Virginia* (1590) included remarkable drawings by John White – the first accurate representations readers would have seen of Amerindians. Between 1598 and 1600 Richard Hakluyt's three-volume *Principal Navigation, Voyages, Traffics and Discoveries of the English nation made by Sea or over land to the most remote and farthest distant quarters of the earth . . . within the compass of these 1500 years* became available to all who could afford it. The author's dedicatory epistle to the first volume carried a pointed reproach. Hakluyt observed that, while the exploits of the adventurers of other nations were proudly related:

The English of all others for their sluggish security and continual neglect of the like attempts, either ignominiously reported or exceedingly condemned . . . and not seeing any man to have care to recommend to the world the industrious labours and painful travels of our countrymen.[4]

He had therefore found it necessary to shoulder the burden himself. How many of Hakluyt's contemporaries read the early editions of his monumental work we cannot know, but his books and those of other advocates – not to mention the travellers' tales recounted in alehouses and marketplaces the nation over – all fed into a growing curiosity, interest and fascination with other lands. Travelogues of all kinds were much in vogue. For example, Thomas Coryat, sometime courtier in the household of King James's elder son, Prince Henry, achieved bestseller status for his *Coryat's Crudities: Hastily Gobbled up in Five Months' Travels* (1611) in which he described a journey largely on foot to Venice. He followed up this success with another book of his observations of foreign customs, before setting out once more on a journey that took him all the way to Surat. Although Coryat died in India and was never to give the world another volume of his experiences, various of his letters home were subsequently published; he is, with good reason, recognized as the originator of the idea of the Grand Tour, which by the mid-century was widely regarded as essential to the education of young English gentlemen. Clearly, the world had become very much smaller. Hitherto unknown lands beyond the western ocean were now within reach of more than imagination.

But if permanent settlements were to be established, something more would be demanded of their instigators than stimulation of the profit motive: vision. If new societies were to be planted and nurtured, they would need more than material resources. They would require political structures, educational facilities, law appropriate to life in a country already inhabited by a very different indigenous population. All this would call for a vision with a religious–ethical framework – in short, a Christian commonwealth. This was the aspiration that had inspired Catholic missionaries in the more southerly regions of the Americas. It was the dream followed by religious émigrés travelling in different directions across the

Narrow Seas in the sixteenth century. It would be the same idealism that drove some colonists to set up specifically Catholic or Protestant settlements in North America in the era just dawning. Despite the eloquent pleading of Hakluyt and other enthusiasts, no such elevated ambitions inspired the Virginia pioneers. The earliest ventures of the new reign continued to suffer from cupidity, unsuitable colonists, poor direction and mixed motives. Some of Raleigh's rights in Virginia had been handed over to other investors, and by 1606 two chartered companies, the London Virginia Company and the Plymouth Virginia Company, had been set up. The Crown kept a watching brief through the Royal Council for Virginia. In the spring of 1605, another venture, backed by the Catholic peers Thomas Arundel and Henry Wriothesley, despatched an expedition under Captain George Weymouth that explored the coastline of Maine. The objective was to establish a haven for Catholic families currently suffering the crippling burden of recusancy fines. Nothing came of this venture, partly because Arundel was briefly imprisoned on suspicion of involvement in the Gunpowder Plot.

The following year witnessed a vital new initiative, the Charter of 1606. King James brought the colonization of America under Crown control. He claimed all the coast between 34 and 45 degrees north and the entire hinterland from there to the Pacific coast. Development of this territory was to be divided between the Plymouth Virginia Company in the north and the London Virginia Company to the south. An area of overlap between the two was up for grabs for whoever got there first. The companies were granted a raft of privileges in return for governing the territory and providing the Crown with a percentage of the profits made by the trade in minerals and agricultural produce. Lip service was paid to more exalted objectives than profit. The pious purpose of any settlement was clearly stated. His Majesty commended the backers of the companies:

> and graciously accepting of, their Desires for the Furtherance of so noble a Work, which may, by the Providence of Almighty God, hereafter tend to the Glory of his Divine majesty, in propagating of Christian Religion to such People, as yet live in Darkness and miserable ignorance of the true Knowledge and Worship of God, and may in time bring the Infidels and Savages, living in those

parts, to human Civility, and to a settled and quiet Government: DO, by these our Letters Patents, graciously accept of, and agree to, their humble and well-intended Desires . . .[5]

The charter did not, however, provide any guidance as to how these humble and well-intended desires were to be achieved. The document went on to specify how settlements were to be governed and, particularly, what share of the profit from the mining of gold, silver and copper should be sent to the king (for still no one doubted that deposits of precious metals would form the mainstay of the Virginian economy).

Yet, with regard to the spiritual welfare of the settlers and Christian missions among the inhabitants of the region, the charter was silent. What kind of religious life did the London Company officials envisage planting in the colony? Insofar as they had any vision at all, we must assume that their pattern of church life for Virginia was modelled on the church life of England. But, as we have seen, church life in England was fractured. Could the projectors ensure that religious divisions were not replicated in the New World – particularly when they were desperately trying to recruit anyone and everyone to populate the colonies they planned to establish? They certainly sent out a chaplain with their first settlement expedition in 1606, but his woeful tale did not augur well for the establishment of a godly commonwealth.

Robert Hunt, vicar of Reculver, Kent, was specifically chosen by Hakluyt and, since the choice was endorsed by the reactionary Archbishop Bancroft, we may assume that he was a 'safe' establishment man. What he was not was a good sailor. During the voyage he was so seasick that his life was despaired of. He was also unpopular with some of his ship's complement (dismissed in a report to the company in London as 'little better than atheists'). They branded the minister as a 'Jonah', bringing ill fortune on the venture, and tried to abandon him on some foreign shore. When the expedition arrived and marked out a place they called 'Jamestown' for their first settlement, Hunt set about his duties, many of which involved making peace between the fractious settlers. He was also charged with overseeing the construction of the first place of Protestant worship to be built in English-governed America. In January 1608, the church was destroyed, along with adjacent dwellings, when an accidental fire broke out. Hunt did not survive to see the completion of its replacement.

His replacement, Richard Bucke, did not arrive until the spring of 1610. Bucke was a 27-year-old Oxford graduate of Leicestershire background who arrived with a wife and two daughters. He came with the strong recommendation of Bishop Thomas Ravis of London, a staunch establishment man who made no bones about his opposition to ministers who did not toe the line. 'By the help of Jesus,' he declared, 'I will not leave one preacher in my diocese who doth not . . . conform.'[6] Bucke seems to have been a popular preacher untainted with Puritanism. As well as attending to his religious duties he was paterfamilias of an expanding family, eventually with six children. He also set about making himself a prosperous settler, acquiring more land and having it worked by indentured servants. By the time of his death in 1624, Bucke was the master of 750 acres of arable land and had a secure place among the elite of Jamestown society. One feels that Bishop Ravis would have approved of his protégé's progress. Yet certainly not all was *couleur de rose* for the pastor and his flock, as the biblical names he gave some of his children may well suggest: Mara ('bitter'), Gershon ('a stranger there'), Peleg ('division') and Benoni ('son of my sorrow').

The early years of Jamestown were perpetually chaotic and intermittently catastrophic. The problems experienced by the immigrants were of three kinds: those springing from their own internal divisions, those arising from their relations with original inhabitants, and those caused by disagreements with the company leaders in London. Every difficulty encountered in the attempt to evolve a stable, civilized and economically viable community was capable of various solutions, each of which had its champions. Most of the pioneers had made the perilous journey in search of 'liberty' – the desire to escape from the religious, social or political restraints of a hierarchic society (some were there as the result of a state policy of using the colonies as dumping grounds for prisoners, vagrants and malcontents). They were not the sort of people who were easily disciplined or prepared to trade some of their freedoms for the kind of compromises vital to the smooth running of any community. But Bucke was not the only kind of Protestant professional living in the colony. As we shall see shortly, more radical ministers without episcopal backing felt the call to Virginia.

Investors in the new colony were not slow in coming forward in the early days. Joint-stock business ventures were flavour of the month. The Levant Company and the East India Company were showing backers good returns. But the difference between them and the new mercantile entity was that they did not rely on the productivity of *permanent* settlers who would develop their own agricultural and industrial economies. Francis Bacon, who became Solicitor General in 1607, was realistic when he advised that investors should be prepared to wait 20 years before recouping their outlay and showing a profit. Sadly, most people were as interested in economic realism as they were in evangelistic mission.

It is not insignificant that the captain chosen by the London Virginia Company council to establish their first settlement was Christopher Newport, a mariner with a – literally – golden reputation. In 1592, he had captured the Portuguese carrack *Madre de Deus*, the most valuable prize taken by an English privateer in the whole of the sixteenth century. In 1606, Newport conveyed to Virginia a mixed human cargo of landless younger sons, released prisoners, and vagabonds, with only a sprinkling of farmers, artisans and practical individuals. The basic weakness of the recruitment of settlers was that it attracted people who, for one reason or another, were unable to achieve a productive and satisfying life in England, and were therefore not likely to make a success of living in a new and hostile environment. Added to this was the fact that the location of the first colony, Jamestown, was poorly chosen, the ground being marshy and ill-suited to agricultural development. The settlers became dependent on supplies brought from England by relief expeditions. The last backward glance into the era of hopeful, quick-profit North American settlement is provided for us by Newport. Having set down his hundred or so passengers in their new environment, he returned to London with various samples of Virginia's potential riches. This included some chunks of rock containing glistening strata. It took English experts very little time to identify it: iron pyrites – fools' gold.

One potentially disastrous incident occurred in the very early days. In the summer of 1609, an expedition of three ships bearing more settlers, fresh supplies and the new interim-governor, Sir Thomas Gates, ran into a hurricane. Gates and his fellow passengers on the *Sea Venture* were driven on to rocks off the Bermudas. Although the ship was lost,

Gates and 150 other survivors made it safely to dry land. Gates now set about devising ways of completing the journey. But some of the company saw no reason to abandon the pleasant and uninhabited island, where they could be their own masters rather than put themselves permanently under Gates's authority. The ringleader of the rebels was an Essex separatist, John Want, who insisted that their survival and their 'guidance' to this favoured isle was God's doing and that he desired the company to live on Bermuda as free people. 'Liberty' and 'freedom' became fashionable words among early American settlers, not infrequently used with a holy aura. Eventually, the party completed their journey to Jamestown on two small ships they had built on the island. Only two of their number elected to remain behind. Want was not one of them.

On arrival in the colony, Gates's party must have wondered whether Want was not right after all. They expected to find more than 200 settlers well established in stockade compounds, keeping themselves fed with the results of their own farming and hunting. They were actually met by 60 half-starved survivors, much of whose remaining energy was given over to faction-fighting and mutual recrimination. Disease, malnutrition and warfare with the local inhabitants had taken a terrible toll. The desperate survivors had sunk to the bestial depths of murder and cannibalism. They thought of only one thing – to cram themselves aboard the little ships from Bermuda and commit themselves once more to the ocean in the hope of getting back to England. Jamestown would have suffered the same fate as earlier settlements had it not been for the arrival, at the last moment, of yet another relief expedition.

The tenth day of June, 1610, was the turning point in the fortunes of Jamestown – and probably of the Virginia Company. Four men may be said to have changed the fortunes and (just as importantly) the perception of the colony.

The first had just come from England and was destined to spend less than a year in Virginia. The newly arrived fleet, as well as carrying life-saving food, and grain for planting, brought with it a new governor, Thomas West, Baron De La Warr (in whose entourage was a certain Edward Brewster), a member of the Privy Council and a long-established servant of the Crown in political and military capacities. His very rank brought a degree of stability to the colony, but the old problems continued.

Europeans were still dying at an alarming rate, Amerindian raids were becoming more frequent, and feuding among the settlers was rife. One victim of these internal disputes was John Smith, a seasoned soldier who had emerged as the leader of the colony. Anyone who assumed command was certain to find himself up against at least one enemy cabal. Smith was unpopular with his compatriots because he imposed a necessary discipline and because he tried to establish friendly relations with the local chief. The arrival of the Europeans had coincided with the emergence of a powerful leader among the Powhatan people. His name was Wahunsonacock, and by 1609 he had become the paramount chief of a large area. Smith established contact with him, by which he hoped to set up a useful trading partnership.[7] Some of the settlers resented Smith's high-handedness and, rather than deal with the Powhatans, preferred to take from them by force whatever food and other goods they needed. In the autumn of 1609, Smith narrowly survived what was probably an assassination attempt, and was forced to return to England where he had to face charges of maladministration sent on ahead by his enemies. It was the conflicting reports coming out of Jamestown that De La Warr was intent on exploring.

His Lordship arrived with a fresh mind but also an acute awareness of how important it was to the Virginia Company, and indeed to England, that the colony should be successful. That meant raising morale and, in particular, not allowing the prevailing despondency to infect the latest batch of settlers. He was not so much a new broom as a new scythe. He dealt ruthlessly with internal dissensions and relations with the indigenes. Gone was any idea of establishing rapport with the Powhatans and Christianizing them. They must be conquered and their land taken over. The colonists must be prevented from brooding on their misfortunes and kept busy by husbandry, by rebuilding damaged homes, barns and churches, by military expeditions, and by exploring beyond the further reaches of current settler activity. The strategy was fine in theory, but the odds were stacked against its success. Amerindian raids were constant and sometimes annoyingly successful. The governor was obliged to hang one of the settlers for leading a group of dissenters who tried to steal a boat and leave Jamestown.

A serious disappointment was the failure to find gold. The dream still persisted in Virginia and England that somewhere in the interior were mines of precious metal, the discovery of which would, overnight, transform the sad Jamestown saga into a triumphant story of brave English pioneers whose heroic exploits led to establishing their native land as the richest in the world. De La Warr entrusted this mission to Edward Brewster. It came to nothing. Brewster's penetration of the interior was blocked by Powhatans, and he had to satisfy himself by venting his anger on the enemy and burning their village.

Nothing went right for De La Warr. The new administration suffered as badly as its predecessors. Disease removed a further third of the settlers during the winter of 1610-1611; the governor himself fell ill, and in the spring he was obliged to return to England. Concerned about how his desertion would be perceived and reported by other members of the colony, De La Warr got in first by penning a report for the company councillors, *The Relation of the Right Honourable the Lord De La Warr, Lord Governor . . . of the Colony planted in Virginia*. It was a whitewash, designed not only to protect his own reputation but also to assure his colleagues that all was well in that settlement that bore the king's own name. The writer knew only too well that several nervous investors were contemplating removing their capital and that every snippet of news from America was avidly read and analysed in London.

The parent body had its own problems. Recruitment was a constant headache. The directors used every tactic they could think of to attract money and settlers – from parliamentary pressure to lotteries (one such, in 1612, raised £25,000 to shore up Jamestown's finances) and from recruiting in Europe (for example, Polish artisans were brought in to make pitch and soup) to buying African slaves from Dutch merchants. They faced a double dilemma. It was not enough to attract people and money; they needed to attract the *right kind* of people and money. Just as get-rich-quick investors were an embarrassment, so were unsuitable settlers. Filling passenger space on ships with criminals, vagrants and fleeing debtors was not the way to establish a vibrant economy and a thriving community. How did the London Company resolve these dilemmas? The short answer is: they didn't. They grasped every gold sovereign and every able-bodied person they could find. And the more committed they became, the more difficult it was for them to back out.

The importance of De La Warr's report was that it offered hope. He gave reassurance that good times were just around the corner. His Lordship deliberately underplayed the losses of manpower from disease. He also dismissed the depredations caused by the Powhatans, many of whom were willing and able to engage in regular trade with the settlers. The soil and the climate, he asserted, were excellent for rearing livestock and raising crops. De La Warr made no mention of gold deposits but explained that there were promising mines of antimony and lead. Offshore fishing was, he said, an abundant source of income. As for himself, De La Warr insisted, he could scarcely wait to get back to Virginia to preside in person over the inevitable flowering of the colony. All in all, the situation at Jamestown was such as to

encourage every good mind to further so worthy a work as will redound both to the Glory of God, to the Credit of our Nation, and to the Comfort of all those that have been Instruments in the furthering of it.[8]

It worked. The company leaders resolved to continue their recruitment drive.

The second person responsible for turning the fortunes of the Virginia enterprise was the man they now sent out (1611) to take charge in De La Warr's absence. Thomas Dale was a career soldier who had established a reputation as an efficient and successful captain fighting in the Netherlands and Ireland. He gained the admiration of Prince Henry and was knighted by King James in 1606. Four years later the council of the Virginia Company decided that Dale was the right person to reorganize colonial life and stiffen its backbone. He was appointed the marshal (the military commander) and despatched to Jamestown with 300 soldiers the following year. This military man, very accustomed to assessing the worth of any recruits, concluded that most of the settlers were 'disordered', 'profane' and 'riotous'. He advised that the king would do better to open the prisons and despatch across the Atlantic men awaiting execution. They, at least, might be glad 'to make this their new country'.[9] Meanwhile, Dale treated the existing colonists like criminals, imposing martial law and setting them to husbandry in disciplined working parties. This was the unpalatable medicine the colonists needed. Proper stockades were built, land clearance and farming were efficiently organized, another village, Henrico, was founded, and workmanlike relations were established with the indigenes at musket point.

Yet this might well have created only temporary stability had it not been for the contribution of John Rolfe. He has gone down in the annals of popular, romantic history as the husband of Pocahontas, the daughter of the powerful Amerindian chief, Wahunsonacock. The story of this marriage certainly had its part to play in the development of good relations with the local community, the impact on the imagination of people back in England, and the religious development of Virginia. Rolfe arrived at the colony in May 1609 as a member of the relief expedition that was scattered by the hurricane and shipwrecked on Bermuda. He was one of the lucky ones who eventually made it to Jamestown. It was well for the colony that he did, for Rolfe was the man who, almost single-handedly, set the colony's economy on a sound footing.

Tobacco had been known in Europe for half a century, since its introduction by Spanish merchants who had brought seeds back from Central America and the Caribbean. Chewing, sniffing or smoking of the dried leaves, which began as a quaint custom with, according to some users, medicinal properties, developed into a valuable fashionable luxury pursuit. Earlier North American settlers had experimented with tobacco as a cash crop, but the only strains available were too strong or coarse for most tastes. The *Nicotiana tabacum* grown in Spain was of a finer variety, and production was kept a closely guarded secret in order to preserve the national monopoly. Rolfe, however, had managed to smuggle some seed out of Spain. He began farming on his land at Henrico, and by 1614 was able to sell his first crop. Other settlers followed his example. By 1617, 20,000 pounds of tobacco was exported. Four years later this had risen to 35,000 pounds. What King James dismissed in his *Counterblast to Tobacco* as 'this filthy novelty' proved to be the salvation of the Virginia settlements. It established that they would be essentially agricultural communities producing tobacco and food crops for their own self-sufficiency and for export.

But man does not live by bread alone, and certainly not by tobacco. The colonists had spiritual needs that had to be met. In all the turbulence and violence that had accompanied European settlement in Virginia, issues more fundamental than survival had not been lost sight of. Some families had travelled thither out of religious conviction. Migration to America was a part of that religious movement that had taken Robinson and Co. to the Netherlands, and would eventually bring some of them to America. That is why we must draw attention to a fourth man who left his mark on New World settlement. Alexander Whitaker was yet another product of that busy Puritan spawning ground, Cambridge University. His father was Master of St John's and, though a loyal supporter of the Elizabethan settlement, his leanings were definitely towards the Puritan elements in this traditionally radical college (something that probably put a stop to his further advancement). He was also, through marriage, part of an extensive network of Puritan families. Alexander, the elder son, went, via Eton and Trinity, to be rector of a Yorkshire parish. He did not stay long because he felt the call to fulfil his ministry in Virginia. He confided in friends that he suffered 'many distractions and combats within himself',[10] and only with difficulty resolved that 'God called him thither, and therefore he would go'.[11] Accordingly, he travelled with Thomas Dale's contingent in 1611. Two years later he was styling himself the minister of Henrico, the offshoot settlement Dale had established 50 miles upriver from Jamestown.

Whitaker's decision is significant in the story of religious migration we are trying to tell. It was a decision reached, 'notwithstanding the earnest dissuasions of many of his nearest friends and the great discouragements which he daily heard of touching the business and country itself'.[12] Colonial propagandists had talked piously about converting the natives, but no one had proposed a mission strategy – not the government, not the church hierarchy, not the company, not the leaders of the separatist assemblies. William Crashaw, a famous Puritan divine and a friend of Whitaker's, commented on the reaction of most contemporaries: 'Men may muse at it; some may laugh and others wonder at it.' But the writer's explanation was twofold. Whitaker had thought through the implications of establishing a godly commonwealth in a pagan land and concluded (in good Calvinist fashion) that 'magistracy and ministry are the strength and sinews; nay the very life and being of a Christian body politic . . . without these all emptying of purses here [that is, in England]

and venturing of persons thither is to no purpose'.[13] It was necessary for devout Christians to fill civil and ecclesiastical roles in the new settlement. Whitaker had heard the call and, whatever the cost, he had to obey. As we have seen, ministers were appointed by the company to pastor the colonists, but Whitaker was the first Protestant missionary in the English American settlements and was soon being called the 'Apostle to Virginia'. He built two churches for the settlers, and began teaching such natives as were prepared to listen. His most famous success was Pocahontas, whom he baptized under the new name of Rebecca.

By 1613, Whitaker had an important mission to the folks back home. In that year, he sent to England for printing a sermon under the name *Good News from Virginia*. Most English people who read this pamphlet would have recognized the *double entendre* of the title: 'good news' was the translation of 'gospel' (*evangelium*), the revelation 'that Christ died for our sins according to the Scriptures, that he was buried, that he was raised on the third day according to the Scriptures' (1 Corinthians 15.3-4 NIV). Whitaker wrote to show how this gospel was playing out in Virginia:

> This plantation, which the devil hath so often trodden down, is by the miraculous blessing of God revived, and daily groweth to more happy and more hopeful success . . . God first showed us the place, God first called us hither, and here God by his special providence hath maintained us.[14]

Whitaker described the religious practices of the natives, which he did not hesitate to call satanic, allied to the witchcraft that still plagued parts of the Old World. Yet the locals had many good qualities and the writer was optimistic about his mission:

> If we were once masters of their country and they in fear of us (which might with few hands employed about nothing else be in short time brought to pass) it were an easy matter to make them forsake the devil, to embrace the faith of Jesus Christ and to be baptized. Besides . . . they would be available to us in our discoveries of the country, in our buildings and plantings and quiet provision for ourselves . . .[15]

From that last sentence it would seem that even the Apostle to Virginia could not avoid a certain Janus-like quality in his approach to preaching the gospel: saving the souls of the indigenes would also prove beneficial for the immigrants. He urged his readers to humble reflection on the plight of the local people who, beneath the skin, were in reality their brothers:

> Wherefore, my brethren, put on the bowels of compassion and let the lamentable estate of these miserable people enter into your consideration. One God created us . . . we all have Adam for our common parent. Yes, by nature, the condition of us both is all one – the servants of sin and slaves of the devil.[16]

Whitaker's immediate objective in this sermon was to encourage fresh investment and settlement. He attacked the short-termism of earlier colonial ventures. He reminded his readers that God's ancient people had wandered for 40 years before being led to the promised land, and urged God's modern people to display the same trust and patience. Spain and Portugal, he observed, had laboured long and at great cost before securing their rewards:

> Shall our nation, hitherto famous for noble attempts and the honourably finishing of what they have undertaken, be now taxed for inconstancy and blamed by the enemies of our protestation, for uncharitableness? Yea, shall we be a scorn among princes and a laughing stock among our neighbour nations for basely leaving what we honourably began; yea, for beginning a discovery whose riches other men shall gather so soon as we have forsaken it? Awake, you true-hearted Englishmen, you servants of Jesus Christ. Remember that the plantation is God's and the reward your country's. Wherefore, aim not at your present private gain but let the glory of God, whose kingdom you now plant, and good of your country, whose wealth you seek, so far prevail with you that you respect not a present return of gain for this year or two but that you would more liberally supply, for a little space, this your Christian work which you so charitably began.[17]

Alexander Whitaker was a remarkable man who certainly deserves more than the footnote he is assigned in many histories of American colonization. He was intelligent, and accurately assessed the situation facing the Virginia Company. He was devout and courageous, willing to follow his vision at great personal cost. There can be little doubt that he would have achieved much more had he been spared. Unfortunately, he drowned in the James River in 1617.

It is not fanciful to suppose that copies of his appeal to Christian charity and national pride will have made their way to the United Provinces, where some of the reluctant émigrés from England were already questioning whether they were in the right place. It was 16 years since Francis Johnson and his little band had arrived in Amsterdam after their ignominious failure to be the first Christian pilgrims to relocate to North America, and only three years since he and his supporters had set up a rival church to that led by Henry Ainsworth (see above, p. 113). The restless gene that was such a powerful component of the separatists' DNA may already have been stirring some to consider responding to Whitaker's appeal. Disquiet was certainly affecting John Robinson, William Brewster and several of their friends. As we have seen, they had various reasons for wondering whether Leiden was the end of their exodus journey. They will have reflected often on the wanderings of their spiritual ancestors of the biblical exodus. Like the Israelites (and indeed like the Christians referred to in Hebrews 13.14) they had no abiding city but had to be ready to fold up their tents and move on. They experienced a very natural desire to settle down, to sink roots into the soil of their chosen habitation. But might it not be that 'settlement' was, of itself, a temptation? As they followed the news periodically arriving from Jamestown and as they were increasingly aware of the fervent appeals by the Virginia Company for yet more colonists, they bethought themselves whether the Lord's beckoning hand was to be seen in these events.

It cannot have been easy for them to discern where they were being led, for conflicting rumours continued to circulate in the years after Lord De La Warr's departure from Virginia in 1611. Although tobacco became the staple of the colony's economy, establishing a plantation economy (and the social stability resting on it) took time, and meanwhile many of the old tensions remained. The men left in charge of the colony knew by now how to rule effectively. The iron hand was kept in the iron glove when dealing with settlers and locals alike. This inevitably provoked conflict among the colonists and reprisals from the Powhatans. Complaints found their way back to London and were particularly vibrant against Samuel Argall, who was deputy governor from 1617 to 1619.

This led to friction among the directors – and two in particular. Sir Thomas Smythe was a companies' man through and through. That is to say that his entire, very considerable fortune was built on investment in overseas trading companies. As well as London Virginia Company he was a leading figure in the East India Company, the Muscovy Company and the Levant Company. Smythe was treasurer of the London Company from 1609 to 1620, and it was towards the end of that time that he was accused by malcontents in Jamestown of misappropriating funds and supporting the regime of Samuel Argall, who was accused of being high-handed and of stirring up trouble with the Powhatans.

The person who vigorously took up the case against Smythe was Sir Edwin Sandys. This son of an Archbishop of York was one of the leading political figures of the day and regarded by many as the 'king of the House of Commons'. He was a staunch upholder of parliamentary privilege and an opponent of anything that smacked of royal autocracy – something that earned him the lasting enmity of James I. Sandys was also something of a theologian and a close friend of Richard Hooker, 'high priest' of what a later age would call 'Anglicanism'. At one point in his career, he tried to steer through Parliament a bill that would have subjected separatists to the same penalties as Catholics. When King James declined to summon Parliament between 1615 and 1621, Sandys diverted his energies to the work of the London Company council, of which he had been a member since 1607. He instituted a rigorous investigation of the administration of the company, succeeded in having Smythe and Argall removed from office, and himself took over the role of treasurer. There was probably too much personal animus involved in the sacking of Sandys' enemies, but what was more important was the complete overhaul of the company's administration that now followed. As a result, the first representative assembly to be held on American soil was convened in Jamestown on 30 July 1619, its procedures being based on those of the House of

Commons. In a remarkably short space of time, Sandys organized a large transhipment of families of new settlers, introduced new manufactures, secured the exclusion from England of all non-Virginian tobacco, and set up a missionary college at Henrico (later abandoned).

It was in the midst of all this activity that Sandys was approached by representatives of the Leiden separatists who wished to go to Jamestown.

12

To boldly go

As we approach the terminal point of this narrative, the departure aboard the *Mayflower* of those who would go down in national mythology as the Pilgrim Fathers, we must be careful to maintain our grasp on historical reality, which is, at several points, at odds with the simple story of a unique band of united, heroic pioneers, fleeing persecution in order to preserve personal liberty in a society based on doctrinal purity and a strict code of ethics. Courageous and dedicated the *Mayflower* passengers certainly were. However, their expedition was not unique. They were far from united and frequently split into opposing factions. There were at least 25 groups of English religious refugees in Holland. Their convictions varied, and while some kept themselves rigidly to themselves, others moved from church to church. The stories of religious persecution have been much exaggerated – it was often they who sat in judgement on their neighbours rather than vice versa. In the process of planning and executing their departure, they frequently compromised their own ethical standards. And they were not above tailoring their religious convictions to fit their changing circumstances. The reality is that they were fallible human beings, desperately and – yes – heroically clinging to a way of life that was increasingly at odds with the mores of the Old World. They were the latest manifestations of those religious enthusiasts, like the Lollards, the Marian exiles and the Brownists, who, rather than engaging with a changing and bewildering society, and labouring to be its salt and light, sought rather to escape from it – internally and, as opportunity presented itself, externally by physically retreating with their families to new havens.

The year 1618 was an ominous date in European history. The continent was teetering on the brink of the worst crisis that had ever overwhelmed it. In May of that year, Bohemian nationalists dramatically asserted their independence from the Holy Roman Emperor by throwing his envoys out of a high window. The Defenestration of Prague lit the fuse of a war that would convulse Europe for 30 years, involve all the major powers, wipe out a third of the population of the empire, reduce hundreds of towns and cities to rubble, trample farmland into uselessness, create economic dislocation that would take a generation to set to rights, and influence people's religious convictions in ways that are incalculable. Of course, no one in 1618 could have foreseen the scale of the catastrophe into which the continent was stumbling but, by the same token, anyone with a sensitive ear to the strident cacophonies being borne on the wind would have been anxious for the future. Events close to home for the English exiles were alarming enough. Politico-religious discord in the Netherlands did not wait for the ending of the Twelve Years' Truce. Conflict between Calvinists and Arminians led to purges that removed from office scores of university teachers and civic leaders. The year 1618 saw the arrest of the 71-year-old Johan van Oldenbarnevelt, the senior statesman of Holland, and a veteran of the fight for independence. The following year he was executed.

In England, James I, pursuing his self-appointed role of universal peacemaker, attempted to link his country to both sides in the religious conflict. In 1613, he married his daughter Elizabeth to Frederick V, Count Palatine of the Rhine, the white hope of the Protestant cause in the empire. In 1619, Frederick was chosen as king by the Bohemian rebels. A year later his forces were crushed by imperial troops. Thereafter, Elizabeth and her husband lived in exile at The Hague. Meanwhile, James I had been negotiating a Spanish, Catholic bride for Prince Charles, his son and heir. The Spanish Match provoked a major constitutional crisis. James stuck stubbornly to his plans for a marriage alliance from 1614 to 1623. They were, over and again, resisted by Parliament and by the public at large. In 1621, the House of Commons actually called for a war with Spain. In response, the king dissolved Parliament. This was a foretaste of the confrontation that would eventually lead to civil war.

Against such a background of events it is not surprising that the prospect of escape to some virgin territory where people could live their own lives, free from the machinations of rival politicians, now seemed particularly attractive. When the Virginia Company offered land grants to groups of settlers, 44 charters were taken up between 1618 and 1624. Not all the charters granted were to religious groups and not all were ultimately realized, but it is obvious that the English settlers in Leiden contemplating emigration to Virginia were part of a wider movement. Robinson and his friends had particularly poignant news of one such party. Francis Blackwell was a Leiden settler who had fallen out with the leadership of the community and had returned to the Ancient Brethren in Amsterdam (evidence that the movements of English separatists in the Dutch Republic were not in just one direction). In 1618, he set off with a band of 180 colonists for Chesapeake Bay. The following spring, John Robinson received alarming news about the Blackwell expedition, which had eventually arrived: 130 of the ship's complement were dead, including Blackwell and the ship's master: 'they were packed together like herrings. They had among them the flux and also want of fresh water, so it is here rather wondered at that so many are alive, than that so many are dead'. Robinson's correspondent was anxious to hear what impact this news would have on the plans of those in Leiden hoping to make a similar voyage.[1] What answer Robinson was able to return we cannot know, but the fate of Blackwell and Co. must have had some effect. Only a minority of the Leiden fellowship eventually set out for America. Of those, some subsequently withdrew. By the time the *Mayflower* set sail, she carried only 37 members of Robinson's flock. Response to life in Leiden was personal. Some migrants assimilated easily enough and put down deep roots. They were fairly successful in business. They were raising large families. Perhaps, in some cases, the hard edges of their religious zeal had softened. They committed themselves to making a future for them-selves and their children. Others, by contrast, clung to their Englishness. They feared contamination by the easy-going Dutch and rarely ventured outside their own community. They were regarded by their neighbours as aliens and they thought of themselves as aliens – superior aliens of course. Occasional xenophobic conflict strengthened their feelings of not belonging. In April 1619, one English couple was attacked by a gang of stone-throwing boys, and it is unlikely that that was an isolated inci-dent. Over the years some families drifted back to England. Then there were the hard-liners. Egged on by their preachers, they were determined to fulfil their destiny of establishing a godly commonwealth. The Bible assured them, 'you are . . . the holy nation, God's own people, chosen to proclaim the wonderful acts of God' (1 Peter 2.9). And proclaim they did. The process of sanctification tends to make the believer aware of other people's sins as well as his or her own. We have probably all come across 'philanthropists' like W. S. Gilbert's King Gama:

> Each little fault of temper and each social defect
> In my erring fellow creatures I endeavor to correct.
> To all their little weaknesses I open people's eyes;
> And little plans to snub the self-sufficient I devise.
> I love my fellow creatures – I do all the good I can –
> Yet everybody says I'm such a disagreeable man!
> And I can't think why![2]

It is unlikely that the locals took kindly to being lectured about their lax sabbatarianism or toleration of 'false religion'. Judgementalism raised social barriers in Holland no less than it did in England. For some – a minority – of the Leiden immigrants, the conviction grew that their wanderings, like those of the ancient Israelites, were not over; that God had prepared for them another land where they could serve him without let or hindrance. There were sufficient numbers of this last group for two of their number, Robert Cushman and John Carver, to be despatched to London in 1617 to explore the possibility of a move to Virginia.

Attempts to discover Carver's origins tentatively assigned him to Sturton-le-Steeple, John Robinson's home village, where others of that name were certainly well established. His first wife, Marie de Lannoy, was a member of the French-speaking community in Leiden who had fled from the Spanish Netherlands. However, she died in 1609, and when the widower married again it was to Catherine White, John Robinson's sister-in-law. That connection suggests that Carver was among the 'elite' of the English community. Certainly, he was sufficiently trusted to be appointed, with Cushman, as their envoy to the Virginia Company directors. Cushman was a dyed-in-the-wool separatist, much of whose adult life had been spent in open rebellion against the state church. In 1603, he had been in trouble for posting scurrilous notices on church doors in Canterbury. That was the first of several offences that earned him short stays in prison. By 1611, he and his family had moved to Leiden. However, by 1617, he was back in England where he became one of the prime movers of the emigration to America.

On 8 May 1619 Cushman wrote from London to one of his friends in Leiden. Passing on his latest news, he reported:

> Master Brewster is not well at this time. Whether he will come back to you or go into the north (Scrooby or Sturton) I yet know not. For myself I hope to see an end of this business, ere I come . . .[3]

We last encountered Brewster and his partner in the Pilgrim Press; Thomas Brewer was trying to avoid discovery by James I's ambassador. It was early in 1619 that Sir Dudley Carleton set his bloodhounds to sniff out the Pilgrim Press. They stuck to their task tenaciously, but Brewer and Brewster stayed out of harm's way for about six months. Not until mid-July did the trail lead their pursuers to Leiden, by which time most of the incriminating material had been destroyed or moved. The ambassador, intent on pleasing his royal master, missed no opportunity afforded by diplomatic pressure or English gold to aid his quest, but the members of the separatist English community were just as assiduous in protecting the publishers. It was several more months before the hunt ended. It had involved the cooperation (doubtless reluctant) of the university council, the municipal authority and the state leaders of Holland, with the Estates General leaning heavily on the other administrative bodies. Brewer was detained and examined. Carleton professed himself astonished (and appalled) at the vast amount of his own money that Brewer had ploughed into the venture. Proceedings against the prisoner dragged on for more months (doubtless slowed by yet more gold Brewer poured in to clog up the machine). Eventually he was released, but King James and his industrious ambassador had achieved their objective. The Pilgrim Press was silenced, though Brewer may have salvaged some of the type and taken it to Amsterdam where another underground press was active.

While all this was going on Brewster was, as Cushman's letter indicates, in London. He was involved in planning the Virginia move (the 'business' referred to in Cushman's letter). But he had other reasons for being in London. He wanted to see his son. Captain Edward Brewster had arrived recently from Jamestown and was probably lucky to be alive. He had remained in the colony after Lord De La Warr's departure and, as captain of the pinnace *Virginia*, had been involved in various sorties against Wahunsonacock's people. The deaths in 1618 of the paramount chief, and also of Lord De La Warr, had led to a radical change of policy by Samuel Argall, who now had a free hand. His actions (backed by the company treasurer, Sir Thomas Smythe) provoked the opposition of the old guard, of whom Brewster was one. As a result, Brewster found himself on a treason charge. He was tried, found guilty and sentenced to death. But the penalty was subsequently commuted to banishment. Thus Edward left Virginia, never to return. He was obviously the bearer of important information about the state of affairs in America. Whether he and his father saw eye to eye about the future prospects for settlement we cannot know. Did the latest news from Jamestown contribute to the indecision Cushman hinted at?

It is interesting to note Cushman's laconic reference to Brewster's immediate plans. It has become customary to think of the transition from England to the New World as a simple, two-stage process: England to the Dutch Republic, and Dutch Republic to America. It has been assumed that the door to the Pilgrims' mother country was fast closed against them by official persecution, and that once they had crossed the sea, there was no going back. Clearly, this was not the case. Some of the Leiden folk had family and/or business concerns in England that necessitated their occasional return, and there were no royal or ecclesiastical agents at the ports ready to pounce on them as soon as they disembarked. Many Leiden folk settled in their new home, but others returned to England after a few years. As for Brewster, in May 1619, 14 months before the American venture was launched, he was calmly deliberating whether to return to Leiden or set out for his ancestral home. This does not give the impression of a man 'on the run' from royal justice. It would seem that we must jettison the representation of these separatists as heroes and martyrs, pursued by a vindictive regime.

By the spring of 1619, discussions were still in progress and Cushman was wearily reporting his hope to 'see an end of this business'. However, the Leiden representatives now acquired a powerful ally to help them shift the logjam. It was on 28 April that Sir Edwin Sandys became the treasurer of the company, determined to be a new broom, sweeping away the incompetence of his predecessor and putting in place policies designed to encourage settlement. He was someone with whom the Leiden envoys thought they could do business, particularly as William Brewster had connections with him from his Scrooby days.

The negotiations that now began in earnest were based on a mix of idealism and pragmatism. Cushman and Carver had come armed with a document that set out their position in a way they hoped would be acceptable to the company and to the government. They knew they would have to overcome religious prejudice against separatism. Virginia might be 3,500 miles away from England, but it was still a colony under English law and owing allegiance to King James. The *Seven Articles* submitted by the leaders in Leiden sought to convince the government that people who had quit their native land and rejected its Church would be good and dutiful subjects. If they were granted the freedom to worship according to conscience, the appellants stated: (1) that they accepted the doctrines of the Church of England; (2) that those doctrines were properly implemented in the life and worship of their church; (3) that they accepted the king's authority, would be fully obedient to his commands that were in accord with the Bible, and would passively oppose any that did not agree with Holy Writ (in which case they would meekly accept the consequences); (4/5) that they recognized all church officials lawfully appointed; (6) that they only accepted the judgements of ecclesiastic tribunals, the authority of which derived solely from the king (a veiled protest against the Court of High Commission); (7) that they would render due honour to all civil and ecclesiastical superiors. Their overwhelming desire, they insisted, was to live in peace and unity with all people who feared God. This was a considerable climbdown and demonstrates how desperate the Leiden group were to find an alternative to the two unattractive choices of continuing in the Republic or returning to the fold of the Church of England. It did not satisfy King James's demand for total obedience and submission, but it did give Sandys a basis for his negotiations with friends in government.

For his part, Sandys was equally anxious to strike a deal. The campaign to oust Smythe and Argall had been acrimonious and divisive.

He had won that contest, but his enemies had by no means lost all their teeth and continued to oppose drastic reforms. Moreover, they had the backing of the king, who still disliked Sandys. More worrying was the company's debt, which mounted steadily year on year. The onus was therefore on the new treasurer and his friends to produce policies that would set the Virginia settlement on a course of stability and prosperity. As we have seen, Sandys initiated an overhaul of the administration in both London and Jamestown (see above, p. 196). This ensured a closer control of day-to-day operations by tightening regulations and the selection of officers.

But no amount of tinkering with the bureaucracy could ensure the survival of the colony. What the settlement desperately needed was cash and settlers. The turbulence of the early years deterred both investors and colonists. However, what the colony had in abundance was land. Sandys and his supporters now came up with ways to exploit this great asset. Instead of offering potential settlers free passage, the company now provided land grants to people who could pay their own costs of getting to the colony. Once there, the settlers were able to lease 50-acre plots at a cheap rental. Agricultural land needs people to work it. So the directors provided cheap labour. They encouraged the importation of slaves and indentured servants. The latter were men, women and even children offering to work for an agreed term of years in return for free transatlantic passage, food and shelter. There were many such unemployed people to be found in England's port towns for whom such an arrangement offered one of the few legal routes out of poverty. Sandys and his colleagues were, thus, proposing an arrangement that not only solved the problems of settlers but also helped to combat England's chronic overcrowding. Every new colonist prepared to hire indentured servants on these terms was providing the colony with landholders and workers without any cost to the company. It had all the makings of a win-win situation.

Shifting the financial burden from shareholders to settlers had the effect of concentrating the minds of the Leiden folk. They had made the emotional commitment to crossing the Atlantic, but were they prepared to raise the necessary cash? Paying for the passage of themselves, their families and as many indentured servants as they could afford would be very expensive. For the majority of them, it would mean selling most of their possessions and probably borrowing extra funds from friends or bankers. And it should be remembered that what they were investing in was frail human lives. The travellers undoubtedly prayed earnestly for divine protection, but they knew full well from the stories coming back from America that a large percentage of settlers did not survive the crossing and the early years. Anyone signing up to the new venture would be risking everything. Their preachers certainly did not conceal this from them. Rather, they emphasized the difficulties the settlers would face as proof that they were true men and women of God, assuring them that he who had called them to this holy task would preserve them:

> though Satan seek to make us desist, and because he cannot, therefore will hurt us, by all his power, yet we have Christ Jesus on our side, whose kingdom we go to enlarge; whose love to his children is such that, even then when Satan sifts them most narrowly, he with his prayers is most near them for their assistance: And therefore we doubt not, but that Satan is now so busy to sift us by all discouragements, and by slanders, false reports, backwardness of some, baseness of others, by raising objections and devising doubts, endeavours to daunt us, and so to betray the business that God himself hath put into our hands: the more I say are we assured that Christ will the more mightily oppose this malice of the devil, and by his glorious intercession, obtain from his father so much the greater blessing both on us and it.[4]

The words are those of William Crashaw from a sermon preached in 1610 (and subsequently printed to put fire in the bellies of those embarking on an earlier voyage to Virginia), but the mood was much the same a decade later among those venturing all in a similar godly crusade. Crashaw had held out to his congregation the vision of a society where the Sabbath was honoured, swearing and other abominations were outlawed, public prayers daily attended and 'idleness eschewed'. The preacher doubted not that such an example of a perfect Christian society would prove to be an inspiration to leaders of Church and State in the mother country and the means of restoring true religion in England. Such, then, were the challenge and the vision facing those exiles who were no longer content to call Leiden 'home'. For some, the cost would prove to be too high. They would be absorbed into Dutch society or return to England. The remainder – about 35 in number – would eventually find themselves aboard the *Mayflower*.

The story of the departure from Leiden, the false starts to the voyage and the Atlantic crossing has usually been told from the perspective of this brave, devoted remnant. But there is more to it than that. If we allow the events to unroll in chronological sequence (as we have done thus far in the narrative) and seek to omit nothing of relevance, we shall discover that the unfolding plot is more complex and that the main players, for all their courage, were fallible human beings whose motives were frequently mixed. Edwin Sandys, for example, shared with most of his fellow countrymen a prejudice against separatists. He took after his father, the archbishop, as a student of theology and an upholder of the established Church. His earliest tutor had been Richard Hooker, whose *Laws of Ecclesiastical Polity* was a detailed apologia for the Church of England. The two remained close friends until Hooker's death, and Sandys contributed handsomely towards the publication of the *Laws*. Several of his contributions to parliamentary debate were devoted to attacks on Presbyterianism and Brownists, and his bill to stretch the anti-recusancy laws to cover separatists was only defeated in the upper chamber. But Sandys' reputation rested on rescuing the Virginia settlements. He had personal enemies – not least of whom was the king. He could not afford to let religious scruples stand in the way. He gave Cushman and Carver his full backing.

They certainly needed his advice when it came to matters of high finance and commercial negotiation. Their inexperience almost wrecked the whole project. In their search for capital, they turned first of all to Dutch bankers. That was before the unscrupulous Thomas Weston scented a money-making opportunity. He was a member of the London Ironmongers' Guild but turned his hand to anything that might show a profit. He was active in Holland as early as 1615, when smuggling seems to have been his forte. He imported alum, vital as a textile dyestuff, purchased in the Netherlands – and omitted paying duty on it. Another speciality was the clandestine trade in banned religious tracts. This gained him the confidence of the separatist communities. When he heard about the projected New England venture, he decided to carve himself a slice of the action. In conversation with Robinson and Carver, this smooth talker suggested that, rather than continue with their Dutch bankers and the Virginia Company, they should entrust their affairs to a consortium he would put together. Weston promised to provide total finance in return for total control of the operation, including the selling of the agricultural produce from the colonists' holdings in America. When the time came for John Carver in London to finalize arrangements, he discovered that only a fraction of the capital was forthcoming. This shattering blow caused considerable hardship to the colonists, many of whom were already financially committed up to the hilt. But worse catastrophes were to come.

First of all, Edwin Sandys lost his position as treasurer of the Virginia Company. His term of office expired in May 1620 and the directors were anxious to re-elect him. The king, however, was adamant that Sandys' influence should be removed. 'Choose the devil if you will,' he said, 'but not Sir Edwin Sandys.'[5] The colonists felt control of affairs slipping out of their hands. And time was passing. Those who had now committed themselves to the enterprise had made their plans, sold property, closed business premises and settled their affairs in the hope of being on board ship before the end of summer, and the threat of autumn gales.

As the migrants waited anxiously in Holland and England for their leaders to finalize arrangements, their chosen agents, Cushman and Carver, were increasingly coming under Weston's sway. He was recruiting for passengers separately, and two distinct groups emerged, both of which expected to be consulted about the details of the voyage. One member of Weston's group was Christopher Martin, a wealthy Essex merchant, who was a Puritan, though not, apparently, a separatist. He had applied to the Virginia Company for a passage to the New World in 1617 before transferring his allegiance to Weston. In the interests of harmony between the two groups, Cushman and Carver involved Martin in the financial detail of provisioning the expedition. Accordingly, he based himself in Southampton and began stockpiling everything from salt beef to muskets and armour to trade goods. But he showed himself to be not only incompetent and wasteful in dealing with chandlers but also arrogant and oversensitive to criticism. If we are to believe a later report of Cushman's, Martin treated the Leiden contingent with contempt and flew into a rage when anyone questioned his authority.[6] Before the *Mayflower* even set sail, the cohesion and common purpose of the voyage were seriously compromised.

The same must also be said about the probity of the leaders. Cushman and Carver were in a difficult position. They were committed to the hilt to the success of their venture, yet increasingly at odds with Weston and his colleagues over the morality of their business dealings. Inevitably this led them to cut corners. Instead of insisting on the ethical principles underlying the whole enterprise, they fell in with the dubious proceedings of Weston and Martin. Instead of being completely honest with their friends back in London, they fudged issues that might have caused Robinson and the church elders to ring alarm bells. There is a sad irony about the fact that people who deserted their native land in the belief that it was decadent and corrupt now lowered their own moral standards in the process of establishing a superior society. Faith exhorted them to embrace moral absolutes. Reason impressed on them that politics is the art of the possible.

The tragic tale often told to illustrate this jettisoning of integrity is that of a great scandal Carver and Cushman got involved in. Familiar it may be, but it illustrates very well the constraints the leaders were under and the difficult choices they had to make. It began as a very common 'eternal triangle' affair. Catherine More and Jacob Blakeway were young people in love, and they became clandestinely engaged. Secrecy was necessary because Catherine's family had other plans for her. The Mores were extensive Shropshire landowners who were running out of male heirs. For this reason, in 1610 Catherine was forced to marry her cousin, Samuel More, who may have been as much as ten years her junior. She and Jacob continued their affair, and by 1616 Catherine had given birth to four healthy children. Their relationship was easy to maintain because Samuel spent much of his time in London as a secretary to Edward, Baron Zouche, a privy councillor and a holder of various offices of state. He was also on the governing body of the Virginia Company.

When the cuckolded husband eventually got wind of his wife's infidelity, he was determined to disentangle himself from Catherine and her bastards. He needed to be free to remarry, sire legitimate heirs and safeguard his inheritance from possible claims by Catherine's children. Easier said than done. English law did not recognize divorce. Marriages could only be dissolved on a few specific grounds. One was pre-contract. Unfortunately, because Catherine and Jacob's betrothal had been secret (and, perhaps, because the witnesses had since died), pre-contract could not be proved in their case. Despite the expense and distress of high-profile court hearings, there was no legal way forward. Samuel, therefore, egged on by his father, devised a more ruthless and permanent solution. It may have been suggested by Lord Zouche, whose own matrimonial history showed him to be callous in the extreme. In 1582, he had abandoned his wife and two daughters and, for the next 29 years, he refused to make any financial provision for them, even after his cruelty resulted in excommunication from the Church of England. The solution was simply to make Catherine's children disappear. First of all, they were removed from their mother's care – to her very great distress. Then, Zouche arranged for them to be added to the list of *Mayflower* passengers as indentured servants.

Someone had to be responsible for the children during the crossing and their early years in the new colony. It was the obnoxious Weston who arranged the fine detail. He persuaded the Leiden leaders to take on the care of the infants, aged between four and eight, thus making them complicit in this sordid affair. The children were apportioned to Brewster, Carver and Edward Winslow (who had joined the Leiden church in 1617). They were to serve out the period of their indenture, after which each was to be granted 50 acres of land. It may be that the reluctant guardians saw it as their duty to help the abandoned children at their own cost. Or perhaps they felt manoeuvred into a situation from which there was no obvious escape. Whatever their thinking, it was borne in on them that they were losing the initiative in planning and executing their grand enterprise. They were dancing to the tune of unscrupulous men driven by the profit motive.

Throughout the summer of 1620, as all parties waited impatiently for the business to be concluded, tempers frayed. Correspondence became acrimonious – a development exacerbated by the fact that messages had to pass between London, Southampton and Leiden. Robert Cushman bore the brunt of most accusations:

here cometh over many . . . complaints against me, of lording it over my brethren and making conditions fitter for thieves and bond slaves than honest men and that of my own head I did what I list (letter to the leaders at Leyden 10 June 1620).[7]

However, others involved in the negotiations suffered their share of blame and accusation. More than once Cushman was on the verge of quitting. Weston swore that he would pull out but for his promise. Some backers and some would-be voyagers did desert the project. Almost as much alarm was caused by a group who sought to *join* the expedition. A request came from Ainsworth and the Ancient Brethren. 'I had thought they would as soon have gone to Rome as with us,' Cushman sourly observed, 'for our liberty is to them as rat's bane and their rigour as bad to us as the Spanish Inquisition.'[8]

One more disaster lay in wait for the Virginia-bound voyagers – one that was almost fatal in its consequences. Warned by the likes of Francis Blackwell, they wanted to ensure that there was adequate accommodation for passengers. They therefore planned to use two ships, one to be hired in Southampton and a smaller support vessel to be bought outright in London. The second ship would remain in the colony at journey's end to be used for fishing and coastal activities. It was a sound scheme and might have worked well had the Leiden folk not been as ignorant of shipbuilding as they were of high finance. The vessel they bought was the 60-ton, two-masted pinnace *Speedwell*. It had been laid down in 1577 and was a veteran of the Armada campaign. At 43 years of age the ship was old and in need of a complete overhaul. It was brought over to Delfshaven in the summer of 1620 for a refit, and its intended passengers at Leiden set about packing their bags. The arrival of the *Speedwell* was an exciting event for them. Here, at last, was tangible proof that the great adventure was imminent. Perhaps they were too eager to be on their way. Perhaps they put too much pressure on the shipwrights to complete their work. Perhaps those shipwrights were not as competent as they should have been (a job for a bunch of troublesome foreigners might not have been high on their list of priorities). For whatever reason, the repairs to the *Speedwell* were not adequate for the transatlantic voyage planned for it.

On 22 July 1620 the Leiden contingent embarked for the journey to Southampton where they would link up with the larger *Mayflower*, carrying the rainbow-hued contingent of migrants gathered there. One notable absentee from the *Speedwell*'s passenger list was John Robinson. Just as years before he had remained in Scrooby, ministering to the majority of his congregation who had not yet departed for Holland, so now he resolved to care for the members of his flock in Leiden until the pioneer émigrés had established a colony ready to welcome them. He did preach a last sermon to his departing friends, either at Leiden or Delfshaven, and followed it up with a letter offering his wise counsel on the setting up of a new community. These both appeared in print several decades later, and questions have inevitably been raised about how well the preacher's words had been remembered and how far they were coloured by the experiences of the settlers during the early years of the colony. Certain themes, however, seem to be original in the thinking of a man who had lived through the fragmentation of Protestant churches in England and the Dutch Republic and who had learned to maintain under constant review those beliefs that were non-negotiable and those that should not be allowed to create barriers between Christians.

Robinson deplored the devotees of Luther, Calvin and other Christian teachers who had closed their minds to fresh divine guidance. He was close to medieval Catholicism in his belief in progressive revelation. Believers must, he urged, be open to receiving fresh truths out of Scripture. He was scathing about the term 'Brownist', which would always evoke for him the painful conflicts at Amsterdam. He understood well that as long as Christians held rigidly to the points of *lexis* and *praxis* that divided them, the new community would be doomed to go the same way as some of the old ones. Addressing himself to politics, he had this advice to give in a final letter sent to its leaders:

whereas you are become a body politic, using amongst yourselves civil government, and are not furnished with any persons of special eminency about the rest, to be chosen by you into office of government; let your wisdom and godliness appear, not only in choosing such persons as do entirely love and will promote the common good, but also in yielding unto them all due honor and obedience in their lawful administrations, not beholding in them the ordinariness of their persons, but God's ordinance for your good . . . the image of the Lord's power and authority which the magistrate beareth, is honorable, in how mean persons soever. And this duty you both may the more willingly and ought the more conscionably to perform, because you are at least for the present to have only them for your ordinary governors, which yourselves shall make choice of for that work.[9]

Robinson had returned to the age-old problem of where authority resides in a Christian commonwealth. Top down or bottom up? The writer tried to hold the two in tension. However, five words in his final sentence left the question of ultimate authority open. Democracy would be an inescapable element in the political life of the new colony – 'at least for the present'.

By the time the *Speedwell* reached Southampton, it was leaking badly. There was no question of an immediate departure. The leaders, seeing their food and water supplies diminishing before the voyage had actually started and impatient to be away before the weather turned, fell to more mutual recriminations. The *Speedwell* was quickly – too quickly – patched up, and on 5 August the two ships weighed anchor. Now the voyagers were only able to get 75 miles through coastal waters before the state of the pinnace forced another halt. The ships put into Dartmouth for fresh repairs to be carried out. It is scarcely possible to imagine the state of morale on board when the ships made a second start. When this, too, had to be aborted due to the *Speedwell*'s unseaworthiness, despair and anger drove many to mutiny as the two ships anchored at Plymouth. There the *Speedwell* was abandoned and as many passengers as possible were crammed onto the *Mayflower*. Twenty people, including Robert Cushman, abandoned the voyage and made their way back to London. When the *Mayflower* once more set sail, on 6 September, she carried 102 passengers. Of these only 37 were from Leiden; 28 constituted other volunteers gathered by Thomas Weston; 19 were indentured servants. The rest were émigrés having no connection with the Christian idealists who had conceived the Christian adventure in the first place.

It was while the ships were docked in Dartmouth after their false start that Robert Cushman wrote to a friend to describe the frustrations and tensions the travellers were enduring. His was the letter of a disillusioned man:

Better the voyage to have been broken off then [at Southampton] than to have brought such misery to ourselves, dishonor to God and detriment to our living friends, as now it is like to do . . . if ever we make a plantation, [it will be because] God works a miracle, especially considering how scant we shall be of victuals, and most of all ununited amongst ourselves and devoid of good tutors and regiment. Violence will break all. Where is the meek and humble spirit of Moses? And of Nehemiah who re-edified the walls of Jerusalem, and the state of Israel? Is not the sound of Rehoboam's brags daily here amongst us? Have not the philosophers and all the wise men observed that, even in settled commonwealths, violent governors bring either themselves or people or both to ruin? How much more in the raising of commonwealths, when the mortar is yet scarce tempered that should bind the walls! If I should write to you of all things which promiscuously forerun our ruin, I should over-charge my weak head and grieve your tender heart. Only this, I pray you prepare for evil tidings of us every day. But pray for us instantly, it may be the Lord will be yet entreated one way or other to make for us. I see not in reason how we shall escape even the gaspings of hunger-starved persons; but God can do much, and His will be done. It is better for me to die than now for me to bear it, which I do daily and expect it hourly, having received the sentence of death both within me and without me. Poor William Ring and myself do strive who shall be meat first for the fishes; but we look for a glorious resurrection, knowing Christ Jesus after the flesh no more, but looking unto the joy that is before us, we will endure all these things and account them light in comparison of that joy we hope for . . . Remember me in all love to our friends . . . whose prayers I desire earnestly, but not till I can with more comfort look them in the face . . . The Lord make me strong in Him and keep both you and yours. – Your loving friend, Robert Cushman.[10]

The writer did not see his Pilgrim friends again. Though maintaining contact by letter and assuring the settlers of his desire to join them, he delayed his departure until, in 1625, death prevented it.

'The raising of a commonwealth'. Had it taken so much suffering, so much division, so much mistrust, so much mixing of incompatible motives, so much hatred, to bring at least one of the 'Pilgrims' to the point of grasping what their whole venture had been about – or should have been about? Commonwealths, nations, human communities of all kinds are built on common purpose, the positivism that enables participants to hold fast to the things that bind them, rather than underscoring the points of difference. The best survive, not only because people cannot be forced into agreement, but also because they realize that toleration and compromise are not indications of weakness. Cushman's God did work a miracle. Against all the odds, the pilgrims reached a safe haven and settled there. Plymouth colony survived – by the skin of its teeth.

The rest (or much of it) is . . . legend.

Notes

Introduction

1 A. P. Putnam (ed.), *Singers and Songs of the Liberal Faith*, Boston, 1875, p. 6.

1 A new world

1 J. Barzun, *From Dawn to Decadence: 1500 to the present*, New York: HarperCollins, 2001, p. 54.

2 'Letter of Amerigo Vespucci upon the isles newly found in his four voyages', in *The First Four Voyages of Amerigo Vespucci*, trans. M. K., London, 1885, p. 19.

3 See Matthew 28.19–20.

4 G. B. Spolorno, *Memorials of Columbus*, London, 1823, p. 234.

5 O. Dunn and J. E. Kelley (eds), *The Diario of Christopher Columbus's First Voyage to America, 1492–1493*, Norman, OK: University of Oklahoma Press, 1988, p. 69.

6 Thomas More, *The Yale Edition of the Complete Works of St. Thomas More, vol. 3, pt 2: Latin Poems*, ed. C. H. Miller, L. Bradner and C. A. Lynch, New Haven, CT: Yale University Press, 1984, p. 103.

7 E. V. Hitchcock (ed.), *The Life of Sir Thomas More Knight, written by William Roper Esquire*, Oxford: Oxford University Press, 1935, p. 21.

8 Thomas More, *Utopia*, trans. R. Robinson, ed. W. A. Rebhorn, New York: Barnes & Noble, 2005, p. 42.

9 More, *Utopia*, p. 93.

10 More, *Utopia*, p. 146.

11 Erasmus, Preface to the *Novum Instrumentum*, Basel, 1516.

12 Erasmus, *The Education of a Christian Prince*, trans. N. M. Cheshire and M. J. Heath, Cambridge: Cambridge University Press, 1997, p. 5.

13 Isaiah 1.14–17.

14 E. F. Rogers (ed.), *St Thomas More: Selected letters*, New Haven, CT: Yale University Press, 1961, p. 178.

15 Thomas More, *The Yale Edition of the Complete Works of St. Thomas More, vol. 8, pts 1–3: The Confutation of Tyndale's Answer*, ed. L. A. Schuster, R. C. Marius, J. P. Lusardi, New Haven, CT: Yale University Press, 1973, p. 590.

16 *Luther's Works*, ed. H. T. Lehmann and J. Pelikan, 55 vols, St Louis, MO, and Philadelphia, PA: Fortress Press, 1955–1986, vol. 31, p. 25.

2 The idea of commonwealth

1 Edmund Dudley, *The Tree of Commonwealth*, ed. D. M. Brodie, Cambridge: Cambridge University Press, 1948, p. 20.

2 Dudley, *Tree of Commonwealth*, p. 31.

3 Dudley, *Tree of Commonwealth*, p. 24.

4 J. H. Lupton, *Life of John Colet*, London, 1887, p. 259.

5 Lupton, *Life of John Colet*, p. 38.

6 John Skelton, *Why Come Ye nat to Courte?*, ed. Richard Kele, London, 1550, lines 654–9.

7 H. Walter (ed.), *Doctrinal Treatises and Introduction to Different Portions of the Holy Scriptures by William Tyndale*, Parker Society, Cambridge: Cambridge University Press, 1848, pp. 102–3.

8 G. Walker, *Writing Under Tyranny: English literature and the Henrician Reformation*, Oxford: Oxford University Press, 2005, p. 410.

9 D. MacCulloch, *The Boy King: Edward VI and the Protestant Reformation*, New York: St Martin's Press, 1999, p. 126.

10 H. Robinson (ed.), *Original Letters relative to the English Reformation . . .*, Parker Society, Cambridge: Cambridge University Press, 1846, pp. 65–6.

3 The genie out of the lamp

1 E. V. Beilin (ed.), *The Examinations of Anne Askew*, Oxford: Oxford University Press, 1996, p. 114.

2 W. Turner, *The hunting and fyndyng out of the Romish fox*, Basel, 1543, n.p.

3 P. Marshall, *Heretics and Believers: A history of the English Reformation*, New Haven, CT: Yale University Press, 2017, p. 295.

4 A pamphlet circulated among the exiled communities and dated 2 August 1554. Cf. G. Beeley, *Church Historians of the English Reformation Period*, vol. 2, pt 1, London, 1870, p. 18.

5 For details of the Frankfurt schism, see below, pp. 48–9.

6 H. Robinson (ed.), *The Zurich Letters . . . during the early part of the Reign of Queen Elizabeth*, Parker Society, Cambridge: Cambridge University Press, 1842, pp. 230-1.

7 Robinson (ed.), *Zurich Letters*, p. 71.

8 D. Mathew, *James I*, London: Eyre and Spottiswoode, 1967, pp. 126-7.

9 Preface to the Douai-Rheims New Testament, 1582.

4 Home truths from abroad

1 H. Robinson (ed.), *Original Letters relative to the English Reformation . . . chiefly from the Archives of Zurich*, Parker Society, Cambridge: Cambridge University Press, 1846, p. 374.

2 J. Calvin, *Institutes*, ed. A. Lefranc, Paris, 1911, p. 755. For further discussion see J. W. Allen, *A History of Political Thought in the Sixteenth Century*, London: Methuen, 1960, pp. 58ff.

3 In 1553 Calvin actually cooperated with Catholic authorities in condemning to death the anti-Trinitarian heretic Michael Servetus.

4 W. Walker, *John Calvin, the Organiser of Reformed Protestantism*, New York: G. P. Putnam's Sons, 1906, pp. 304f; cf. F. Wendel, *Calvin: The origins and development of his religious thought*, trans. P. Mairet, London: Collins, 1963, p. 84.

5 W. S. Reid, *Trumpeter of God: A biography of John Knox*, New York: Scribners, 1974, p. 132.

6 John Milton, *On the New Forces of Conscience under the Long Parliament*, London, 1646, lines 6-7, 20.

7 Robinson (ed.), *Original Letters*, p. 134.

8 J. Petheram (ed.), *A Brieff discours of the troubles begonne at Frankford*, London, 1845, p. 77. This was another issue of principle destined to raise its head in the American colonies decades later.

9 Cf. C. H. Garrett, *The Marian Exiles*, Cambridge: Cambridge University Press, 1966, pp. 158-9; K. Gunther, *Reformation Unbound: Protestant visions of reform in England, 1525-1590*, Cambridge: Cambridge University Press, 2014, p. 115.

10 *Two sermons preached, the one at St Maries Spittle . . . the other at the court at Windsor the Sunday after the twelfth day, being the viii of January, before in the yeare 1569 by Thomas Drant Bachelor of Divinitie*, London, n.d.

11 H. Robinson (ed.), *The Zurich Letters* (second series), Parker Society, Cambridge: Cambridge University Press, 1845, p. 25.

12 Robinson (ed.), *Zurich Letters* (second series), p. 152.

13 D. Laing (ed.), *The Works of John Knox*, Edinburgh, 1895, vol. 3, p. 198.

14 Laing (ed.), *Works of John Knox*, vol. 2, p. 227.

15 G. Parker, *The Grand Strategy of Philip II*, New Haven, CT: Yale University Press, 1998, p. 101.

16 L. S. Marcus, J. Mueller and M. B. Rose (eds), *Elizabeth I: Collected works*, Chicago, IL: University of Chicago Press, 2000, p. 169.

17 C. Read, *Lord Burghley and Queen Elizabeth*, London: Cape, 1965, p. 24.

18 *Dictionary of National Biography*, London: Oxford University Press, 1921-1922.

19 John Whitgift, 'The Defence of the Answer to the Admonition . . .', in J. Ayre (ed.), *Works of John Whitgift*, Parker Society, Cambridge: Cambridge University Press, 1851, vol. 1, p. 3.

20 P. Collinson, *The Elizabethan Puritan Movement*, London: Cape, 1967, p. 246.

21 H. Robinson (ed.), *The Zurich Letters . . . during the early part of the Reign of Queen Elizabeth*, Parker Society, Cambridge: Cambridge University Press, 1842, p. 295.

5 Lollardy to lectureships

1 R. Edgeworth, *Sermons very fruitful, godly and learned . . .*, London, 1557, fol. xliiii.

2 G. E. Corrie (ed.), *Sermons by Hugh Latimer*, Parker Society, Cambridge: Cambridge University Press, 1844, p. 70.

3 P. Marshall, *Heretics and Believers: A history of the English Reformation*, New Haven, CT: Yale University Press, 2017, p. 140.

4 Cf. R. Whiting, *The Blind Devotion of the People: Popular religion and the English Reformation*, Cambridge: Cambridge University Press, 1989, p. 240.

5 Marshall, *Heretics and Believers*, p. 50.

6 Marshall, *Heretics and Believers*, p. 50.

7 J. Longland, Bishop of Lincoln to Thomas Cromwell, 5 May 1536, in J. Gairdner (ed.), *Letters and Papers Foreign and Domestic of the Reign of Henry VIII*, London, 1887, vol. 10, p. 804.

8 J. Strype, *Ecclesiastical Memorials relating chiefly to religion . . .*, London, 1822, vol. 1, pt 2, p. 180.

9 J. Foxe, *Acts and Monuments*, ed. G. Townsend, London, 1837, vol. 4, p. 623.

10 D. MacCulloch, *Reformation: Europe's house divided, 1490–1700*, London: Allen Lane, 2003, p. 501.

11 H. Robinson (ed.), *The Zurich Letters . . . during the early part of the Reign of Queen Elizabeth*, Parker Society, Cambridge: Cambridge University Press, 1842, p. 295.

12 J. C. Cox (ed.), *Records of the Borough of Northampton*, Northampton, 1898, vol. 2, p. 387.

13 Cf. P. Collinson, *Archbishop Grindal, 1519–1583: The struggle for a reformed Church*, London: Cape, 1979, pp. 240–5.

14 L. S. Marcus, J. Mueller and M. B. Rose (eds), *Elizabeth I: Collected works*, Chicago, IL: University of Chicago Press, 2000, pp. 178–9.

15 W. Dillingham, *Laurence Chaderton, D.D. First Master of Emmanuel*, trans. E. S. Shuckburgh, Cambridge: Macmillan & Bowes, 1884, p. 4.

16 P. Stubbs, *The Anatomy of Abuses*, London, 1595 edition, p. 10.

17 T. G. Crippen (ed.), *A Treatise of Reformation without Tarrying for Anie by Robert Browne*, London, 1903, p. 18.

18 Marshall, *Heretics and Believers*, p. 545.

6 Mission and money

1 J. Gairdner (ed.), *Letters and Papers Foreign and Domestic of the Reign of Henry VIII*, London, 1861–1863, vol. 19, pt 2, 766.

2 B. S. W. Vaux (ed.), *The World Encompassed by Sir Francis Drake . . . collated with an unpublished manuscript of Francis Fletcher, chaplain to the expedition*, Hakluyt Society, London, 1854, p. 118.

3 Quoted in D. Carey and C. Jowitt (eds), *Richard Hakluyt and Travel Writing in Early Modern Europe*, Abingdon: Routledge, 2016, p. 199.

4 R. Lemon (ed.), *Calendar of State Papers, Domestic Series, of the Reigns of Edward VI, Mary, Elizabeth 1547-1580, preserved in the State Paper Departments of Her Majesty's Public Record Office*, London, 1856, vol. 118, 12.

5 See Mark 16.15-16.

6 J. Hemming, *The Conquest of the Incas*, London: Macmillan, 1970, pp. 448-9.

7 C. Deane (ed.), *History of Plymouth Plantation by William Bradford*, Massachusetts Historical Society, Boston, 1856, p. 7.

7 Divided we stand

1 William Shakespeare, *Twelfth Night*, Act 3, Scene 2, lines 30-1.

2 Book of Common Prayer 1662, 39 Articles, Article 24.

3 H. Robinson (ed.), *The Zurich Letters . . . during the early part of the Reign of Queen Elizabeth*, Parker Society, Cambridge: Cambridge University Press, 1842, pp. 201-2.

4 B. Reay, 'Popular Religion', in B. Reay (ed.), *Popular Culture in Seventeenth Century England*, London: Croom Helm, 1995, pp. 94-5.

5 A reference to the widespread Puritan dismay that James VI, reared by Presbyterians, did not order a more radical reform of the Church; Ben Jonson, *The Alchemist*, Act 1, Scene 1, lines 166-8.

6 Ironically, one of Browne's descendants, Edward Brown (the 'e' had by now been dropped), probably a grandson, was one of the founding settlers of Maryland in 1633-1634. The colony, established by Lord Baltimore, was designed as a haven for Catholics, but it became the first of the American territories to pass an act of religious toleration (1645).

7 J. Calvin, *Institutes*, quoted in F. Wendel, *Calvin: The origins and development of his religious thought*, trans. P. Mairet, London: Collins, 1963, pp. 296-7.

8 Cf. P. Marshall, *Heretics and Believers: A history of the English Reformation*, New Haven, CT: Yale University Press, 2017, p. 547.

9 E. Zinner (ed.) and E. Brown (trans.), *Regiomontanus: His life and work*, Amsterdam: Elsevier, 1990, p. 130 (my translation).

10 Cf. D. B. Hamilton, *Shakespeare and the Politics of Protestant England*, Lexington, KY: University Press of Kentucky, 1992, p. 95.

11 H. Chisholm (ed.), 'Penry, John', *Encyclopaedia Britannica*, 11th edn, Cambridge: Cambridge University Press, 1911, p. 117.

12 H. Gee and N. J. Hardy (eds), *Documents Illustrative of English Church History*, London: Macmillan, 1896, pp. 492-8.

13 C. Burrage, *The Early English Dissenters*, 2 vols, Cambridge: Cambridge University Press, 1912, vol. 1, p. 233, vol. 2, pp. 172-3.

14 J. Strype, *Annals of the Reformation and Establishment of Religion . . .*, Oxford: Clarendon Press, 1824, vol. 3, pt 2, p. 613.

8 The Midlands nursery

1 J. Gairdner (ed.), *Letters and Papers Foreign and Domestic of the Reign of Henry VIII*, London, 1861-1863, vol. 15, pt 1, 295.

2 *Calendar of State Papers, Henry VIII*, London, 1830-1852, vol. 1, 463.

3 E. V. Beilin (ed.), *The Examinations of Anne Askew*, Oxford: Oxford University Press, 1996, p. 142.

4 Beilin, *Examinations of Anne Askew*, p. 99.

5 Cf. P. Collinson, *The Elizabethan Puritan Movement*, London: Cape, 1967, pp. 48-9.

6 P. Collinson (ed.), *Letters of Thomas Wood, Puritan 1566-1577*, London: University of London, Athlone Press, 1960.

7 Cf. Collinson, *Elizabethan Puritan Movement*, p. 145.

8 *Principal Probate Registry*, 43 Welles.

9 Cf. P. W. Hasler (ed.), *The House of Commons, 1558-1603*, 3 vols, London: Secker & Warburg, vol. 3, 1981, p. 656.

10 Hasler, *House of Commons*, p. 656.

11 George Gafford, *A sermon on the parable of the sower*, quoted in P. Collinson, *The Religion of Protestants: The church in English society, 1559-1625*, Oxford: Oxford University Press, 1982, pp. 201-2.

12 Cf. Collinson, *Elizabethan Puritan Movement*, pp. 384-5.

13 See Acts 16.9.

14 The Dudley Papers at Longleat, vol. 2, fol. 60.

15 P. Collinson, *Godly People: Essays on English Protestantism and Puritanism*, London: Hambledon Press, 1983, p. 77.

16 Cf. W. J. Sheils, *The Puritans in the Diocese of Peterborough, 1558-1610*, Northampton: Northamptonshire Record Society, 1979, p. 30.

17 Cf. M. Gibson, *Possession, Puritanism and Print*, London: Pickering & Chatto, 2006, p. 7.

18 Collinson, *Letters of Thomas Wood*, p. 10.

19 P. Collinson, *Archbishop Grindal, 1519-1583: The struggle for a reformed Church*, London: Cape, 1979, p. 240.

20 Beilin, *Examinations of Anne Askew*, p. 142.

9 New king, old problem

1 Cf. P. Collinson, *The Elizabethan Puritan Movement*, London: Cape, p. 449.

2 J. Craigie (ed.), *The Basilikon Doron of King James VI*, Edinburgh: William Blackwood and Sons, 1944, p. 70.

3 *Cobbett's Complete Collection of State Trials . . .*, vol. 2, London, 1809, pp. 71-2.

4 *Cobbett's State Trials*, p. 80.

5 P. Clark, *English Provincial Society from the Reformation to the Revolution*, Hassocks: Harvester Press, 1977, p. 304.

6 P. Collinson, 'Antipuritanism', in J. Coffey and P. C. H. Lim (eds), *The Cambridge Companion to Puritanism*, Cambridge: Cambridge University Press, 2008, p. 23.

7 Collinson, 'Antipuritanism', p. 24.

8 P. Lake, 'A Charitable Christian Hatred', in C. Durston and J. Eales (eds), *The Culture of English Puritanism, 1560-1700*, Basingstoke: Macmillan, 1996, p. 182; Collinson, 'Antipuritanism', p. 30.

9 Cf. Collinson, 'Antipuritanism', p. 28.

10 *Bartholomew Fair*, Act 1, Scene 1, Everyman's Library, London: J. M. Dent and Sons, 1910, p. 194.

11 *Dictionary of National Biography*, London: Oxford University Press, 1921-1922.

12 P. Collinson, *From Cranmer to Sancroft: Essays on English Religion in the Sixteenth and Seventeenth Centuries*, London: Bloomsbury, 2007, p. 126.

13 'A Fruitful Meditation – containing a plain and easy exposition . . . of the vii, viii, ix and x verses of the 20 chapter of the Revelation', in *Works of the Most High and Mighty Prince, James, by the Grace of God, King of Great Britain . . .*, London, 1616, pp. 79-80.

14 'A Declaration concerning the Proceedings with the States General . . . in the cause of D. Conradus Vorstius', in *Works of the Most High and Mighty Prince, James . . .* , pp. 347-8.

10 John Robinson and Co.

1 *Wiggenton's Visitation: A series of articles ministered in a Mock Visitation . . .* , Transactions of the Congregational Historical Society, London, vol. 3, 1907, p. 31.

2 C. Deane (ed.), *History of Plymouth Plantation by William Bradford*, Massachusetts Historical Society, Boston, 1856, pp. 8-10.

3 Cf. E. Parsons (ed.), *Neal's History of the Puritans*, 2 vols, London, 1811, vol. 1, pp. 317-18.

4 J. Robinson, *Works*, ed. R. Ashton, London, 1851, vol. 2, p. 52.

5 P. Collinson, *The Religion of Protestants: The church in English society, 1559-1625*, Oxford: Oxford University Press, 1982, p. 278.

6 *Dictionary of National Biography*, London: Oxford University Press, 1921-1922.

7 Deane, *History of Plymouth Plantation*, p. 12.

8 Deane, *History of Plymouth Plantation*, p. 15.

9 Deane, *History of Plymouth Plantation*, p. 14.

10 Deane, *History of Plymouth Plantation*, p. 15.

11 Collinson, *Religion of Protestants*, p. 274; see also E. H. Shagan, *The Rule of Moderation: Violence, Religion and the Politics of Restraint in Early Modern England*, Cambridge: Cambridge University Press, 2011, pp. 170-2.

12 In 1618 he became one of the first ex-Amsterdam exiles to settle in Virginia on land near Jamestown. It was the experiences of Lawne and other Puritan pioneers that encouraged some members of the Leiden congregation to consider heading for America.

13 T. Whetenhall, *A Discourse of the Abuses now in Question in the Churches of Christ of their Creeping in, Growing up and Flourishing in the Babylonish Church of Rome. How they are Spoken against not only by the Scriptures*, Leiden, 1617, pp. 75-6 (emphasis original).

11 America 1600–1620

1 W. C. Sellar and R. J. Yeatman, *1066 and All That: A memorable history of England*, London: Methuen, 1930, p. 75.

2 R. Hakluyt, *Discourse Concerning Western Planting*, ed. C. Deane, Cambridge, 1877, p. 67.

3 T. Wyatt, *The Voyage of Robert Dudley, afterwards styled Earl of Warwick and Leicester and Duke of Northumberland to the West Indies 1594-1595*, Hakluyt Society, London, 1899, p. 34.

4 R. Hakluyt and E. Goldsmid (eds), *The Principle Navigations*, Edinburgh, 1885, Epistle Dedicatory of the first edition.

5 W. W. Hening, *Statutes at Large: A collection of all the laws of Virginia*, Richmond, 1803, vol. 1, p. 573.

6 *Dictionary of National Biography*, London: Oxford University Press, 1921-1922.

7 The story, as reported by Smith himself, of how he was captured by the Powhatans and threatened with death but saved by the intercessions of Wahunsonacock's daughter, Pocahontas, is well known. She later married John Rolfe and travelled to England with him. The accuracy of Smith's account has been much debated.

8 *The Relation of the Right Honourable the Lord De-La-Warre, Lord Governur and Captaine Generall of the Colonie, planted in Virginea*, London, 1611, Encyclopedia Virginia transcript, 2011, pp. 11-12.

9 Cf. J. Horn, *A Land as God Made It: Jamestown and the birth of America*, New York: Basic Books, 2005, p. 196.

10 A. Whitaker, *Good News from Virginia*, 1613, Epistle Dedicatory by William Crashaw.

11 Whitaker, *Good News*, Epistle Dedicatory.

12 Whitaker, *Good News*, Epistle Dedicatory.

13 Whitaker, *Good News*, Epistle Dedicatory.

14 Whitaker, *Good News*, p. 23.

15 Whitaker, *Good News*, p. 40.

16 Whitaker, *Good News*, p. 24.

17 Whitaker, *Good News*, p. 33.

12 To boldly go

1 J. B. Boddie, *Seventeenth Century Isle of Wight County, Virginia*, Chicago, IL: Chicago Law Print Co., 1938, pp. 25-6.

2 From *Princess Ida*, written by W. S. Gilbert, composed by Arthur Sullivan, 1884.

3　L. C. Hills, *History and Genealogy of the Mayflower Planters and First Comers to Ye Old Colonie*, Washington, DC: Hills Publishing Co., 1936, p. 40.

4　W. Crashaw, *A sermon preached in London before the right honourable the Lord Lawarre*, London, 1610, n.p.

5　T. Rabb, *Jacobean Gentleman: Sir Edwin Sandys, 1561–1629*, Princeton, NJ: Princeton University Press, 1998, p. 349.

6　N. Philbrick, *Mayflower: A story of courage, community and war*, New York: Viking Press, 2006, pp. 26-7.

7　A. Ames, *The Mayflower Ship's Log*, 6 vols, Madison & Adams Press, 2018, Appendix IV.

8　Cf. R. D. Habich (ed.), *Lines Out of Letters: Essays on American literary biography and documentation*, Cranbury, NJ: Fairleigh Dickinson University Press, 2004, p. 38.

9　'Farewell Letter to the Pilgrims', in *Works of John Robinson . . .*, *Old South Leaflets 142*, Online Library of Liberty, Boston, 2018.

10　Ames, *Mayflower Ship's Log*, Appendix VIII.

Select bibliography

Alford, S., *Burghley: William Cecil at the court of Elizabeth I*, New Haven, CT: Yale University Press, 2008.

Allen, J. W., *A History of Political Thought in the Sixteenth Century*, London: Methuen, 1960.

Aston, N. and Cragoe, M. (eds), *Anticlericalism in Britain, c. 1500-1914*, Stroud: Sutton, 2001.

Bangs, J. D., *Strangers and Pilgrims, Travellers and Sojourners: Leiden and the foundations of Plymouth Plantation*, Plymouth, MA: General Society of Mayflower Descendants, 2009.

Barzun, J., *From Dawn to Decadence: 1500 to the present*, New York: HarperCollins, 2001.

Beilin, E. V. (ed.), *The Examinations of Anne Askew*, Oxford: Oxford University Press, 1996.

Brigden, S., *New Worlds, Lost Worlds: The rule of the Tudors, 1485-1603*, London: Penguin, 2000.

Bruce, J. (ed.), *Correspondence of Robert Dudley, Earl of Leycester during his government of The Low Countries, in the years 1585 and 1586*, Camden Society, London, 1844.

Calvin, J., *Institutes*, ed. A. Lefranc, Paris, 1911.

Childs, D., *Tudor Sea Power: The Foundation of Greatness*, Barnsley: Seaforth, 2009.

Coffey, J. and Lim, P. C. H., *The Cambridge Companion to Puritanism*, Cambridge: Cambridge University Press, 2008.

Collinson, P., *Archbishop Grindal, 1519-1583: The struggle for a reformed Church*, London: Cape, 1979.

——, *Elizabethans*, London: Bloomsbury, 2003.

——, *Godly People: Essays on English Protestantism and Puritanism*, London: Hambledon Press, 1983.

——, *The Elizabethan Puritan Movement*, London: Cape, 1967.

____, *The Religion of Protestants: The Church in English society, 1559-1625*, Oxford, 1982.

Corrie, G. E. (ed.), *Sermons by Hugh Latimer*, Parker Society, Cambridge: Cambridge University Press, 1844.

Cox, J. C. (ed.), *Records of the Borough of Northampton*, Northampton, 1898, vol. 2.

Culpepper, S., *Francis Johnson and the English Separatist Influence*, Macon, GA: Mercer University Press, 2011.

Delaney, C., *Columbus and the Quest for Jerusalem: How religion drove the voyages that led to America*, New York: Free Press, 2012.

Dillingham, W., *Laurence Chaderton, D.D. First Master of Emmanuel* (trans. E. S. Shuckburgh), Cambridge: Macmillan & Bowes, 1884.

Doran, S., 'Elizabeth I's Religion: The Evidence of Her Letters', *Journal of Ecclesiastical History*, vol. 51, no. 4, October 2000.

Duke, A., *Reformation and Revolt in the Low Countries*, London: Hambledon & London, 2003.

Dunn, O. and Kelley, J. E. (eds), *The Diario of Christopher Columbus's First Voyage to America, 1492-1493*, Norman, OK: University of Oklahoma Press, 1988.

Edgeworth, R., *Sermons very fruitful, godly and learned . . .*, 1557, ed. J. Wilson, Cambridge: Brewer, 1993.

Elton, G. R., *Policy and Police: The enforcement of religion in the age of Thomas Cromwell*, Cambridge: Cambridge University Press, 1972.

____, *Reform and Reformation: England 1509-1558*, Cambridge, MA: Harvard University Press, 1977.

Erasmus, Preface to the *Novum Instrumentum*, Basel, 1516.

____, *The Education of a Christian Prince*, trans. N. M. Cheshire and M. J. Heath, Cambridge: Cambridge University Press, 1997.

Evenden, E. and Freeman, T. S., *Religion and the Book in Early Modern England: The making of John Foxe's 'Book of Martyrs'*, Cambridge: Cambridge University Press, 2011.

Faulkner, R. K., *Richard Hooker and the Politics of a Christian England*, Berkeley, CA: University of California Press, 1981.

Foxe, John, *Acts and Monuments*, ed. G. Townsend, London, 1837.

Garrett, C., *The Marian Exiles*, Cambridge: Cambridge University Press, 1938, 1966.

Gray, A., *From Here We Changed the World: Amazing stories of pilgrims and rebels from North Nottinghamshire and West Lincolnshire*, Retford: Bookworm, 2016.

Gunther, K., *Reformation Unbound: Protestant visions of reform in England*, Cambridge: Cambridge University Press, 2014.

Helgerson, R., *Forms of Nationhood: The Elizabethan writing of England*, Chicago, IL: University of Chicago Press, 1992.

Hitchcock, E. V. (ed.), *The Life of Sir Thomas More Knight, written by William Roper Esquire*, Oxford: Oxford University Press, 1935.

Höpfl, H., *The Christian Polity of John Calvin*, Cambridge: Cambridge University Press, 1982.

Horn, J., *A Land as God Made It: Jamestown and the birth of America*, New York: Basic Books, 2005.

Howarth, D., *Images of Rule: Art and politics in the English Renaissance, 1485-1649*, Berkeley, CA: University of California Press, 1997.

Israel, J. L., *The Dutch Republic: Its rise, greatness and fall, 1470-1806*, Oxford: Oxford University Press, 1995.

Ives, E., *The Reformation Experience: Living through the turbulent sixteenth century*, Oxford: Lion Hudson, 2012.

Laing, D. (ed.), *The Works of John Knox*, Edinburgh, 1895.

Loades, D. M., *Politics and the Nation, 1450-1660: Obedience, resistance and public order*, London: Fontana/Collins, 1974.

Luther's Works, ed. H. T. Lehmann and J. Pelikan, 55 vols, St Louis, MO, and Philadelphia, PA: Fortress Press, 1955-1986, vol. 31.

MacCulloch, D., *Reformation: Europe's house divided, 1490-1700*, London: Allen Lane, 2003.

——, *The Later Reformation in England, 1547-1603*, Basingstoke: Palgrave, 2001.

——, *Thomas Cranmer: A life*, New Haven, CT: Yale University Press, 1996.

MacCulloch, P. E., *Sermons at Court: Politics and religion in Elizabethan and Jacobean preaching*, Cambridge: Cambridge University Press, 1998.

Marcus, L. S., Mueller, J. and Rose, M. B. (eds), *Elizabeth I: Collected works*, Chicago, IL: University of Chicago Press, 2000.

Marshall, P., *Heretics and Believers: A history of the English Reformation*, New Haven, CT: Yale University Press, 2017.

——, *Reformation England, 1480-1642*, London: Hodder Arnold, 2003.

____, *Religious Identities in Henry VIII's England*, Aldershot: Ashgate, 2006.

Marshall, P. and Ryrie, A., *The Beginnings of English Protestantism*, Cambridge: Cambridge University Press, 2002.

Martin, J. W., *Religious Radicals in Tudor England*, London: Hambledon, 1989.

McConica, J. K., *English Humanists and Reformation Politics under Henry VIII and Edward VI*, Oxford: Clarendon Press, 1965.

Milton, J., *On the New Forces of Conscience under the Long Parliament*, London, 1646.

More, Thomas, *The Yale Edition of the Complete Works of St. Thomas More, vol. 3, pt 2: Latin Poems*, ed. C. H. Miller, L. Bradner and C. A. Lynch, New Haven, CT: Yale University Press, 1984.

____, *The Yale Edition of the Complete Works of St. Thomas More, vol. 8, pts 1-3: The Confutation of Tyndale's Answer*, ed. L. A. Schuster, R. C. Marius and J. P. Lusardi, New Haven, CT: Yale University Press, 1973.

____, *Utopia*, trans. R. Robinson, ed. W. A. Rebhorn, New York: Barnes & Noble, 2005.

Parker, G., *Spain and the Netherlands, 1559-1659*, Glasgow: Fontana/Collins, 1979.

Petheram, J. (ed.), *A Brieff discours of the troubles begonne at Frankford*, London, 1845.

Porter, H. C., *Reformation and Reaction in Tudor Cambridge*, Cambridge: Cambridge University Press, 1958.

Read, C., *Lord Burghley and Queen Elizabeth*, London: Cape, 1965.

Reid, W. S., *Trumpeter of God: A biography of John Knox*, New York: Scribners, 1974.

Robinson, H. (ed.), *Original Letters relative to the English Reformation . . . chiefly from the Archives of Zurich*, Parker Society, Cambridge: Cambridge University Press, 1846.

____ (ed.), *The Zurich Letters . . . during the early part of the Reign of Queen Elizabeth*, Parker Society, Cambridge: Cambridge University Press, 1842.

____ (ed.), *The Zurich Letters* (second series), Parker Society, Cambridge: Cambridge University Press, 1845.

Robinson, R. (trans.), *Utopia – Sir Thomas More with The Life of Sir Thomas More by William Roper*, New York: Barnes & Noble, 2005.

Rogers, E. F. (ed.), *St Thomas More: Selected letters*, New Haven, CT: Yale University Press, 1961.

Ryrie, A., *Being Protestant in Reformation Britain*, Oxford: Oxford University Press, 2013.

Scarisbrick, J. J., *The Reformation and the English People*, Oxford: Oxford University Press, 1984.

Seaver, P. S., *The Puritan Lectureships: The politics of religious dissent, 1560–1662*, Stanford, CA: Stanford University Press, 1970.

Sharpe, K., *Selling the Tudor Monarchy: Authority and image in sixteenth-century England*, New Haven, CT: Yale University Press, 2009.

Sheils, W. J., *The Puritans in the Diocese of Peterborough, 1558–1610*, Northampton: Northamptonshire Record Society, 1979.

Spolorno, G. B., *Memorials of Columbus*, London, 1823.

Strype, J., *Ecclesiastical Memorials relating chiefly to religion . . .*, London, 1822.

Stubbs, P., *The Anatomy of Abuses: containing a Discovery or Brief Summary of such Notable Vices and Imperfections as now reign in many Countries of the World but especially in a famous Island called Ailgna . . . together with examples of God's Judgements*, London, 1595.

The First Four Voyages of Amerigo Vespucci, trans. M. K., London, 1885.

Thornton, T., *Prophecy, Politics and the People in Early Modern England*, Woodbridge: Boydell Press, 2006.

Turner, W., *The hunting and fyndyng out of the Romish fox*, Basel, 1543.

Walker, G., *Writing Under Tyranny: English literature and the Henrician Reformation*, Oxford: Oxford University Press, 2005.

Walker, W., *John Calvin, the organiser of Reformed Protestantism*, New York: G. P. Putnam's Sons, 1906.

Wendel, F., *Calvin: The origins and development of his religious thought*, trans. P. Mairet, London: Collins, 1963.

Whitgift, J., 'The Defence of the Answer to the Admonition . . .', in J. Ayre (ed.), *Works of John Whitgift*, Parker Society, Cambridge: Cambridge University Press, 1851, vol. 1.

Whiting, R., *The Blind Devotion of the People: Popular religion and the English Reformation*, Cambridge: Cambridge University Press, 1989.

Wilson, D., *A Brief History of the English Reformation: Religion, politics and fear*, London: Robinson, 2012.

___, *A Tudor Tapestry: Men, women and society in Reformation England*, London: Heinemann, 1972.

___, *Sweet Robin: A biography of Robert Dudley, Earl of Leicester, 1533-1588*, London: Hamish Hamilton, 1981.

Zweig, S., *Erasmus and the Right to Heresy*, London: Condor, 1979.

Index

233

Index

Index

Index

Gilby, Anthony 119
Golden Hind (ship) 88
Good News from Virginia (Whitaker) 193–4
Greenham, Richard 77
Greenwood, John 109, 110, 135
Gregory XIII, Pope 54
Grindal, Archbishop Edmund 74–5, 103, 123, 133
Grindal, Bishop 99–100
Guise, Mary of 104
Gunpowder Plot 156, 159

Hakluyt, Richard (b. 1530) 89
Hakluyt, Richard (b. 1552)
  expansionism of 89, 90–1
  mission to the New World 96–7
  on the New World riches 176
  The Principle Navigations . . . 90–1, 181–2, 183
Hampden, John 124
Hampton Court Conference (1604) 39, 138
Harington, Sir James 120
Harriot, Thomas
  colonizing Virginia 89, 91, 92–3
  A Report . . . of Virginia 92, 181
Harrison, Robert 77, 80
Harwick, Stephen van
  Chancewell 111
Hastings, Henry, Earl of Huntingdon 119
Hawkins, John 57, 96–7
Heberden, William 66
Hebrews, Letter to the 195
Helwys, Thomas 152, 157
  A Declaration of Faith 163
  return and imprisonment 161, 163
Henry Grace à Dieu/Great Harry (ship) 85
Henry VII of England 18
Henry VIII of England
  break with Rome 17, 65–6, 117
  Cromwell, Thomas, and 22–3
  death of 23, 118
  A Defence of the Seven Sacraments 14
  as Defender of the Faith xi
  development of navy 84–5
  dissolution of monasteries 86
  Dudley, Edmund, and 20

effect of Bible-reading 33
English Bible and 21–2, 31, 32
expectations of ministers 85
on fenland folk 115
intolerance of 118
maritime plundering 86–7
More, Thomas, and 7–8
Tyndale, William, and 21–2
heresy
  as 'choice' 12
  Colet, John, on clergy 20
Heretics and Believers (Marshall) 99
Hickman, Sir William 157
Historia Regum Britanniae (Geoffrey of Monmouth) 89
History of Plymouth Plantation, The (Bradford) 166–8
Hooker, Richard 73, 196
  Laws of Ecclesiastical Polity 70, 207
Hooper, John, Bishop of Gloucester 25–6
Hopkins, John 38
Horne, Robert 48–9
Huguenots
  Calvin and 44
  relocation of 43, 55
  St Bartholomew's Day massacre 54, 129
Hunt, Robert 184–5

iconoclasm 69
individualism, Bible exegesis and 30
Institutes of the Christian Religion (Calvin) 44
Introduction to Cosmography (Waldseemüller) 3
Ireland 36, 91, 93
Islam 4–5

Jacob, Henry 149–50, 169, 173
James VI and I 78
  authorized Bible and 39
  Basilikon Doron 136
  colonial policy 180, 183–4
  Counterblast to Tobacco 191
  declines to summon Parliament 196
  defending the faith 147–50
  ends hostility with Spain 178
  hopes of Puritans on accession of 135–7

Index

Index

Index

Printed and bound by CPI Group (UK) Ltd, Croydon, CR0 4YY

13/04/2025

14656469-0001